EVERYBODY'S WINE GUIDE

EVERYBODY'S WINE GUIDE

A MINE OF INFORMATION FROM PETER DOMINIC

Anthony Hogg
with decorative maps by
Diana Hoare

Quiller Press

The Author

After thirty years in the Royal Navy, where he became a specialist in mines, Anthony Hogg has now served a second thirty year term, pen in hand, promoting wines. From 1959 to 1974, as a Director of Peter Dominic, he became well known as the creator of *Wine Mine*, that amusing half yearly mine of wine information which was the only wine periodical in those days. Since retiring at 65 his books have included the following:

Cocktails and Mixed Drinks

The Hamlyn Publishing Group 1979/80/81/82/83/84. (108,000 copies sold . . . royalty about 0 · 7 per cent.)

Guide to Visiting Vineyards

Michael Joseph 1976-81-82-84.
'No other remotely comparable guide exists: and anyone with an interest in wine who proposes to travel in Europe should carry a copy.'
John Arlott in the *Guardian*

Off the Shelf

Gilbey Vintners' Guide to Wines and Spirits 1973/77/78

Travellers' Portugal

Solo Mio Books 1983
'Every conceivable piece of information you will ever require – I cannot praise it too highly.'
Tom Stevenson *British Airways High Life*

Everybody's Wine Guide
First published 1985 by
Quiller Press Ltd
50 Albemarle Street
London W1X 4BD

ISBN 0-907621-53-8

Designed by Jim Reader.
Design and production in association with
Book Production Consultants, Norfolk Street,
Cambridge.

Printed in Italy by Poligrafici Calderara (Bologna).

Contents

Acknowledgements

As may be seen from the text and the bibliography, the works of many authors have been indispensable to the author of this one. I am glad to mention them because, except once a year in November, wine books get little press publicity and it would benefit the trade and the public more if they did.

My thanks go also to Alison Pendree of the Champagne Bureau, Helen Chardin of Moët & Chandon and Catherine Manac'h for their factual help. Likewise to my German-speaking friend, Peter Longhurst and to Keith Warren of Her Majesty's Customs for their advice.

A team of typists, Judith Moore, Anna Best, Sarah Dabrowski and Elizabeth Godfrey, has transformed heavily corrected manuscripts into 350 sheets of legible typescript, individually read and corrected with great care at International Distillers & Vintners, Harlow by Don Lovell M.W., M.B.E., Charles Eve M.W. and Allan Simpson M.B.E., the Group's oenologist, who deserves a bar to his medal. Finally Diana Hoare's decorative maps give the book unusual distinction.

I record my thanks to them all, and not least to two old wine trade friends, Leslie Seyd and James Long, who readily agreed to contribute themselves to Part 2, The Wine Merchants.

The initials M.W. stand for Master of Wine, the highest professional qualification in the British Wine Trade. The M.W. Institute has over a hundred members. The annual theoretical and practical examinations are held in May, passes being about one in five.

Introduction

Mines to Wines

On reading Saturday's *Times*.

> No tonic for the man depressed
> By news of earthquakes, 'Mr K'
> And Ike, and Mao, and all the rest
> That fills the paper day by day . . .
> No Lapper-Litre quip or jest
> No chat of rosé, rouge or blanc
> *The Times* front page remains
>   unblessed . . .
> How long, O Dominic, how long?

Was there a Mr Dominic?

I am frequently asked two questions. The first is 'Was there a Mr Dominic?' to which the answer is 'Yes'; and the second 'Do you still do *Wine Mine*?' to which the answer has been 'No' for ten years, but becomes 'Yes' again with the completion of this book, though I have called it *Everybody's Wine Guide*, because in 1984, from Yorkshire to the Persian Gulf, we have all had enough of mines in any shape or form.

Peter Dominic's real name was Paul Dauthieu, a Scotsman, whose French parents ran their own Hotel Banavie in Fort William. With little more than a short conventional education at the Perth Academy and a three-year kitchen apprenticeship at the Caledonian Hotel, Edinburgh, he came to London in 1930 after this family hotel, under-insured, burnt down. He died in 1967, aged 63, twenty-eight years after he and his wife, Blanche, had opened their first wine shop in Horsham, with a capital of £120 and the War barely three months old. Inspired by a family game of dominoes, Paul named it Peter Dominic as being easier to pronounce and remember than his own name.

Having weathered the War, thanks in no small measure to Blanche, who ran the business with a growing team of women while her husband was in the RAF, Paul had managed to add another nine branches in southern market towns by 1956. This was no small achievement: licence applications were almost always opposed, often successfully, by established holders, and with whisky rationed, Peter Dominic — non-existent before the war — received an inadequate quota of the leading brands.

This was when I arrived after some months as an apprentice in the City of London cellars of Brown, Gore & Welch (also destined like Peter Dominic to join International Distillers & Vintners later) and a few more behind the counter of Peter Dominic's Worthing branch. In the Navy since I joined the Royal Naval College, Dartmouth as a cadet of 13, I had been selected to specialise in torpedoes, which

1

included mines and electrics, principally because HMS Vernon, the Torpedo School, thought I might help them beat HMS Excellent, the Gunnery School, at rugger. Unfortunately instead of a football match there was a war, in which I became an early victim of Hitler's dive bombers off the Dutch coast in a 1940 version of 'Casabianca'.* Though I recovered to fight again, the role of Captain Brown playing his ukelele as the ship went down in some future imbroglio lost its appeal, so I opted for a pension and a quite life in the wine trade.

How dull that would have been! Looking back from the thirtieth year of promoting Peter Dominic with my pen, there has rarely been a dull moment, the whole world of wine changing completely.

Peter Dominic's Wineyard

At Horsham in 1956 every empty Vermouth bottle was being collected in which to sell Lemaire's three Bordeaux ordinaires: red, rosé and white, afterwards called Carafino. Holding 91 centilitres — as opposed to 75 centilitres for table wines — the use of these larger bottles in conjunction with no capsules and plain black and white labels, reduced their prices by a few pence. The wines themselves, drunk by the Dauthieu family daily, were good because Lemaire was pioneering a new technique of quicker maturing by refrigeration, later to be widely adopted.

My job was to start a mail order department; though there was little money, we began classified advertisements in the weekend *Epicure* columns, which *The*

Times and *Sunday Times* had just started, offering: 'BIG value in BIG bottles. Trial Three by post 23s 6d'. After rewriting textbooks on naval mines during the previous four years, describing Peter Dominic's less explosive missiles and receiving nearly two hundred cheques that first Monday morning was rather exciting.

But what can one say week after week about 'plonk'? My search for inspiration became as desperate as the one for BIG bottles. However, with characters like Disraeli's Mr Mountchesney (who only liked bad wine) and Pollard, the architect who, suffering from Wine Starvation,

PETER DOMINIC
VINEYARD
VISITING GUIDE

---

* 'The boy stood on the burning deck, whence all but he had fled.' Felicia Dorothea Hemans 1793—1835.

forgot the staircase in the 49-storey hotel, winning (thanks to vin ordinaire) a bronze medal later for his revolutionary design of a one-storey house with three staircases, Peter Dominic's Wineyard became well known.

When eventually we took a rest from advertising, a postcard arrived from 'The Housemaster, The Cathedral School, Truro'. On it was the verse at the beginning of this chapter.

The Trial Threes, followed by the same wines in half-gallon jars by rail, established a mail order department serving the DOVODs (Dominic's Own Vin Ordinaire Drinkers) with Lord Lapper-Litre (a precursor of John Wells's Denis perhaps) volunteering as colonel, even though he had yet to hear a bottle drunk in anger. These ordinaires − 'the cheapest wines you will drink with pleasure' − were eventually named Carafino, by which time France as a source had become too expensive; none the less their popularity is still as great as ever.

Having described vin ordinaire in light-hearted fashion, we turned in similar vein to other wines, blossoming forth with as many leaflets as time permitted, including a tabloid called *The Daily Quaff (Forward with the Bottle).** With the first *Wine Mine, A Mine of Wine Information* (described in *Punch* as '100-odd pages illustrated by a chap who really does know that Botticelli is not a drink, and written by another who thinks it ought to be') the blossom turned to fruit just in time for Christmas 1959.

The Wine Mine Club

The main reaction to this descriptive,

---

* The *Daily Mirror* was 'Forward with the People' in those days.

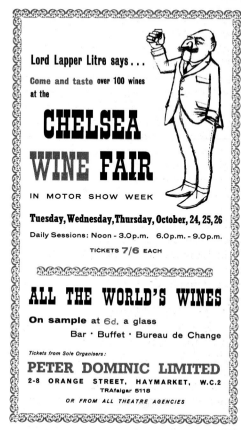

Lord Lapper Litre says...

Come and taste over 100 wines at the

CHELSEA
WINE FAIR

IN MOTOR SHOW WEEK

Tuesday, Wednesday, Thursday, October, 24, 25, 26

Daily Sessions: Noon - 3.0 p.m.   6.0 p.m. - 9.0 p.m.

TICKETS **7/6** EACH

ALL THE WORLD'S WINES

On sample at 6d. a glass

Bar · Buffet · Bureau de Change

Tickets from Sole Organisers:

PETER DOMINIC LIMITED
2-8 ORANGE STREET, HAYMARKET, W.C.2
TRAfalgar 5118
OR FROM ALL THEATRE AGENCIES

pocket-sized price list was 'How we'd like to try them all!' So in May and June 1960 the Wine Mine Club held its first meeting to taste and compare six 1953 and six 1955 clarets, with a buffet meal and post-prandial port all for ten shillings a head. This was, we believed, the first tasting, in the United Kingdom, of fine wines offered to the public on payment. Two evenings and one lunch time a week, it ran for five weeks, acquainting eight hundred people with both the wines and Peter Dominic's 2−8 Orange Street shop-in-a-cellar, recently opened.

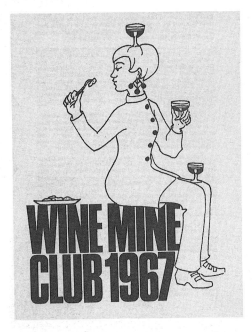

Thenceforward until 1974 the meetings continued at the rate of five a year, so that the Club became a repertory theatre of wine tasting, praised by the *Evening Standard* for not being 'esoteric gatherings of bouquet-swishing experts'. The meetings, subsequently less frequent, have continued without a break, numbers 111 to 114 being held in 1984 at the Royal Festival Hall.

In 1974 there was a welcome merger for the Wine Mine Club with the Directors' Wine Club, founded by Cyril Ray in 1959 and also part of International Distillers and Vintners since 1963. This gave members not only tastings but their own wine list, special offers and social events.

The firm was Paul's life and he was a fine man to work for and to learn from, with a sense of humour that transformed occasional disagreements into a grin when

he said, 'You've got to remember all bosses are bastards' when this was precisely what you were thinking.

There was often talk of Peter Dominic becoming a public company. Had Paul's health been better perhaps we would have done and then, who knows, Peter Dominic might have taken over Grand Met?

Three Chelsea Wine Fairs

By 1961 we had persuaded W. H. Smith & Sons to sell our 'bar bible, students' primer and drinkers' guide' on their bookstalls for one shilling a copy and the new edition announced that Peter Dominic would hold the Chelsea Wine Fair, with three hundred wines on sample at sixpence a time, during the 1962 Motor Show. Meeting a number of buyers from brewery wine departments at the Fair, educating their palates on Château Latour at sixpence a glass, *Wine Mine*

The Peter Dominic marquee at the 1984 C.L.A. Game Fair.

remarked, with uncanny prophecy, 'They'll be taking us all over tomorrow so we must have our quip today'. The series ended with the third Fair in 1963 'promoted not pensioned' from Chelsea to the larger Seymour Hall, north of Oxford Street, where 1500 people congregated each night, all now skilled in holding a glass, a programme, a pencil and a sample of cheese at one and the same time.

These three Chelsea Wine Fairs, so efficiently run by my co-director, Richard Boon and staffed by almost the whole company, brought to London for a week from twenty shops, were the climax of Peter Dominic enterprise as a privately-owned independent family firm. An agreement with International Distillers & Vintners (principally Gilbeys, Justerini & Brooks and Twiss & Brownings & Hallowes, the Hennessy agents) selling Peter Dominic for around threequarters of a million pounds was signed soon afterwards.

For a small privateer sailing independently, it had been a memorable first commission.

Mergers and takeovers
1964–1973 was a decade of mergers and takeovers. At first many small wine merchants and small retail chains had to merge with bigger concerns because the ending of resale price maintenance,

5

permitting price cutting, made their profits on spirits inadequate. At the outset Gilbeys had some 180 retail outlets, trading as T. Foster & Co, a firm they had bought in 1928. By 1968 when there were 354 outlets trading variously as Peter Dominic, Hunter & Oliver, Fosters & Camerons, it was time for unity and the Chairman of International Distillers & Vintners announced that they would all become 'Peter Dominic, the best name we've got' — under the popular J. K. Peppercorn, another experienced wine merchant who had spent his life in the trade. His son David Peppercorn was already the Dominic wine buyer. Offices at Wembley and Horsham duly closed and in 1969 the management was ensconced as the retail arm of International Distillers & Vintners in the restored Regency splendour of 12 York Gate at the southern entrance to Regent's Park. Here we were joined by Don Lovell M.W. and others from Brown & Pank, Watney's wine and spirit company, Watney's having bought a 25 per cent stake in International Distillers & Vintners to stave off a bid from Showerings.

The association was not to last long. In 1972 Watney's took over International Distillers & Vintners having learnt, like other brewers, that selling wine could be more profitable than selling beer. But within a few months both companies found they were part of Grand Metropolitan, with Watneys instructed to be the brewer and International Distillers & Vintners the vintner.

Wine Mine 1959–1974

Since 1963 *Wine Mine,* to please the bookstalls, had become a biennial, half-magazine and half-catalogue, with a few advertisements to reduce the cost of giving copies to customers and a circulation of 100,000 to 150,000 copies. Somebody had coined another sub-title *Wine, Wit and Wisdom for the Million* and I'm sure the magazine side lived up to this title, with such contributors as James Cameron, Richard Church, Peta Fordham, Robert Gittings, James Laver, Eric Newby, John Oaksey, Anthony Powell, Edmund Penning-Rowsell, Cyril Ray and B. A. Young. Quite an XI for that cricket fixture against the publishers!

As a wine list, in the early 1970s with the help of David Peppercorn sending information from his buying travels, *Wine Mine* was at its best. Fulfilling the company's policy of not listing clarets until they were ready, there were no less than thirty-six 1962 *crus classés,* each with its descriptive note, in the issue of Summer 1971.

The penultimate issue, no. 25, reverted to being an annual, with the compensation of *Invitation to Italy,* in sixteen pages of colour. Currency fluctuations now made the inclusion of prices difficult and with a new management insisting on a new format twice the size of the old one the series ended in 1974 with no. 26. Doubtless there were pecuniary gains but this left a gap for competitors to fill. Today the Wine Society's 96-page list and 60,000 members shows who filled it.

In 1972, soon after the Grand Metropolitan takeover, what had now become International Distillers & Vintners Home Trade moved out of 12 York Gate to long-prepared new warehouses and offices at Harlow. Our export colleagues, feverishly creating new brands such as Bailey's Irish Cream, remained in London at headquarters, No. 1, the twin Nash building across the road. And there they all remain after twelve productive years of

WineMine

Number 25   **1973**   **15p**

Invitation to Italy

Elizabeth David   Eric Newby   Georgina Masson

Published by Peter Dominic, All the World's Wines

'Educating 'em our way' clearly continues in very good hands. In 1961, when the USA named (without our leave!) its last nuclear explosion in the atmosphere 'Operation Dominic', this was a winning entry by a Mrs. Ambler. Let us all drink to its fulfilment!

> Old words like wine-bottles retain their shape:
> Meanings like clarets change with age. Today
> The once so warlike phrase 'a whiff of grape'
> Merely suggests a mellowed wine's bouquet.
>
> Years hence, when this *new* Dominic so alarming
> Has petered out, all radiation spent,
> Still shall *old* Peter Dominic, disarming, 'Radiate'
> his wines to make the heart content.

Off the Shelf 1967–1984

In 1971 Brown & Pank, Watney's wine and spirit company, had become part of International Distillers & Vintners bringing many Westminster wine branches with them and their excellent *Off the Shelf*, a guide to the sale of wines and spirits by Robin Don M.W. published in 1967. With copies scarce I was asked, as a director of Peter Dominic and editor of *Wine Mine*, to provide a second edition for Gilbey Vintners. Though primarily for the food and drink trade the public liked it too, so that since 1971 I have written three revised and reset editions printing 60,000 copies, many of them bought at around £2 a copy until stocks must now be exhausted.

Everybody's Wine Guide 1985

With the publication of *Everybody's Wine Guide,* Peter Dominic will have for the first time a guide to wines in book form written specifically — as the title implies — for everybody. My wine-drinking life, however, has by no means been confined to Peter Dominic. Home on leave in the 1930s my father's table was seldom without the decanter of St. Julien he bought from Furze

largely wholesale trading by Gilbey Vintners and retail by Peter Dominic.

With only five years to go to my retirement, I went back to work from my home town, Chichester, conveniently close to the David Paul Design Group, Art Editors of *Off the Shelf* and *Wine Mine* besides numerous passports to visiting vineyards and Peter Dominic newsletters. 'Educating 'em our way', as one old Branch manager called it.

Chris Foulkes, Hugh Johnson's *Wine Companion* editor, now edits *The Peter Dominic Magazine,* in which authors and Masters of Wine, Jancis Robinson and Michael Broadbent contribute fascinating articles on such matters as how wine came to television and when to decant.

The author (right) with André Simon

& Jones in the City at 3s 2d a bottle. A £1 wedding present from my father-in-law in 1940 made me a member of the Wine Society (I.E.C. 1874). And after the War George Delaforce and John Boys M.W., of Harveys on the Hard at Portsmouth, kindly took my practical instruction in hand.

For this book my publishers' only instruction has been 'a guide to wines in not more than 90,000 words', which precludes it being encyclopaedic. British table (i.e. light wine) consumption is now roughly France 39 per cent, Germany 31 per cent, Italy 13 per cent, Spain 7 per cent, Yugoslavia 4 per cent, Portugal 2 per cent, Hungary 1 per cent, Cyprus 1 per cent. Bulgaria, Austria, Australia, New Zealand, the United States and others share the remaining 2 per cent. I have tried to be guided by these figures. France inevitably gets more than her share; there is so much to explain and to see in the country itself. Developments in California, Australia and New Zealand anticipate fine wines to come, leaving me no space for the continents of South America and Africa.

Measurements

Though EEC countries now use the metric system, acres still convey more to English-speaking readers than hectares and cases of 12 bottles more than hectolitres. Moreover, more English-speaking people live outside the EEC than in it. I have therefore given British measures where appropriate.

1 hectare $= 2 \cdot 47$ acres
1 hectolitre $= 100$ litres $= 11$ cases.
To convert litres to 12-bottle cases, divide the former by 9.

Part 1

The Wine-makers

The year in the vineyard*

January Pruning officially starts on St Vincent's day, 22 January but usually brought forward to December. If there is no snow the ground is often frozen hard. Vines will survive temperature down to minus 18°C.

February Continue pruning. Take cuttings for grafting. Make grafts on to root-stock putting them indoors in sand. Prepare machines for the year's work. Order copper sulphate for spraying.

March Ploughing. About mid-month the vine awakes from winter: sap rises, brown sheaths on buds fall off. Finish pruning. Work the soil deeply to aerate it and destroy weeds.

April Finish ploughing. Clear up vineyard, burning remaining prunings and replacing rotten stakes. Plant one-year-old cuttings from the nursery. Pray for late vegetation, as frosts are frequent and hail possible.

May Frost danger at its height. On clear nights stoves may be needed among the vines, with watchkeepers to fuel them. A

*From an International Distillers & Vintners' calendar. Reproduced by kind permission of Hugh Johnson from *The World Atlas of Wine*.

second working of the soil to kill weeds. Spray against oidium and mildew. Every ten days remove suckers to encourage sap to rise in the vines.

June The vines flower early in June when temperature reaches 10°–20°C. Weather is critical, the warmer and calmer the better. After flowering thin the shoots, tying the best to the wires. Spray against oidium with powdered sulphur dioxide.

July Spray the vines regularly with Bordeaux mixture (copper sulphate, slaked lime and water). A third hoeing of the soil against weeds. Trim long shoots so that vines spend their energy on making fruit.

August Keep vineyards weeded and vines trimmed. Black grapes begin to turn black. Check and prepare any gear needed for the vintage.

September Vintage. Keep small boys and birds out of the vineyard. Keep vines trimmed, pray for sunshine. Vintage usually begins in the third week when grapes are ripe.

October The vintage continues for perhaps two weeks. On completion spread manure (pressed grape skins are good) and fertiliser over the vineyard. Deep plough any land for new plantations.

November Cut off long vine shoots and collect them for fuel. Finish manuring. Plough the vineyards to move soil over vines' roots to protect from frost.

December Soil washed down slopes by rain must be carried back and redistributed. Pruning can start before Christmas about 15 December.

Climate and micro climate

Though there are now many successful vineyards in Southern England, its climate is almost beyond the wine-making fringe. The vine does best in a warmer climate, thrusting its roots downwards in search of nourishment in a light soil. We meet it all round the Mediterranean planted in patches by peasants where little else will grow. The effort of bearing great bunches of grapes in the autumn exhausts the plant, which needs a winter's rest and plenty of rain at the roots to repeat the cycle year after year.

Approaching the equator winters become too short for this recovery; approaching the Poles — North or South — the temperature, ideally averaging 15°C/58°F, becomes too low and the average daily sunshine drops below the six hours needed to ripen the grapes.

Thus wine-makers are restricted to two bands of latitude as shown opposite, the parallels passing through, or close to, the places named below.

Northern Hemisphere
33°N   Los Angeles — Madeira — North Africa — Bagdad — Central China — Japan
to
50°N   Land's End — Mosel and Rheingau — Vancouver — Newfoundland

Southern Hemisphere
23°S   Southern Chile — Northern Argentina — Republic of South Africa — Queensland
to
40°S   Melbourne — New Zealand North Island

Then come the exceptions, little regions outside these bands with micro-climates equivalent to being inside. Southern England, able to make white wine but not red so far, is one. Marlborough 42°S on the north-east corner of the South Island of New Zealand is another, making a good red wine what is more. Being close to the sea — and the Gulf Stream in the case of England — often creates a favourable micro-climate.

In the tropics the Mexicans have tried plantations on the cooler mountain slopes, their experiments recalling that there was once talk of trying a vineyard in Tanzania up Mount Kilimanjaro 19340 ft./5895 m., only 3° south of the equator.

There is no particular soil that makes the greatest wine; quality is much more a matter of the right variety of vine being found to suit the soil and the climate (see page 12). Thriving in these soils the roots draw into the plant the trace elements as oenologists call them, traces of minerals that include boron, cobalt, copper, iodine, manganese, molybdenum, nickel, selenium, vanadium and zinc. These nourish the vine and ultimately improve the taste and aroma of its wine as seasoning improves the work of a chef.

The plant that drinks mineral water.

Like other plants the vine needs water, carbon dioxide, light and heat as well as minerals. Its main water supply is tapped by the roots deep in the soil; the leaves also

World Wine Production

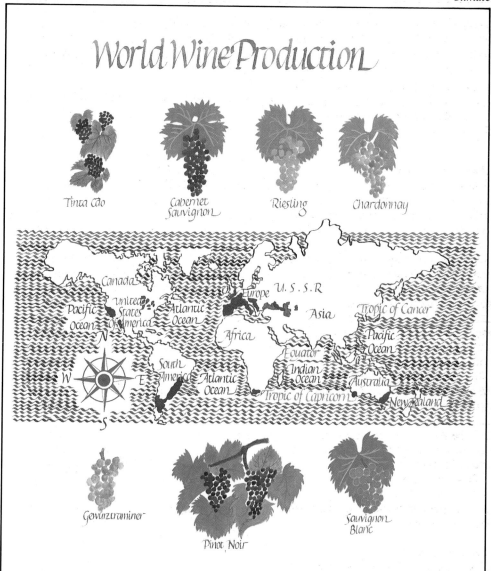

Tinta Cão

Cabernet
Sauvignon

Riesling

Chardonnay

Canada

Pacific
Ocean

United
States
Of America

Atlantic
Ocean

Europe

U.S.S.R

Asia

Tropic of Cancer

Africa

Pacific
Ocean

Equator

South
America

Atlantic
Ocean

Indian
Ocean

Australia

Tropic of Capricorn

New Zealand

Gewürztraminer

Pinot Noir

Sauvignon
Blanc

MATCHING VINES WITH SOILS

Soil	Region	Vine
Chalk	Champagne	Chardonnay, Pinot Noir
	Chablis	Chardonnay
	Sherry (Jerez)	Palomino
Gravel (well drained)	Médoc	Cabernet Sauvignon
	St. Emilion	Merlot
	Pomerol	
Loess and loam	Rheingau	Riesling
Schist (crystalline rock)	Port (Douro Valley)	A dozen varieties unique to Portugal
Volcanic	Madeira	(Various)
	Italy, Etna and Vesuvius	

absorb water from rain. In sunlight chlorophyll (the colouring matter of the leaves) draws carbon dioxide from the air combining it with the water from the soil to make the carbohydrate, sugar. The circulating sap then delivers the sugar to the grape for storing. To avoid dissipation *en route*, in summer the grower — having already reduced the main stems in the winter — cuts back any long shoots, pruning them so that the sun's energy is concentrated on the sugar-making process.

Sites and slopes
Since all plant life gives off carbon dioxide during the night, it is wise to make sure that the sugar-making process starts as soon as the sun appears at dawn, before its rays are hampered by the haze and dust of the day. This is why many vineyards are planted on south-eastern slopes. It explains why up the Douro they say that those on the side of the river that gets the morning sun make the best port. And if, driving south through France on N6, you care to visit Montrachet, greatest of the white burgundy vineyards and marked on Michelin Map 69, I fancy you will find it is so cunningly orientated

that it gets just a little more sun than its adjacent neighbours above and below, Chevalier-Montrachet and Bâtard-Montrachet.

Slopes are invaluable to the wine-maker. Not far to the north-east of Burgundy, on the borderline parallel of 50°N where the Mosel twists and turns, the vine-clad gradients have to be seen to be believed. Without these stately slopes we should have no Mosel, for the Riesling grape would never ripen there on the flat.

The books say sites best avoided are those near woodland (humid), on high ground (windy) and in valleys (possible frost pockets). Yet we find many vineyards in river valleys, because the rivers were the only means of transport when they were planted; the results do not seem to be too bad.

Distinction with age
The age of vines has a considerable influence on the quality of a fine wine. In a new vineyard for the first three years the aim is to develop the roots and to form shapely plants with strong branches. A commercial crop may take five years and

even then, in the world of *grand cru* clarets, a vine may not be thought good enough for the château label until it is eight to ten years old.

The working life of a vine is from twenty to fifty years. Most of the great vineyards are large enough to replant small sections at a time, except in Burgundy. I remember how in 1946, all $4\frac{1}{2}$ acres of Romanée-Conti, the greatest jewel in the crown, had to be ploughed up. There was no more Romanée-Conti until 1952. Age, however, does pose a problem because as the quality improves the quantity declines; in practice about thirty years must be the average in fine wine vineyards.

The perfect vintage

Sap begins to rise in the spring, followed by foliage and buds five to six weeks later, taking up to ten weeks. In Bordeaux, flowering *(floraison)* lasting two weeks usually begins early in June, fine weather being vital to prevent *coulure*, a condition in which the flowers, flower clusters or little green berries are washed or blown away by bad weather and grapes do not develop.*

The fruit slowly matures; green with chlorophyll the grapes assimilate carbon dioxide in the manner of the leaves, with a slight rise in acidity. *Véraison*, the stage where they change colour towards a final reddish-purple or a greenish-white when fully ripe, is in August. In Bordeaux, the interval between the first flowers and the first gathering is reckoned at 110 days.

After *véraison* the acidity decreases and the sugar content increases. When the sugar ceases to increase, the order to start the

---

*This condition has been a disaster for Pomerol and St. Emilion in 1984.

vintage is given. If left to become overripe, water content evaporates; in certain places (e.g. Sauternes and the Rheingau) the *Botrytis cinerea* mould will appear, giving rise to selected late pickings and luscious sweet dessert wines.

Almost everywhere in Western Europe the vintage of 1982, yielding a large quantity of the highest quality, was so good that it will be talked about for decades. April, May and June in Bordeaux were unusually warm and dry, leading to an early flowering with an exceptionally large number of grapes developing throughout July. At the end of the month there was a little much-needed rain that continued intermittently during a cool August. In September the hot dry weather returned, enabling the white grape vintage to begin about 9 September and the red by 15 September, at least a week earlier than usual. Warmth and some light rain to swell the grapes and increase the quantity at the right time, made this the perfect vintage, something that may happen in France every fifteen years or so.

Sometimes prospects look good and suddenly cold, sunless days or heavy rainstorms with hail put paid to a bountiful harvest. Other years — as in 1983 — a warm August and September, ripening backward grapes quickly, lead to wines of high quality when all seemed lost.

In this annual struggle, which may have a happy or a tragic ending, the stage manager is undoubtedly the Clerk of the Weather, the players the victims of his mood. But in the higher latitudes of the two wine bands where the Clerk creates the most difficulties — in France, Germany, the Napa Valley, Victoria, New South Wales and New Zealand — the rewards of achievement are table wines greater than can be made elsewhere. The reasons for this can be summarised in one word 'balance'. When conditions are good, as in 1982, the increased sugar balances the acidity, which is never quite enough in the hotter zones.

And its enemies

The enemies bent on disrupting orderly progress towards the wine-maker's first goal — the maximum quantity of healthy ripe grapes — are three-fold. First come the weapons in the Clerk of the Weather's armoury — late frosts to kill the new growth, clouds to hide the sun, rain and hail to create general havoc and reduce the size of the crop. Drought too can kill the vines if the wine-maker cannot reply with irrigation.

Secondly, there are the fungi, spreading disease such as *Plasmopara viticola*, known as downy mildew, and *Oidium*, known as powdery mildew, doing their worst when rain and damp are present. These have to be controlled by frequent preventative sprayings, costly in materials and labour, whether done on foot or from a vehicle or helicopter, using the blue Bordeaux mixture (copper sulphate) for the former and sulphur dioxide for the latter.

Thirdly, there is the bug brigade whose captain *phylloxera*, the burrowing vine louse, is non-playing because the American rootstock, on which all European vines have been grafted for almost a century, are too tough for his technique. The other subterranean bug, eelworm, is neutralised by sterilising the soil. Above the soil ground predators — various mites, moths and beetles — are killed with insecticides.

Guyots and Gobelets

Ways of training vines vary from region to region. In Bordeaux and Burgundy relatively cool weather dictates a shapely bush two feet high close to the earth which releases its heat at night. Their Double Guyot has two wires stretched horizontally, to which the shoots are tied. In the Rhône valley, to combat the hated Mistral wind, the Gobelet, a single vertical stake, holds each vine; the Echellas uses several.

In northern Italy the plain of the Po is so hot that the need is to preserve acidity, consequently Valpolicella and Soave vines are grown upwards to be supported six feet above the ground, ideally with the leaves shielding the grapes at midday. For less prosperous places — southern Italy and northern Portugal — this high system permits vegetables to be grown underneath.

Men, women and machines

Any lascivious male under the delusion that grapes are gathered by scores of merry matrons and maidens dressed as if they were off to the beach at Bali Bali is in for a shock. The sherry vintage it is true, does begin with the town of Jerez *en fête*; further north there is no near certainty of sunshine all through September, such as Spaniards enjoy under their Andalusian sky. In France, Germany and England (where October is the month) the rig of the day can be 'wellies or woollies'. Lest rain should come, diluting the grapes' juice or rotting them completely, speed is vital, dawn to dusk daily being normal hours of work for two to three weeks.

Since the 1960s mechanical harvesters have been tried in many parts of the world including the Médoc.

These harvesters have protruding arms, which vibrate the bushes as they pass; the grapes are shaken off (not cut), falling undamaged into tanks built into these vehicles, leaving the stems attached to the vines. Unripe grapes are not shaken off and the latest tanks can be given an injection of inert gas that protects the grapes from oxidation.

Wet grapes make insipid wine. Picking has to be abandoned between showers until the sun has dried them. Though the machine, like the pickers, may stand idle, unlike the pickers engaged for the duration of the vintage, it does not have to be paid. In the Médoc it takes 42 people 3 hours and 40 minutes (154 hours of work) to pick one hectare (2.47 acres). With only one mechanical monster the figure could be 2 to $2\frac{1}{2}$ hours. Moreover, the monster needs no sleep; in California, working with teams in relays, it will harvest forty acres in twenty-four hours. Its disadvantage is that trellising has to be very robust.

The year in the cellar*

January   Topping up. Barrels of new light wine must be kept filled to the top, their bungs wiped every other day with a solution of sulphur dioxide. In fine dry weather older wine can be bottled, labelled and packed.

February   Racking. In fine weather with a new moon and a north wind (i.e. when there is high atmospheric pressure) start 'racking' the new wine into clean barrels to clear it. Rack some new wine into a vat for topping up these barrels.

March   Finish first racking before end of the month. When the sap rises a mysterious sympathy between vine and wine is said to start the latter's second fermentation, scientifically known as 'malolactic'. Keep

*From an International Distillers & Vintners' calendar. Reproduced by kind permission of Hugh Johnson from *The World Atlas of Wine*.

A mechanical harvester

casks topped up. Finish bottling white wines.

April   In a wooden cask five per cent of the wine per annum evaporates through the staves. There must never be any empty space (ullage). Topping up must continue.

May   Despatch orders. Just before the vines flower towards end of May, begin a second racking of the new wine off the lees into clean barrels.

June   Finish second racking of new wine and rack all wines in the cellar. Evaporation increases with warmer weather. Check all casks for weeping. Keep topping up.

July   No shipping of wines in hot weather. Concentrate on keeping cellar cool. When close weather requires cellar doors to be closed at night, burn a sulphur candle. Heat slows down vine growth. Bottling can re-start.

August Inspect and clean vats and casks needed for the vintage. Vine growth (and fermentation) start again about mid-month so bottling must stop. Watch low strength wine, less stable and liable to turn in hot weather.

September Scour out the *cuvier* where the wine will be made. Put anti-rust varnish on all metal working parts of presses etc. Fill fermenting vats with water to swell the wood.

October The new wine is fermenting. Year-old wine should be given a final racking, the barrels bunged tight and rolled a quarter turn so that the bung is at the side. Move barrels to second-year cellar to make room for new wine.

November Rack and fine (filter by pouring in whisked egg-white, which sinks to the bottom of cask) any older wines to be bottled. After rich and ripe vintages, rack new wine now; in poor years leave it on the lees another month.

December Casks must be topped up frequently. More bottling of older wine can be done. Start tasting the new wine with old friends.

Alcoholic fermentation

All wines whether apple, barley, ginger or grape are alcoholic beverages and alcohol can only be obtained from sugar or from a product which can be changed into sugar. To make beer, for example, warm water has to be sprinkled on to barley, causing the grain to sprout and grow. This creates a chemical change, brought about by diastase the principal enzyme present in maltose, as the barley, becoming sugar or maltose, is

mixed with hot water in mash tuns at strictly controlled temperatures, fermentation of this liquid (induced by brewers' yeast) making the beer. Malting, mashing and fermentation are the first three stages in making whisky; maturing and possibly blending follows.

Initially, making wine is simple, because the sugary liquid for fermentation is already there in the grapes. The vine starts events by making starch through a biological change involving glycero-phosphoric acid and carbon dioxide, which as we have seen has been absorbed through the leaves from the atmosphere. When the grapes are gathered, the starch has already reached them in the form of sugar.

On the grape skins there are millions of invisible microscopic moulds, bacteria and yeasts, the majority hostile to the wine-maker. The yeasts, however, are his allies. Once the skins are crushed they become the agents of fermentation, though the work of converting the sugar to alcohol is done by enzymes, proteins forming part of the yeast cell. Enzymes are catalysts — chemical substances that change other substances without changing themselves.

One group, the *Saccharomyces apiculatus* or 'wild' yeasts, start the fermentation, dying after making only 4 per cent of alcohol by volume. By this time the true wine yeasts, *Saccharomyces ellipsoideus*, have begun to operate and will continue until the ethyl alcohol overpowers the yeasts at 15 to 16 per cent by volume. With light wines the sugar will probably

---

*Enzyme is derived from the Greek *zymotic*, derived in turn from *zume* leavening, yeast or other substance used to make dough ferment and rise.

have all been converted when the strength reaches 8 to 13 per cent.

All this presupposes that the wine-maker has created the right conditions. The wild yeasts and acetobacter, 'the vineyard bug' needing oxygen, can only work in the fresh air and are termed aerobic. The true wine yeasts work with or without air and are termed anaerobic. But they cannot operate below 5°C/40°F, nor above 35°C/98°F. Outside this band fermentation stops. In a southern European September it has to be restarted by cooling; in an English or German October by heating.

Modern wineries are equipped with pumps for many purposes. The must can be cooled by pumping it from bottom to top through pipes outside a vat, or through cooling radiators. Water can be pumped to form a constant spray over vats of stainless steel inside the winery; and in the United States the cooling medium is often pumped through jacketed tanks.

As a result of fermentation, the grape sugar is split up into ethyl alcohol and carbon dioxide by the enzymes contained in the yeast cells. One molecule of sugar yields two molecules of ethyl alcohol and two of carbon dioxide. The conversion is never perfect as the yeast takes some of the sugar to feed itself, leading to other by-products contributing to the flavour of the wine. During fermentation the carbon dioxide escapes, though some, which can be detected by taste, remains dissolved in the new wine.

This first fermentation, converting sugar to alcohol, is now called the alcohol fermentation to distinguish it from secondary fermentations, notably malo-lactic fermentation, that may take place later or even simultaneously.

Besides water and grape sugar, grape juice does contain a variety of sugars, acids minerals and vegetable matter in small quantities. Some of these pass to the wine with perhaps a little unfermented grape juice. Fermentation, however, creates by-products not found in the juice — other acids and alcohols and combinations of these, known as esters, all of them thought to bring about subtle differences in the flavours of wines.

Until Pasteur (1822-1895) born at Dole in the Jura and now described as the world's first bacteriologist, declared about 1857, 'No fermentation without life' the process that made wine and beer was a mystery.

To the Ancients this transformation of a sweet innocuous fruit juice, 80 per cent water, into a delectable beverage that made them merry as a grig, tight as a tick or laid them blissfully flat out under the *mensa* was a miracle attributed to one or more gods. This mystery was not wholly solved until 1903 when Edward Buchner, the German chemist awarded the Nobel prize in 1907, had discovered *enzymes.*

In recent years there has been this American (Amerine-Joslyn) definition of fermentation: 'Essentially a process of a series of reversible inter- and intra-molecular oxidation reductions, phosphorylations and an irreversible decarboxylation'.

Had I appreciated this aged 10, when pedalling two miles into Altrincham to fetch for baking the bread, 'Two penny worth of barm please' which invariably my mother had forgotten, or descending to the cellar to fill my father's beer jug from Threlfall's firkin, who knows I might now be seated in a chair of Oenology. In simpler English:

Wine is the alcoholic beverage obtained from the juice of freshly gathered grapes, the fermentation of which has been carried through in the district of its origin, and according to local tradition and practice.

Wine and Spirit Association of Great Britain

The grape

Whereas 'local traditions and practices' make the names of grapes confusing, their composition (being pulp, stalks, pips and skins), irrespective of variety or colour, simplifies wine-making.

Pulp Pulp is in three layers, outer, middle and inner. The middle one, not in contact with either pips or skins, yields the bulk of the first pressing, always held to be the best. Pulp is the same whether the grapes are red or white.

Stalks Formerly left on, the stems or stalks can make the wine bitter and for red wines are now removed by modern crushing machines. Mechanical harvesters leave them on the vine. Making white wines they remain with the skins after pressing. The *marc* is then allowed to ferment under a plastic film and is distilled in order to produce *les prestations d'alcool vinique*. This means the residues; their quantity has to be declared to guard against excessive production.

Pips If crushed, pips will also make the wine bitter. Neither the human foot when treading, nor the machine, crushes them and with red wines, they go through to the fermentation vat.

Skins Red and rosé wines acquire their colour entirely from the skins of black grapes during fermentation. Together with the juice and pips they comprise the *vendange foulé*, or in America the crush, pumped from the press to the fermentation vat. The must is the freshly pressed juice itself.

White wines need no colouring and are made by fermenting the juice alone. The skins and pips remain in the press to be removed for distilling into either *eau-de-vie de marc* or commercial spirit.

Wine-making old and new

The grapes were brought down the slopes in baskets and jettisoned into a huge open vat where four or five men trod them. It is so vividly engraved in my memory that it could well have been yesterday that the cellar master lifted me up the ladder and I jumped into the must with the juice up to my knees. I trod my first and last grape.

Edward Ott *Tread of Grapes, The Autobiography of a Wine Lover*

Switzerland 1925

Edward Ott is 'my vintage' — 1912. In this engaging little book he describes how in 1925, aged thirteen, he was sent from Sheffield to learn French in the family of a village pastor near Vevey in Switzerland. Apart from members of port shippers' families, I imagine few of my readers will have actually taken part in this, the oldest method of making wine. The slow, exhausting 'knees-up-Mother-Brown' action applying the weight of the human body to extract the juice without cracking the pips or bruising the stalks, which supply tannin, is still preferred to auto-vinificators at some *quintas* making port. In Vevey, centre of the Vaud district along the northern shore of Lac Léman, the trodden juice became the *tête de cuvée* and the second pressing, done with a wooden board and a screw, became the second best, *vin de presse*.

France 1984

Forced to accept the risks from bad weather in viticulture, present wine-makers leave nothing to chance in vinification. From the world's vineyards the laden lorries must not be delayed on the journey to the wineries lest the weight should damage the skins and start an uncontrolled fermentation. At the winery each load is weighed and the sugar content recorded. Buying from their members, the Co-operatives pay in proportion to sugar content and competitive member farmers await the results anxiously as the lorries come and go in quick succession.

The grapes — red or white — first pass through an *egrappoir-fouloir*, a stemmer-crusher in which a power-operated revolving screw moves them along having first removed the stalks. As a rule sufficient tannin — that astringent substance found in tea leaves left in your teapot — is derived from the skins and pips. Tannin — an essential component — enables wine to grow old gracefully from rough youth to 'grand old seigneur mellowed but not bent with age', a fanciful phrase that once embellished a Glyndebourne wine list, written by that grand old seigneur himself, André Simon.

The *egrappoir-fouloir* expels the stalks in a separate heap likely to be returned to the land in the form of fertiliser. The *pomace* — the pulp that remains after extracting the juice — can be distilled into that fiery spirit called *marc, grappa, aguardente* and *bagaçeira* in France, Italy, Spain and Portugal respectively.

White grapes pass on for pressing in a

A horizontal press. The mechanism rotates drawing the two end-plates together to crush the grapes. As the mechanism is reversed, chains break up the squashed mass of grape skins, so that they are ready to be pressed several more times.

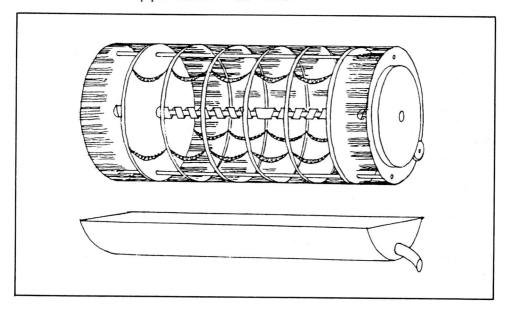

horizontal press, which is essentially a hollow metal cylinder that revolves around its horizontal axis. Two circular steel plates, one at each end, are free to move towards each other along a threaded steel shaft. The closing plates apply pressure to the mass of revolving grapes between them, squeezing concertina-fashion. As they open again an arrangement of hoops and chains breaks up any caking of the grapes. This gentle pressure extracts the juice, now called must, which collects in a trough below and is then pumped to a fermenting vat after being 'cleaned up a bit' by *débourbage*.

After the stemmer-crusher there is a parting of the ways.

White wines   Only the juice is fermented. The skins and pulp left behind will be used for distilling potable spirits or commercial alcohol.

Red wines   To make red and rosé wines the skins must be fermented with the juice to impart colour and tannin, for as long as three weeks in the case of a great long-lived claret like Château Latour. On completion of the alcoholic fermentation, 75 per cent − the 'free run wine' or *vin de goutte* (tasty wine) − is freely run into another vat or a set of casks. The residue, mainly grape skins, is then taken out and pressed in a horizontal press or a vertical press, yielding a further 25 per cent called 'press wine' or *vin de presse*, less good and kept separately so that the two qualities can be blended.

Rosé wines
For rosé wines a matter of hours suffices for the skins to achieve that delicate shade of pink.

Macération carbonique
To meet the demand for fruity, potable wines that require no ageing and to save the cost of ageing in casks, many red wines are now being made by this new method. Whole bunches of grapes, with no de-stalking, go straight into the fermentation vats, which are closed after pumping in carbon dioxide at the top. Deprived of oxygen the yeasts on the grape skins are less effective so that the enzymes inside the uncrushed grapes at the top begin their fermentation. The unbroken skins impart no colour or tannin to the wine while the lack of oxygen greatly increases its fruity flavour. Simultaneously, the grapes at the bottom of the vat, crushed by the weight of those above, undergo a normal alcoholic fermentation.

I suppose musicians might call this process a compound binary form with a tonic and a dominant key. At any rate it has led to many harmonious, light, fruity compositions from Beaujolais, the Rhône and Languedoc-Roussillon, on sale and ready to drink in a matter of months after the vintage.

Malolactic fermentation
The significance of secondary fermentation, apt to take place naturally in cask or vat after the alcohol fermentation usually in the spring when the weather became warmer, has only recently been understood. Improving wine by turning sharp malic acid (as in apples) into soft lactic acid (as in milk), it has now become an induced feature of wine-making.

A special bacteria has been developed that changes one gram of malic into 0.6 grams of lactic acid and 0.33 grams of carbonic acid. Added to the alcoholic fermentation both can proceed together; leaving it till later is less convenient, because the bacteria need warmth to operate, which may mean delaying the job until the spring. In Europe, by keeping the wine in large vats in a warm *cuvier* for some time after the yeast fermentation, it is usually made to happen naturally without any outside agency.

In the hotter places, where wines do not have much malic acid to be changed, this fermentation is pointless. But in France, to improve fine red wines and some white wines, it is being widely used. In *The Wines of St-Emilion and Pomerol,* Jeffrey Benson and Alistair Mackenzie describe malolactic fermentation as 'a necessary stage' in the development of these great clarets. In Australia, New Zealand and USA the story is the same for the finer red wines. In Germany, however, they think the fruity acidity of Mosel is best left alone, yet after a succession of poor years between 1976 and 1982, it would be interesting to have an oenologist's opinion as to whether 'Dr Malolactic's treatment' could help there.

H for Hygiene

Hygiene is as important to wine-making as to surgery. Left alone, exposed to the air, whether in a glass at home or a winery in far-flung Wangaratta, it soon becomes sour and undrinkable turning eventually to *vinaigre* (which means sour) or vinegar. And of course the hotter the temperature the greater the danger.

For wine, the great disinfectant is sulphur dioxide ('the Dettol of the wine trade', said the irrepressible Jancis Robinson) and the must will receive an early sprinkling as a precaution against oxidisation and bacteria. Occasionally after opening a bottle a strong whiff indicates the dose has been overdone; if this occurs in a restaurant, just twirl the wine around before tasting, the smell should soon go. Sulphur dioxide is now generally added in the form of a liquid

or as a powder such as potassium metabisulphite.

A winery at vintage time nowadays is no place for the spectator, who is liable to be ushered out. Most fermentation vats of wood, stainless steel, plain concrete, concrete lined with glass, tiles or enamel, are closed compartments. The temperature inside – usually 28°C/82°F to 30°C/86°F for red wines, 15°C/59°F to 20°C/68°F for white – tends to rise as the gas forces the grapes, skins and pips to the top forming a cap, the *châpeau.* In the open this attracts bacteria as it dries and it should be kept in contact with the fermenting juice by *remontage,* that is, pumping must from the bottom of the vat over it.

Each vat has a control chart on which the specific gravity is plotted, recording the rate of conversion of the sugar to alcohol. Another line records the temperature; if allowed to go under or over the required temperature range above, the fermentation will stop, a practice known as 'sticking' and sometimes as difficult to re-start as a recalcitrant lawn-mower.

S for Sugar and Strength

In the cooler regions after a poor summer the sugar in the grapes can be insufficient to make wine of normal standard. Adding sugar, to the must before or during fermentation, may then be authorised. This makes the wine stronger, but not sweeter because fermentation converts all the sugar into alcohol.

Grape, beet or cane sugar may be used, but adding water to reduce excessive acidity has been prohibited. In France permission can only be given by the Minister of Agriculture after application by the Institut National des Appellations d'Origine (INAO). The rules are strict: in

St-Emilion, for example, the maximum is three kilograms of sugar per hectolitre of must and 200 kilograms per hectare of vineyard. This practice is named chaptalisation after Jean Anton Chaptal (1756–1832) the distinguished chemist and statesman, who also introduced the metric system of weights and measures to France.

Dry, sweet and sparkling

By these methods one wine-maker can produce a surprising number of wines for different purposes. By fermenting all the sugar there are dry wines, white, red and rosé. Yet another dry white wine, made for champagne, is obtained from red grapes by separating the skins before they impart their colour to the juice.

Sweet wines can be made by applying sulphur dioxide to lower the temperature and stop the yeasts working while sugar still remains. Another way is to filter out the yeasts. With enough sugar left to start a secondary fermentation in bottle, white wine can be made into sparkling wine.

Free-run wine and press wine, white, red or rosé, can be blended in different proportions to suit different tastes at different prices. Surplus press wine can be distilled to make brandy. Perhaps Portugal should be given the last word; only there — running it free from a stone *lagar* into a part-filled tonnel of brandy — can they make port, 'the Englishman's wine', as well as those already mentioned.

With the wines safely in sterilised cask or container, like babes in cradle or cot, the wine-maker now has to look after them very carefully until they are bottled, a stage which the French appropriately call *élevage* or 'bringing up'.

Maturing in wood or glass

Traditionally wines have always been matured in wooden casks because there was no suitable alternative, This is no longer so and light wines made to be drunk within a few months can be matured in glass or tile-lined tanks and vats, with a covering of nitrogen or carbon dioxide to protect them from the air.

Most properties making fine claret and red burgundy retain the 225 litre oak *barrique**. The wines, taking tannin from the oak and air through the staves, mature slowly, their purple colour mellowing towards ruby and tawny during the customary two years before bottling. Properties like Châteaux Pétrus, Margaux and the other *premier grands crus* buy their *barriques* new each year. In 1984 each one cost 1800 francs (about £180) and Pértus, the smallest property, would have needed 700, costing £126,000. In the second-hand market they could be bought for 600 francs when two years old and 360 francs when three years old. Some proprietors buy some new each year, others second-hand. A few experiment with cement vats which are not porous. Trials have already found that wines from machine-picked grapes are not inferior to those from hand-picked grapes; others are now needed to evaluate wood and concrete.

To prevent oxidisation, casks must be meticulously topped up, adding wine of the same quality and year through the bung-hole at the top to replace losses. The glass stoppers in the bung-holes allow carbon dioxide to escape but no air to enter. Tilting the cask *bonde de côté*, left or right through 20° or so bringing the bung from the top to the side, lessens the evaporation

---

*228 litre *pièce* in Burgundy.

and the frequency of topping up, which normally is necessary two or three times a week. The losses occur because new wine contains carbon dioxide from the fermentation and new wood absorbs two or three litres of wine in each cask.

Racking
Transferring the wine to a clean sterile cask is usually necessary after three months by which time a potentially harmful sediment (lees) will have collected at the bottom of the first cask. Forcing the wine out by applying air pressure to the old cask gives a better result than a suction action. An old superstition demands a full moon, a north wind and clear weather, a combination consistent with high atmospheric pressure when the wine is least cloudy and is likely to 'fall bright'. For the modern wine-maker, coping with a programme of four rackings a year from many casks, this timing is not paramount and he is unlikely to watch the weatherman on breakfast television to alter his plans.

Fining or collage
This treatment, ridding the wine of impurities and improving stability, usually follows racking. The fining agents are gluey substances known as colloids, which attract impurities to themselves as they sink to the bottom of the cask. For wine they include bentonite, a special clay from Wyoming USA, gelatine, egg white for red wine and isinglass for white.

Filtration
Almost universally adopted, filtration is complementary to fining, not necessarily a replacement. It clarifies wine physically, removing by direct sieving or absorption the turbid material present. There are two main types of filtration. The first clarifies at a relatively early stage, removing most of the turbidity by feeding *kieselguhr* (diatomaceous earth) into the wine as it enters the filter. The second, which may follow or be used at a later stage for bottling, relies on pre-formed sheets or pads made of cellulose fibres, diatomaceous earth and other materials.

Refrigeration
From time to time potassium bitartrates and calcium tartrates appear in bottles of wine in the form of crystals looking like a small dose of Epsom salts. Wine-makers are greatly distressed that they have failed to persuade the drinkers that these are a harmless indication of robust health, which will dissolve if the bottles are stored upright in a warm place. Wine-makers now chill and filter before bottling so that the tartrates, however beneficent, do not appear at all.

Blending
It is important to understand that, at a guess, 90 per cent of wines made for sale are blended; blends of different years or from different grapes. Châteaux clarets are blends of three different grapes grown on one estate; burgundies blends from one specified grape from several estates; champagne blends of up to forty different still wines. Branded wines are blends from wherever their classification permits.

There is no stigma attached to blending; indeed the Christian Brothers, the religious body with the largest cellars in California, rightly declared long ago that, blending being an art to be perfected, they would market none other than blended; only very recently has this policy been modified.

The French term for blending is *assemblage*. How much *vin de presse* to put with the *vin de goutte*, how to give his *cuvée* uniformity when wines fermented in different vats differ — these illustrate the day-to-day problems the wine-maker has to solve. Much of course is experience, but there are some who have 'green-fingers' in the vineyard and 'purple' in the cellar. (*Coupage*, implying the sort of blending likely to benefit the blender more than his customer is a term best avoided.)

Bottling

It was 1956 when I learnt how to bottle, sitting on an upturned box in front of a hogshead of Bouchard Père et Fils Beaune in Seething Lane cellars under the Corn Exchange in London with Sid, the Cockney cellarman. His stories made me laugh so much that the Beaune must have received an extra ester or two from the tearful tartrates that rolled down my cheeks. One needs to compare the spick and span, fast, spacious Queen Elizabeth 2 and that dirty British coaster with the salt-caked smoke stack, to judge the difference between bottling now and bottling then.

Today's bottles are delivered to the winery sterilised. Bottling lines are automated; the empties move along to sterilised filling machines where the wine arrives too, possibly via a filtration plant. The supply to each bottle cuts off at the right point below the top and they move on down the line for labels, corks and capsules — all done, of course, by machines.

The human eye, aided by a bright light, is needed to spot any foreign bodies that have evaded all the wonders of modern science invented to keep them out. And believe it or not, like the gentleman in the Queen's bedroom, some inebriated earwig manages to make it now and then.

Bottling can be either hot or cold. Hot bottling involves a form of pasteurisation and is not used for fine wines which are required to age. Either heating very briefly to 80°C/176°F and then immediately cooling, or filling wine in its bottle at 50°C/122°F, kills living matter, preventing disorders such as a secondary fermentation after bottling. Cold bottling during the spring and early summer is the normal method for fine wines to ensure they develop to the best of their capability.

In a book of this size it is only possible to give an outline of 'wine: what it is, how it is made'. For a more thorough study there is a chapter with this title in Alexis Lichine's *Encyclopedia of Wines and Spirits*. Listing in detail thirteen constituents of a ripe grape, twenty more to be found in musts and another thirty-six contained in wine itself, it says that scientists have actually isolated and measured over one hundred different compounds in wine accounting for 97 to 98 per cent of its constituents. With 2 or 3 per cent still to be accounted for, this great book nevertheless concludes that final judgement of the living blood of the grape can only be made in a glass not a test-tube.

Vine nomenclature

What with countries, communes, châteaux etc. newcomers to wine may think that there are quite enough names already, without adding a set of grape names and a new term 'varietal'. Varietal is an American term for wine made wholly or chiefly (at least 75 per cent) from the grape named on the label, for example, California Chenin Blanc, New York State Chardonnay. Legislation was recently introduced requiring varietal labelling in order to combat generic labelling, which in the view of the Bureau of Alcohol, Tobacco and Firearms (the three must have been equally lethal when allotted to the same Bureau) arises when a name is so widely used that its place of origin has become irrelevant, for example, California Chablis, Australian Burgundy. Most of the best American wine-makers now follow this practice and, says Alexis Lichine's *Encyclopedia of Wines and Spirits,* 'the day when American producers cease entirely to use misappropriated and misapplied European place names and adopt varietal names for wines that are strictly American will be a bright day indeed for American wine lovers'. That day has already dawned.

All over the world in the last fifteen years new vineyards planted with European vines have sprung to life, producing and exporting wines of high quality. Some are from one sort of grape, others a blend of two or more grapes, a few from crosses of one species with another. Their producers are only too keen to describe them in terms of both the locality and the grape variety, the two main factors that determine the quality of the wine. Some examples are Australia: Semillon (Glen Elgin); Bulgaria: (Cabernet Sauvignon); California: Chardonnay (Joseph Phelps); New Zealand: Chenin Blanc (Cook's).

The new varietals make exciting news. To what extent will quality improve as their vines age, thrusting their roots deeper into 'the mineral water' that nourishes them? Tastings comparing wines of the same grape from half a dozen different countries, already bringing new interest and knowledge, will answer these questions in the fullness of time.

Grapes making white wines

Aligoté The number two white burgundy grape, making a perfumed but rather acid version of a Chardonnay except in a hot summer. Much of this wine becomes sparkling.

Blanc Fumé *see Sauvignon.*

Bual Makes rich Madeiras similar to Malmsey. Said to be the Pinot Noir from Burgundy.

Chasselas Sound wine, dry. Fendant in Switzerland, Gutedel in Germany, Knipperlé in Alsace.

Chardonnay Classic grape for white burgundy called *Beaunois* in Chablis. Variations in flavour between Chablis, Meursault and the Montrachets are due to their soils and weather. Similar but stronger wines, in bouquet and in alcohol, are being made in California, Australia and New Zealand.

Chenin Blanc (Pineau de la Loire) Classic grape of Anjou and Touraine, making the light, Sauternes-style wines of Layon and Vouvray, dry and sweet *steen* in South Africa, where results are better than in California.

Gewürztraminer (Traminer) Grown best in Alsace and Germany but doing well round the world from Yugoslavia to Australia and California; the bouquet is unique and its full, spicy, aromatic flavour goes well with smoked fish.

Grüner-Veltliner (Veltliner) Native vine of Austria disinclined to emigrate. In Vienna, its frisky wine, made by an aristocrats' co-operative, pleases the proletariat.

Johannisberg *see Rhine Riesling*

Kerner Not a familiar name on labels as yet, this is a cross between Riesling and the German red grape Trollinger, which we call Black Hamburger and visit at Hampton Court. Rather similar to Riesling it is superior in yield and must weight.

25

Malvasia (Malmsey) Best known for Malmsey Madeira, longest lived of all wines. Small crops are grown for Chianti blends, and for ordinary wines elsewhere in Italy and in Greece.

Marsanne and Roussanne Related varietals planted on the hill of Hermitage by the Rhône, making those superb dry white wines which used to be aged for at least four years and kept for ten.

Müller-Thurgau While Dr Muller's 1882 cross between Riesling and Sylvaner or Riesling and Riesling is still being disputed, growers have been planting away until his creation occupies almost a third of Germany's area under vines. Riesling is the great grape, Müller-Thurgau more prolific; blending them together more profitable. A success in New Zealand, in England the pattern is uncertain; does well in West Sussex but not necessarily elsewhere.

Muscadet Said to have been brought from Burgundy, this grape gives its name to the dry white wine of Nantes, inexpensive and so good with Atlantic sea-foods. (A lesser wine is made there from Gros Plant vines called Folle Blanche in Cognac, where it is distilled into the finest of all brandies.)

Muscat (many varieties) Grown in all the Mediterranean countries, the result is invariably sweet smelling and tasting dessert wines. In southern France some are mis-named *vin doux naturel*, having been fortified with brandy. The really distinguished exception, Muscat d'Alsace, is dry and truly natural.

Palomino (Listan) The sherry grape planted extensively around Jerez.

Pedro Ximénez Makes the dry Montilla-Moriles in this district south of Cordoba. Planted too at Jerez, where its wine is sweetened and used for making dry sherries sweeter. Also found in Australia, California and South Africa for sherry-type wines.

Pinot Blanc (Pinot Bianco in Italy) Better than Aligoté, not as good as Chardonnay, makes a cheap wine in Alsace and in Italy. Grown too in Champagne, California and Eastern Europe.

Pinot Gris (Tokay d'Alsace) Named Tokay in Alsace, Tocai in north-east Italy and Rülander in Germany, its fruity wines of Baden-Württemberg are popular locally.

Pinot Noir This, with a little Pinot Meunier, is the black grape that makes white wine for champagne, but it is rightly far more famous as the classic grape for red Côte d'Or burgundies. Planted in Sancerre the resultant reds and rosés are far from exciting. Called Spätburgunder or Blauburgunder it yields indifferent red wines to the Germans at Assmannshausen and to the mixture of Germans and Italians of the Alto Adige south of the Brenner Pass. Elsewhere to date results do not compare with Côte d'Or burgundy.

Riesling (Rhein or Rhine) This (Rhine) Riesling, cultivated in Mosel-Saar-Ruwer, Rheingau, Rheinhessen and Rheinpfalz, is a different and markedly superior grape to all other Rieslings. Three alternative names are Johannisberg, Riesling Renano (Italy) and White Riesling (California), where good wines, some late-harvest, can now be made. Australian and New Zealand prospects are promising.

Riesling Italico, Laski or Welsch Riesling. A poor relation of the real Riesling above, this variety makes sound medium dry wines in northern Italy, Yugoslavia and Eastern

Europe. (Although pronounced 'Rees-ling' none of these names are related to the inmates of that pre-1915 Castle Coch vineyard near Cardiff.)

Sauvignon (Blanc Fumé) Dry, crisp and 'smokey' Sancerre and Pouilly-Fumé of the Loire all manner of Graves and the luscious sweet Sauternes of Bordeaux — suffice to call Sauvignon the white rose of the white wine garden. Increasingly successful in the new wine countries too.

Savagnin Met only in the Jura making the golden, sherry-like *vin jaune.*

Scheurebe Herr George Scheu crossed Riesling with Sylvaner in 1916 but Scheurebe wines took until the 1950s to reach Britain. The tremendous bouquet astonished the trade. Plantings, mostly in the Rheinpfalz, occupy about four per cent of the country's vineyard area and are used to sweeten and strengthen other wines.

Semillon Invaluable as a late-harvest grape to blend with Sauvignon for white Bordeaux, especially Graves and Sauternes. Produces full dry wines on its own in Australia.

Sercial Thought to be a Riesling, makes the dry, aperitif Madeira with this name.

Seyval Blanc Franco-American hybrid that does well in England and on the eastern coast of USA.

Sylvaner (Silvaner in Germany) Apart from Spain and Portugal I cannot think of a wine country that makes no wine from this grape. Inexpensive and good in Alsace and Rheinpfalz; very good in the Alto Adige. In California, where they are in need of *Appellation Contrôlée*, they call it Franken Riesling.

Tokay d'Alsace *see Pinot Gris.*

Traminer *see Gewürztraminer.*

Trebbiano (Ugni Blanc) Principal white grape in the Veneto (Soave), for Tuscan white wines, and in Umbria (Orvieto). Known as Ugni Blanc in France, and as St. Emilion in Cognac, where its wine is distilled.

Verdicchio Italian grape of the Marches, inland from Ancona, making the fresh fragrant Adriatic wine of this name.

Vernaccia Italian grape met in Verona, Sardinia and above all in Siena as the dry 12° Vernaccia do San Gimignano, the hill town with the towers that every tourist loves.

Viognier Rhône valley grape making the dry white wines of Condrieu, south of Vienne, including the famous Château Grillet, $4\frac{1}{2}$ acres and the smallest appellation in France.

Weissburgunder *see Pinot Blanc*

Grapes making red wine
Barbera Grown principally on the hillsides from Asti to Cuneo giving its name to Piedmont's popular Turin 'tipple'.

Blauburgunder *see Pinot Noir.*

Cabernet Alone on a label could be a blend of the two great varieties below, which increasingly are making fine red wines in many parts of the globe. (From lesser wine countries it could denote no more than a red wine.)

Cabernet Franc Fruity and perfumed, this is the sole grape for Bourgueil, Chinon, the best Anjou rosés and some lesser Loire wines. In Bordeaux its fruity second fiddle to Cabernet Sauvignon's violin and Merlot's cello performs the great claret concerto. Known as Bouchet in St. Emilion, it contributes about one third to Merlot's two thirds.

Cabernet Sauvignon Great grape of the

Médoc and Graves supplying the characteristics and the tannin that achieve claret's incomparable excellence with age. In California, Australia, South Africa, New Zealand (probably) and Bulgaria it appears to have no rivals.

Carigan(e) Widely planted in Languedoc-Roussillon with good results from *Macération carbonique.*

Cinsault Fruity Rhône grape making a fair wine added in small quantities, with Syrah and others, to blend many red Rhône wines. In South Africa, Pinotage (the Cinsault-Pinot Noir cross) now extensively planted, ages well and is highly esteemed.

Dolcetto Dry red wines of fair quality from Asti, Cuneo, Canelli and other Piedmont places.

Gamay Rightly renowned for Beaujolais but not elsewhere. Gamay de la Loire and Gamay de l'Ardèche are relatively very ordinary; and in California Gamay Beaujolais is Pinot Noir not even Gamay.

Grenache A good constituent of Château-neuf-du-Pape, associated with Banyuls on the Mediterranean Franco-Spanish frontier, grown in the Midi, and in Spain as Alicante.

Grignolino (Kadarka in Eastern Europe) Red and rosé wines in northern Italy. Red wines in Hungary and further east are apt to have an earthy flavour.

Merlot Secondary grape in the flat Médoc and in Graves with a 20 per cent share; primary grape in hilly St-Emilion and Pomerol with about 70 per cent. Makes a good local wine in Italy and Switzerland but nothing remarkable reported as yet from the Southern hemisphere.

Mourvèdre Met — often with Cinsault — in the Rhône valley, the Midi and Provence;

important component, with Grenache, Syrah and Cinsault, in the nine different grapes that go to make the best Châteauneuf-du-Pape.

Nebbiolo (Spanna) The best red grape of northern Italy making Barolo and Barbaresco. Slow growing, late to ripen, imparts these two qualities to these two wines.

Pinot Noir The sole permissible black grape for true red burgundy from the Côte d'Or and the Côte Chalonnais. Used quite differently in Champagne to make a white wine from red grapes to blend with Chardonnay, a white wine from white grapes. (See also white grapes, page 26.)

Portugeiser Poor quality red and rosé from Germany. A Rhine maiden, it seems, reminiscent of Wordworth's poor Lucy: 'A maid whom there were none to praise and very few to love.'

Pinotage A black South African grape, from a 1922 cross between Pinot Noir and Cinsault, having some success in Australia and New Zealand.

Sangiovese The mainstay of Chianti (70 per cent) and of lesser wines in Central Italy.

Spätburgunder *see Pinot Noir.*

Syrah (Shiraz) Classic grape of the Rhône valley giving solid character and long life to Côte Rotie and Hermitage in the granite soil from Vienne to Valence. In the lighter stony soil of the southern half needs augmenting with Grenache to bring distinction similar to Châteauneuf-du-Pape. Blending with Cabernet Sauvignon shows promise in Australia.

Zinfandel California's black grape found nowhere else; makes a sound, red fruity table wine of fair to fine quality.

France

I would not yet exchange thy sullen skies,
And fields without a flow'r,
For warmer France
With all her vines.
William Cowper (1731-1800)

A patriotic old person the author of John Gilpin! One wonders what he would say to his compatriots riding in today's horseless carriages for the Channel ports and the land where those vines have reigned supreme ever since the Romans first encouraged their cultivation. Not until 1976, at that now historical tasting in Paris where, tasting blind, an expert French panel pronounced the Cabernet Sauvignons from California superior to the finest first growth clarets of Bordeaux had that supremacy ever been challenged. Always logical, the Frenchmen must have muttered, 'If you can't beat 'em, join them', for Moët & Chandon were soon ensconsed in the Napa Valley and Baron Philippe de Rothschild of Château Mouton-Rothschild formed an *entente cordiale* with his erstwhile competitor, Robert Mondavi, which has now born potable fruit as Opus One, see page 190.

Matchless wine-maker

Making wines in over eighty of her ninety continental *départements* to the tune of seventy-five million hectolitres a year, some of them of unmatched quality, France's position is unlikely to be seriously challenged. Italy's output is much the same. Their combined 150,000 million hectolitres are about half the world's annual production. While Italy's best wines do not seriously rival those of France, a fair proportion of her seventy-five million hectolitres crosses the frontier to make up Jean Pierre's daily litre, formerly supplied by Algeria and Tunisia before their independence. EEC law now forbids blending wines of a third country with EEC wines.

Three-quarters of the French total is *vin ordinaire, vin de consommation courante* – ordinary wine for current consumption, 'plonk' to the Australians, pleasing gullet more that palate, now officially designated *vin de table* in EEC legislation. Labelled *vin rouge* or *vin blanc,* with strengths printed alongside (9°, 10° or 11°) litre bottles abound in French supermarkets and increasingly in our own. The remaining quarter are the fine wines, now designated quality wines in EEC legislation.

Making the rules

A hundred years ago there were no rules; even in Bordeaux, Rhône wines being

France General

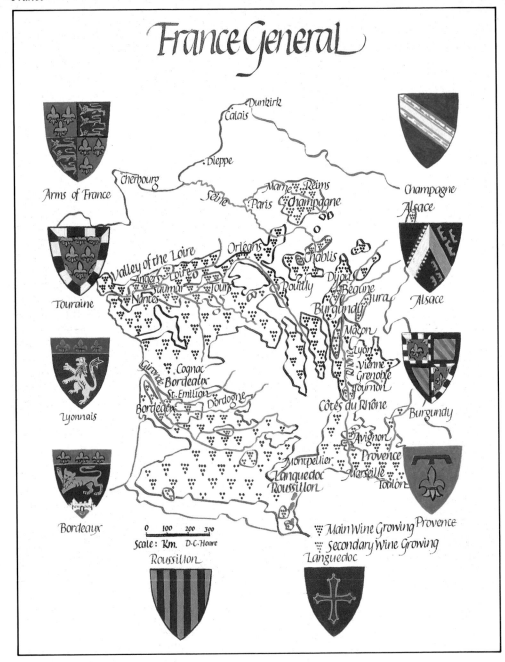

Arms of France

Touraine

Lyonnais

Bordeaux

Champagne

Alsace

Burgundy

Provence

Roussillon

Languedoc

Dunkirk
Calais
Dieppe
Cherbourg
Marne · Reims
Paris Champagne
Seine
Valley of the Loire Orléans Chablis
Angers Loire Dijon
Saumur Tours Pouilly Beaune
Nantes Burgundy Jura
Mâcon
Lyon
Cognac Vienne
Gironde Bordeaux Grenoble
St. Emilion Tournon
Bordeaux Dordogne Côtes du Rhône
Avignon
Provence
Montpellier Marseille
Languedoc Toulon
Roussillon

0   100   200   300
Scale : Km.   D.C.Hoare

🌿 Main Wine Growing
🌿 Secondary Wine Growing

plentiful were openly blended with claret because the public were alleged to like that. But after the destruction of the vineyards by oidium and the phylloxera and of the French economy by the First World War, reconstruction was so costly that makers of fine wines needed protection from imitators. The growers of Châteauneuf-du-Pape first made a start which led, in July 1935, to the establishment of the *Institut National des Appellations d'Origine des Vins et Eaux-de-Vie*, (INAO) a government body charged with controlling all aspects of the best French wines and spirits. It is composed of representatives from the ministeries of agriculture, customs, finance and justice together with growers and others from all sides of the trade. Some of its inspectors watch for fraud, others for abuses of its decrees on viticulture and vinification, virtually laws of the ministry of agriculture. INAO finances come from a small levy on every hectolitre made in France. Other countries, Germany and Italy, have since introduced their own controls adapting this system to their different circumstances.

In practice INAO's *Appellation d'Origine Contrôlée* (AC or AOC) system defining where the best wines must come from and how they should be made, worked so well that by 1945 a similar system, with less exacting rules, *Vin Délimité de Qualité Supérieure* (VDQS), could be introduced for the next best. Then, in 1973, all the rest were put under a new body, the *Office National Interprofessionel des Vins de Table*, known as the *Office du Vin*. These are also divided into two, *Vins de pays* and *Vins de table*.

The overlapping nomenclature of these four sorts (usually drunk at table they are all Vins de Table) is confusing. It needed to be acceptable to all EEC countries, hence perhaps the anomalies.

Appellation d'Origine Contrôlée (AC or AOC) this is the rating for France's first-class wines which amount to about 25 per cent of her total production. The laws specify area of origin, grape varieties, methods of production, alcoholic strength and maximum quantity per hectare. The area of each AOC varies. In Champagne it is the whole demarcated region. In Burgundy it can be the region, a part of the region, a commune or village, a vineyard or just one part of one vineyard. In Bordeaux it also starts with the region, with quality likely to increase as the appellation diminishes in size to a commune. Permissible quantity varies from region to region and can be increased or decreased by INAO locally as the year's weather may require. Forty hectolitres a hectare (445 cases of one dozen bottles) is a basic figure. The system does not guarantee quality; attempts to do this through panels of tasters are made but the supply of expert palates is insufficient for wide application and the job takes up a lot of time. There are 469 *Appellations d'Origine* all told.

Vins Délimités de Qualité Supérieure (VDQS) There are about fifty-five of these, created in 1945 for the protection and satisfaction of wine-makers in secondary localities worth identifying. Controls are less strict than for AOC, to which promotions can take place if INAO is convinced of higher quality over a long period.

In EEC terms these two classes together constitute *Vins de Qualité produits dans les régions déterminées* or VQPRD.

The appellations must be printed on

every French AOC wine label except champagne, where the word itself is both the wine and its region.

Vins de pays Created in 1973 *Vins de pays* constitute the better half of *vin ordinaire,* for which there were no laws or controls. The quality could not help being an improvement with the following requirements. The wine must now come wholly from the demarcated region named, from grape varieties specified and have a minimum alcoholic strength from 10° (Mediterranean vineyards) to 9° (Loire Valley and eastern France). But perhaps the most important step in achieving quality when making wine is to restrict the yield. In the Bordeaux AOC region, for example, red grape yield is restricted to fifty hectolitres a hectare (Haut-Médoc lower still at forty-three). The *vins de pays* figure is ninety hectolitres (just under 12,000 bottles) a hectare. Since a yield of 150 hectolitres was not unusual from one hectare, this is a notable improvement.

For daily drinking — or for drinking as often as inflation and taxation permit — *vins de pays* are to be commended.

Vins de table This is the lowest category — blended and branded wines which do not meet the standards required for *vins de pays.* The same principles of control now apply to table wines as to quality wines, though each has a different governing body. Quality wines come under INAO, table wines under the *Office du Vin.*

France's best wines, the quality wines (AOC and VDQS) represent about 25 per cent of her whole output, *vins de pays* about 10 per cent. The remaining 65 per cent is *vin de table,* mainly for making vermouth and distilling into grape brandy. Some, however, are quite good enough for the French family's daily litre, or for you and me. The red and white Piat d'Or brands in that Mâcon company's pot-shaped bottles are highly successful because the wines are carefully selected and blended.

To move an AOC or VDQS wine anywhere, from growers' to buyers' cellars for example, requires a certificate giving the quantity and full details. Though there is always the ingenious rascal bent on evading the law, INAO's controls now treat wines of different appellations in trade cellars quite separately, making it difficult to get them mixed up. Adding some Rhône wine to a Côte de Beaune appellation, an illegal practice known as 'stretching', has been known to happen in these times when demand for the latter far exceeds supply.

The following sections on the regions of France begin with Bordeaux (the most important) and move next to the Loire (the most visited), thence, roughly clockwise, to Champagne, Alsace, Burgundy, the Jura, Savoie, Provence, Languedoc - Roussillon and the South-west.

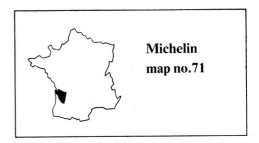

Michelin map no.71

Bordeaux ÷ The Wine Region

Médoc Landscape

Bordeaux

Angoulême Cathedral

Bordeaux Cathedral

Gironde

Médoc

St.Estèphe

Pauillac
St.Julien

Blayais

Blaye

Margaux

Bourgeais
Bourg

Haut
Médoc

Charente Marianne

Château Lafite-Rothschild

Scale in Kilometres
0 5 10 15 20 25

Coutras

St.André
de Cubzac

La Grosse Cloche

Garonne

Entre-Deux-Mers

4 1 2 6
3
14   5
7

Dordogne

St.Foy-La
Grande

Bordeaux

Léognan

14

Graves

Cérons 8
Barsac 9
10   13
Saumes

Loupiac 12
Ste.Croix
du Mont

La Réole

St.Macaire

11

Key
— roads
— wine
areas

N
W   E
S

D.C.Hoare

1 Lalande de Pomerol   8 Loupiac
2 Néac   9 Ste.Croix du Mont
3 Pomerol   10 Cérons
4 Fronsac   11 Sauternes
5 Côtes de Castillon   12 Côtes de Bordeaux
6 Appellation St Emilion 13 Barsac
7 Saint Emilion   14 Premièrs Côtes de Bordeaux

Ruined 14 Abbey at St Emilion

33

Bordeaux

Land under vine   100,000 hectares (248,000 acres) of which 78,000 AOC. Black grapes 57,000, white grapes 21,000
Number of vineyards   20,000
Production (Annual Average)   4 million hectolitres (41.7 million cases, 500 million bottles)
Fillings   Red 65 per cent, white 35 per cent
Exported   Red 22 per cent, white 17 per cent (Of all French wines about 20 per cent are exported and about 20 per cent of all AOC wines are exported)
Employed in wine   60,000 people (1 in 6 of Gironde workers)
Bottlings   About 70 per cent of wines exported leave the region in bottles
Reserves   About 13 million hectolitres (1,625 million bottles) lie in the region at any one time; 11 kept by growers, 2 by shippers.

Best Customers
1   Belgium
2   Netherlands
3   USA
4   Great Britain
5   West Germany
6   Switzerland

The Bordeaux Barrique holds 225 litres = 25 dozen cases of 75-centilitres bottles.
A Tonneau = 4 Barriques = 100 cases.
The wooden Tonneau no longer exists but the term remains as the traditional sales measure. In Burgundy it is a *pièce*, a hogshead of 228 litres.

Bordeaux is the world's most important wine region. No other can match the combination of so compact a region with the variety and overall quality of its wines. Imagine planning a dinner party. There is an enormous choice at different prices for every course: dry white wines from different parts for the aperitif and the first course, whether it be hors d'œuvres or oysters, château clarets by the thousand (and all manner of white wines too) for poultry, game or butcher's meat, and finally incomparable sweet Sauternes as good with cheese as it is with a pudding or dessert.

Lying on the left bank of the Garonne, some forty miles inland from the Atlantic, Bordeaux is the city of the Gironde, the largest French *département*. The Gironde is also the tidal estuary, 37 miles long by up to 7 miles wide from the confluence of the two rivers, Garonne and Dordogne, to the open sea beyond Royan. Gironde is derived from *hirondelle* a swallow and although André Simon described the inhabitants as 'close on a million, a large number of them ever-thirsty souls', I think *hirondelle* refers only to our feathered friends. The rivers' confluence is said to trace a swallow's tail and it is around the two rivers and their estuary that most of the great châteaux are to be found. Notice too on the map how the Gironde flows roughly north; if an east to west line is drawn through the centre of Bordeaux, the red wines nearly all lie to the north and the white to the south.

Conseil Interprofessional des Vins de Bordeaux (CIVB) is the region's governing body, operating from Cours de XXX Juillet. Tel: (56) 44.37.82, known as the *Maison du Vin* on the corner of the Allées Tourny facing the theatre. Open to the public. Visits can be arranged and wines tasted.

New bottles From 1984 the word Bordeaux and the city's emblem will be embossed on a new 75 centilitres official bottle, light green for white wines, dark for red wines. Its use however, is not compulsory until 1 January 1989.

GRAPES AND THEIR PROPORTIONS – SOME EXAMPLES

Ch. Mouton-Rothschild *1er Cru Pauillac*	Petit Verdot I	Cab Sauv 77	Cab Franc 10	Merlot 12
Ch. La Mission Haute-Brion *1er Cru Classé Graves*		Cab Sauv 70	Cab Franc 5	Merlot 25
Ch. Ausone *1er Cru St-Emilion* (Côtes)			Cab Franc 52	Merlot 48
Ch. Pétrus *1er Cru Pomerol*			Cab Franc 5	Merlot 95
Ch. Giscours *3eme Cru Margaux*		Cab Sauv 66		Merlot 34
Ch. Soutard *Grand Cru St-Emilion* (Côtes)		Cab Sauv 5	Cab Franc 30	Merlot 65
Ch. L'Endos *Grand Cru Pomero*			Cab Franc 20	Merlot 80

DISTRICTS AND APPELLATIONS

It is not surprising that wines like Bourg and Fronsac were preferred to those of the Médoc in the eighteenth century, when wines were not aged in bottle, but drunk after cask maturation. I, for one would much prefer to drink a mature Fronsac, a young Bourg or Blaye, even a young Premières Côtes, than an immature Médoc.

— *Bordeaux,* David Peppercorn

Discussing red wines in his prize-winning paperback, David Peppercorn's opinion is consoling. His preference has become a necessity for many claret lovers now that the classed growths of Bordeaux cost at least £6 a bottle. The right bank of the Gironde was in fact a thriving vineyard long before the Médoc was even planted, so it is appropriate to begin any survey with its northernmost appellation, *Premières Côtes de Blaye.* Then, circling upstream in more of a U than a circle, we can make the U-turn at Sauternes, finally reaching the Médoc, two miles across the estuary from the point where we started. First, however, there are the two lowest appellations.

Bordeaux, Bordeaux Supérieur

Red wines can be either of these, minimum strengths 10° and 10.5° respectively. In a good year all red Bordeaux reaches 11° so Supérieur is likely to depend on the skill of the *négociant-eleveur,* whose name is on the label. Price really is the only guide. For dry white wines the appellation is only Bordeaux; for sweet white wines there is no Bordeaux only Bordeaux Supérieur.

Bourg and Blaye (red)

Usually considered together these are primarily red wine districts, Côtes de Bourg and Premières Côtes de Blaye. Bourg, though minute compared to Blaye, is thick with Merlot and Cabernet Franc particularly on the slopes near the Gironde surrounding the old port. The town of Blaye is also an old port where a car ferry crosses to Lamarque in the Médoc. Wines from the better Châteaux with modern equipment are good drinking when three to four years old. Among the best I personally recall was Château l'Escadre 1979 from Peter Dominic at £3.95 in 1983.

Blaye (white)

Blayais production of dry white, fresh and fruity wines augments that of Entre-deux-Mers and the more aromatic

BOURG AND BLAYE

Bourg	Tayac
de Barbe	Verger
Guerry	
du Bousquet	**Blaye**
Coubet	Barbé
Croute-Charlus	Bourdieu
Eyquem	Chante-Alouette
Guionne	Grand-Barrail
Haut Combes	des Graves
Mendoce	Les Gruppes de Pivert
Mille-Secousses	Haut Sociondo
Plaisance	L'Escadre
Poliane	Loumede
Rouselle	Le Menaudat
Rousset	Puy-Benet-Boffort
de Samonac	Segonzac
Sauman	Videau

FRONSAC AND CANON – FRONSAC

Cotes de Canon-Fronsac	Mazeris
Canon	Mazeris Belle Vue
Canon de Brem	Moulin Pey Labrie
Junayme	**Fronsac**
Vrai-Canon-Bouché	Bourdieu-La-Valade
Vray-Canon-Boyer	La Dauphine
Belloy	Jeandeman
Coustelle	La Lagüe
Gaby	Mayne Vieil
du Gazin	Rouet
Grand Renouil	Tasta
Haut Mazeris	des Tonnelles
La Marche	Trois Croix
Mausse	Villars
	Vincent

Graves. All three appear in Bordeaux light green bottles.

Fronsac and Canon-Fronsac (red)

Writing in 1951 H. Warner Allen described the Fronsacais wines as 'attractive in their honest simplicity', before moving smartly on to Pomerol and St. Emilion. The wooded hill by the Dordogne and its tributary the Isle, makes robust clarets prescribed by old time physicians to restore their patients to rude health. Hugh Johnson's *Wine Companion* lists some thirty châteaux with owners names, acreage and production in cases.

St. Emilion

At Libourne on the Dordogne, twenty miles east of Bordeaux, the Petits Châteaux are left behind as we meet the Grand Crus of St. Emilion and Pomerol. The gentle hills 200 feet high above the Dordogne make these districts more attractive than the flat scrubby Médoc. Libourne is the commercial centre, originally built in 1268 by Roger de Leyburn as a fortified town, whence wines were shipped from the quays by the

bridge until motor transport took over.

The charming old walled town of St. Emilion is only four miles to the west surrounded by vineyards, some coming up to the walls.

To the nineteenth-century Bordeaux merchants the Médoc and Graves were accessible and chic, leaving Pomerol and St. Emilion virtually out of sight, out of mind. Thus, when the 1855 classification was made for the Paris Exhibition, their omission was partly snobbery and partly that the *courtiers* (brokers) basing their order of merit on prices paid for the respective châteaux wines over many years, all came from the Médoc and knew nothing of matters eastwards of Bordeaux. When in 1954 a St. Emilion classification was

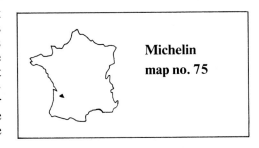

Michelin map no. 75

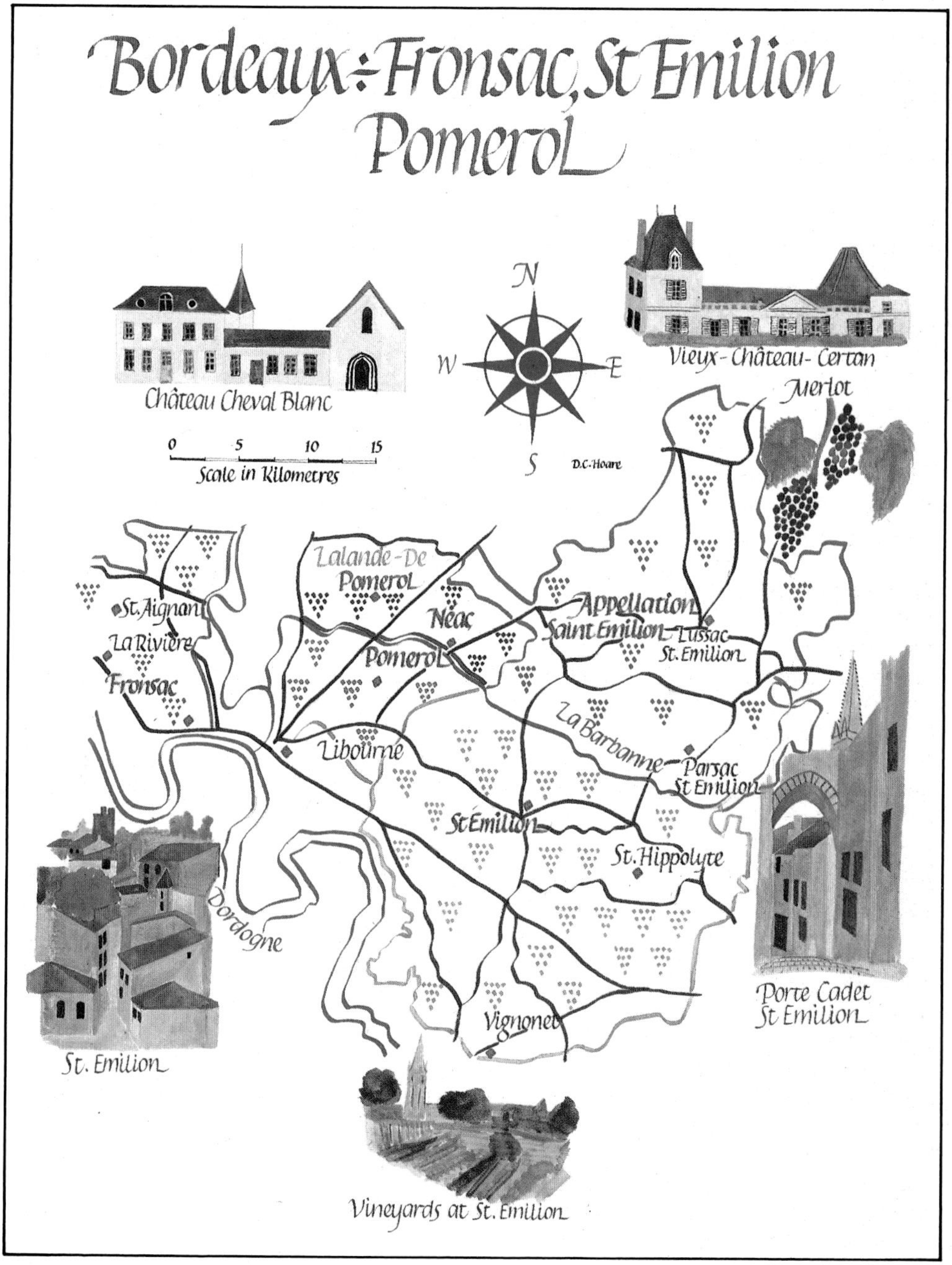

Bordeaux: Fronsac, St Emilion Pomerol

Château Cheval Blanc

Scale in Kilometres
0   5   10   15

N
W   E
S

D.C. Hoare

Vieux-Château-Certan

Merlot

St. Aignan
La Rivière
Fronsac

Lalande-De Pomerol

Néac
Pomerol

Libourne

Appellation
Saint Emilion — Lussac St. Emilion

La Barbanne

Parsac St Emilion

St Émilion

St. Hippolyte

Vignonet

St. Emilion

Dordogne

Porte Cadet St Emilion

Vineyards at St. Emilion

made, prices fetched at auctions between the wars had established Châteaux Ausone and Cheval Blanc as the equals of the Médoc *Premier Grands Crus*. In the St. Emilion classification they are a separate part of the *Premiers Grands Crus Classés*, which precedes some seventy *Grands Crus Classés*. Add to these the wines of outlying parishes — Puisseguin-St. Emilion, Lussac-St. Emilion, Montagne-St. Emilion, St. George-St. Emilion, Parsac-St. Emilion — and the total reaches five million cases, half from these parishes, equal to that of the Médoc and Graves combined.

To the expert, St. Emilion wines taste different. Apart from soil and climate, the Merlot (not the Cabernet Sauvignon) is the principal grape. Moreover, those on gravel (Graves St. Emilion) at the western end differ from those on the slopes (Côtes St. Emilion) at the eastern end.

Pomerol

After St. Emilion's five million cases, Pomerol's 330,000 represent the output of a small commune such as St-Julien in the Médoc. The modest châteaux cluster together on either side of N89 running north-east from Libourne. If there was a classification it might comprise forty *Premiers Crus*, twenty *Grands Crus* with perhaps a dozen more at Lalande-de-Pomerol, leaving out as many again, which are as small as one hectare.

Grown in 80 per cent clay/20 per cent gravel, the 'mineral water' for these old Merlot vines has a touch of stony iron oxide causing the wines to be variously described as 'the burgundies of Bordeaux', 'velvety fatness', 'rich and gentle', while the bouquet which was truffles in Warner Allen's day has become blackcurrants, grilled almonds, roasted coffee, cocoa, ripe plum, honey and even cream. Good travellers it would seem! Collecting smells world wide from the woods of Perigord to the farms of south Devon that used to fill Dartmouth cadets with cream teas.

Château Pétrus, now the world's most expensive claret, has climbed to world fame from its 1878 Paris exhibition gold medal, yet in 1959, when Calvet in Bordeaux gave us the last bottle of their 1929 at a memorable lunch, its fame had gone little further than Bordeaux. The late owner, Madame Loubat, with the highly professional aid of Pierre Moueix, who added four hectares making 11.5, brought Pétrus to the top. The story (and that of its neighbour Trotanoy) is told and illustrated in Serena Sutcliffe's *Great Vineyards and Winemakers*.

Côtes de Castillon (Red).

East of St. Emilion, where the English lost the battle to stay in France in 1453, these Dordogne slopes provide good red wines for blending. A few proprietors bottle, and Côtes de Castillon on a label usually indicates good value. Côtes de Francs is an extension to the north.

Entre-Deux-Mers (White).

'Between two seas', the seas being the rivers Garonne and Dordogne, this region has an appellation only for dry white Bordeaux.

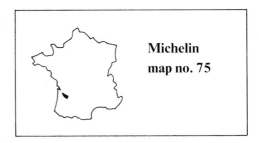

Michelin map no. 75

Bordeaux ÷ Entre-Deux-Mers

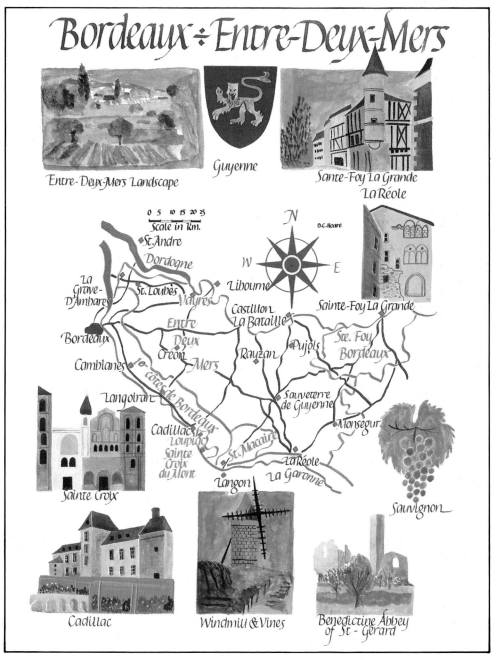

Entre-Deux-Mers Landscape

Guyenne

Sante-Foy La Grande
La Réole

0 5 10 15 20 25
Scale in Km.

St.Andre

Dordogne

La
Grave-
D'Ambares

St.Loubès

Velyres

Libourne

Castillon
La Bataille

Sainte-Foy La Grande

D.C.Hoare

N

W   E

Bordeaux

Entre

Deux

Créon

Mers

Rayzan

Pujols

Ste. Foy
Bordeaux

Camblanes

Côtes de Bordeaux

Langoiran

Sauveterre
de Guyenne

Monsegur

Cadillac
Loupiac
Sainte
Croix
du Mont

St.Macaire

La Réole

Langon

La Garonne

Sauvignon

Sainte Croix

Cadillac

Windmill & Vines

Benedictine Abbey
of St - Gerard

By road Libourne on the Dordogne to Cadillac on the Garonne is about forty miles, a pretty run via Créon through wooded hills and vineyards. In the 1970s the sales of these dry white wines more than doubled, largely because having joined the EEC, British importers had to sell the fresh, fruity dry wine in place of the medium sweet with which the name Entre-Deux-Mers had become associated when previously they had disregarded the AOC laws. The best are blends of Semillon and Sauvignon grapes, bottled in the spring after the vintage for drinking within a year. Other appellations are: Graves Vayreys on the western bank of the Dordogne — dry white wines; Ste-Foy-Bordeaux, an extension of Entre-deux-Mers eastwards along the south bank of the Dordogne — sweet white wines; St-Macaire, an extension eastwards along the north bank of the Garonne from St-Croix-du-Mont — sweet white wines.

Premières Côtes de Bordeaux (Sweet white and red)

This narrow strip, thirty miles long and only two wide, clinging to the right bank of the Garonne from Cadillac downstream to a point just beyond Bordeaux, has two appellations, one for red, the other for sweet white wines. The sweet white wines are excelled by those of Loupiac and St-Croix-de-Mont, neighbours on the same bank upstream, which can be as good as wines labelled Sauternes from the other side of the river. The black grape plantings, however, have been increased, making good drinking from wines three to seven years old. The advice of David Peppercorn in *Bordeaux* is that any bottle with a property name (for example Château Roquebrune CB *1er Côtes de Bordeaux* 1987) could be a pleasant surprise at a modest price.

Cerons (Sweet white and dry wines)

Crossing the Garonne over the bridge from Cadillac leads immediately into the village of Cerons, permitted to make sweet white wines under that name, which are not as good as those of Loupiac or St-Croix-du-Mont across the river. Being in the Graves region it prefers to make dry white wine instead, which can be labelled Graves.

Sauternes

'If Graves is the chocolate, then Sauternes is the cream in the Bordeaux whipped cream walnut', declared the first *Wine Mine* in 1959. To which the Château proprietors today might add, 'Pretty sour cream too, judged solely by our lack of profits'. Five minutes in a car from Cérons, Sauternes has five communes: Barsac, Bommes, Fargues, Preignac and Sauternes occupying an area only seven miles by four. The district is an enclosure within Graves; Barsac, which was famous before the Sauternes appellation was introduced, can be labelled as such, or as Sauternes.

Sauternes, the finest sweet wine of France, if not the world, is made — like Bordeaux's dry white wines — from Semillon and Sauvignon grapes, the yield being restricted to 25 hectolitres a hectare

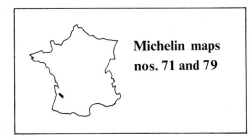

Michelin maps nos. 71 and 79

Bordeaux ÷ Graves, Sauternes

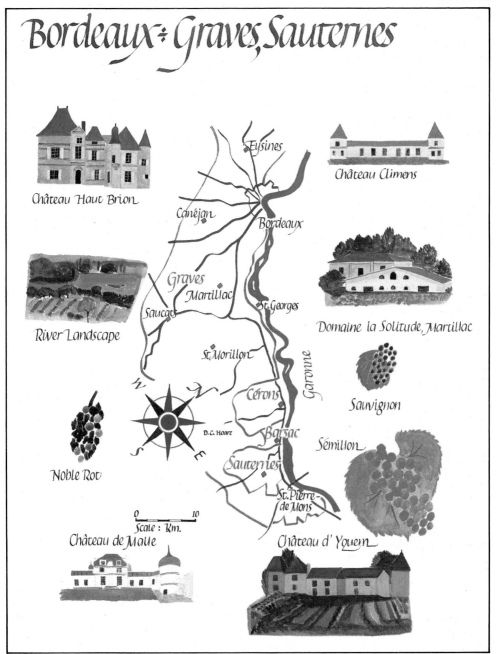

Château Haut Brion

Château Climens

Canéjan

Eysines

Bordeaux

Graves

Martillac

St. Georges

Saucats

River Landscape

St. Morillon

Domaine la Solitude, Martillac

Sauvignon

Garonne

Cérons

D.C. Hoare

Barsac

Sémillon

Noble Rot

Sauternes

St. Pierre
de Mons

0   10
Scale : Km.

Château de Malle

Château d' Yquem

against forty hectolitres for the other white wines, whether Graves or Loupiac. Autumn warmth in conjunction with some humidity from the Garonne and Ciron, its little tributary, gives rise to a mould, called *pourriture noble*, the noble rot which disfigures the grapes that are purposely left unpicked when fully ripe. *Botrytis cinerea*, this mould or fungus, penetrates the skins to feed on the juice without actually breaking them, combining with the sun to concentrate the sugar in the grapes as they slowly turn to mouldy raisins.

At Château d'Yquem 120 pickers are divided into three groups. In a bad year when the grapes over-ripen and rot unevenly, they may have to go through the vineyard ten times; in good years perhaps only five. Working in pairs, an old hand takes a learner to show which ones to pick, for there can be grey rot too, caused by rain.

The grapes are pressed three times, the third (22/23 per cent alcohol) being better than the first (around 19 per cent). Must from these three pressings then ferments for four to five weeks in new oak casks, finishing at 13.5 per cent with 300 to 350 grams of sugar per litre left in the wine. Then comes three and a half years of maturing in 225 litre casks, racked every three months and topped up weekly to replace evaporation loss which could reach 22 per cent. Other châteaux follow the same procedure less meticulously; a minimum strength of 13°, with Baumé scale sweetness 2.5° to 5°.

This perfect combination of alcohol and sweetness, unique to Sauternes, partly explains why the growers accept the risk of failure three or four years in ten, instead of allotting only 5 or 10 per cent of their vineyard to this great dessert wine (as the Germans do with Beeren-Auslese and Trockenbeeren-Auslese). The other reason is that there is already enough white Bordeaux from the normal harvest without a contribution from Sauternes.

In the EEC true Sauternes must be made by the method described. Do not expect this to apply to wines from outside France labelled Sauternes; indeed, even in France chaptalisation of normally ripe grapes will make sweet wines, which the unscrupulous might illegally describe as Sauternes.

My own reaction to my first visit to Château d'Yquem was sheer astonishment that grape juice could be transformed into such a luscious, non-cloying golden nectar; and I give my guests Coutet, Climens, Suduiraut with almost the same satisfaction. Fine, cold Sauternes, best drunk between five and twenty years old, can begin with the cheese and continue with dessert; but two glasses at most per person! I recall advising a friend to take a sea-sick pill if he contemplated half a bottle of fine Sauternes to himself. He forgot, vowing later always to share a bottle between six to eight people.

In recent times only 1961, 1962, 1966, 1967, 1970, 1971, 1975, 1976, 1982 and 1983 have been satisfactory and dessert wines a luxury few felt like affording. *Crus classés* auction prices have been those of *Cru Bourgeois* clarets. Now, with great vintages in 1982 and 1983, the future looks much better for Sauternes.

Graves

Graves means gravel and from Sauternes a gravel soil runs along the left bank of the Garonne past Bordeaux and on through the Médoc. The district, some thirty-five miles long and a dozen wide, ends where the Médoc begins on the northern outskirts of the city. It is the oldest of Bordeaux's vineyards; Château Pape-Clément first belonged to the fourteenth-century bishop, who became Clement V, first of the Avignon Popes; Samuel Pepys (1633–1703) drank in London 'a sort of French wine called 'Ho-Bryen', which was the claret of Château Haut-Brion, easy to export from its position less than two miles from the city centre, and so good that those compiling the Médoc classification of 1855 felt compelled to add this great Graves to their three first growths, Margaux, Latour and Lafite-Rothschild.

Eighty years later an American banker, Clarence Dillon, was needed to rescue it from dereliction. Today a football fan could rightly call Haut-Brion the Liverpool of the Red Graves league and La Mission-Haut-Brion across the road, the Manchester United, whose Matt Busby was the late Henri Woltner. Of the thirteen châteaux, next would come Domaine de Chevalier, Pape-Clément and Haut-Bailly ranking with Médocs like the Léovilles; the others being comparable in merit and price with the third, fourth and fifth growths. They are all about a dozen miles south of Bordeaux marked on Michelin Map 71. Most other red wines of Graves are relatively ordinary, or the properties rather small. One exception – close to Haut Bailly and Carbonnieux – is La Louvière, a fine eighteenth-century château where replantings have led on average to 4000 cases of excellent white and 2000 of red a year.

Among the wine in the white 'league' quality is high but individual production low, except for Carbonnieux (14,400 cases) and Olivier (7680 cases). These dry Semillon-Sauvignon wines age well and are very pleasant alternatives to white burgundy, Haut-Brion and Laville-Haut-Brion being the counterparts of Puligny and Chassagne-Montrachet's best sites.

The Médoc
Classification 1855. (Page 46)
So we reach the land of the greatest clarets running along the left bank of the Gironde from Bordeaux to the Atlantic at Pointe de Grave opposite Royan. 'More delicate and harmonious, bouquet, aroma, body all blending into a whole that transcends its component parts, claret achieves the highest perfection of all wines ever made. Its charms are never sensationally obvious, yet all the more fascinating for their elusive nature. The connoisseur must be gifted with, or try to develop the acutest senses to enjoy fully those subtle shades of taste and fragrance which elude definition.'

That is a precis of H. Warner Allen's masterly 1951 introduction to the Médoc when a mere handful of people wanted to be connoisseurs. Now thousands do. The majority, finding the *Crus classés* beyond their means, may think it a load of 'claret-wallop'. But Warner Allen goes on to stress how the fame of the Médoc also rests on 'a vast abundance of palatable beverage wines that accompanies the select production of the finest *crus*'. In short the *bourgeois supérieurs, bons bourgeois* and *bourgeois ordinaires*, categories since classified together as one.*

The viticultural Médoc, rather smaller than the geographical, runs from Blanquefort on the outskirts of Bordeaux to

---

*H. Warner Allen CBE (1881–1968), son of a Captain RN and Editor of *The Morning Post* 1925–1928 was a distinguished 1914–1918 war correspondent, who covered the wine front with at least ten erudite books between 1924 and 1954. He lived at a place called Sotwell.

Bordeaux : Médoc

Merlot

Soulac

Bordeaux

Cabernet Sauvignon

Church of St. Estèphe

Queyrac

Médoc

Béggdan

St. Christoly-de Médoc

Blaignan

Lesparre

Potensac

St. Yzans

Saint Seurin de Cadourne

Château Siran

Vertheuil

Cissac

Saint Sauveur

Saint Estèphe

Pauillac

Scale : Kms.

0   5   10

Saint Laurent de Médoc

Haut Médoc

Saint Julien

Beycheveille

Cussac

Château Branaire - Ducru

Lamarque

Listrac

Moulis

Arcins

N

Avensan

Margaux

Cantenac Labarde

Château Latour

W   E

Arsac

Macau

Lydon

Dordogne

Garonne

Le Pian Médoc

S

D.C. Hoare

Château Margaux

Médoc Landscape

Church at Moulis

Soulac in the north. It is subdivided into two parts: Haut Médoc, Blanquefort to St-Seurin, and Médoc (formerly Bas-Médoc) St-Seurin to Soulac. Hardly more than three miles wide, the best châteaux (the term in Bordeaux implies a wine-making property with or without a house) lie close to the Gironde on the gravel ridges above the general marshy level. There are eight appellations, all for red wine. Haut-Médoc, in which are situated the communes Margaux, Moulis, Listrac, St-Julien, Pauillac and St-Estèphe, and Médoc north of St-Seurin.

The vineyards, largely established between 1650 and 1750 and sadly disrupted during the Revolution when properties were confiscated and owners guillotined, were either *crus bourgeois* or *crus artisans* until 1855, according to the status of their owners. By 1855 the brokers of Bordeaux had formed their own list of merit, which became the 1855 official classification at the Paris Exhibition.

Though still adequate, with surprisingly few changes, the properties are all Haut-Médoc, plus Haut-Brion, the leading Graves. Omitting St-Emilion, Pomerol and other Graves means that there is still no single classification of Bordeaux clarets as a whole. Alexis Lichine produced one with five classes, but proprietors no more relish relegation than football club managers, so it is likely to remain an excellent unofficial guide.* Another guide, of course, is *At the wine auctions — latest prices* in *Decanter* magazine published monthly.

During the 1970s the AOC area under vine increased by about 40 per cent, while the number of growers declined due to mergers and purchases by the big firms. Thus, Baron Philippe de Rothschild owns Mouton-Rothschild, Mouton-Baronne Phillipe, Duhart-Milon and La Baronnie, his company also marketing his Mouton-Cadet (AOC Bordeaux). M. Jean-Eugène Borie owns Haut-Batailley, Grand-Puy-Lacoste, and a *Cru Bourgeois* called Lalande-Borie as well as his 'flagship', Ducru-Beaucaillou. So many châteaux e.g. Léoville-Poyferré market a second wine that a Bordeaux, 'Who owns who' would be rather useful. Meanwhile Hugh Johnson's 1983 *Wine Companion* is a great substitute and, appearing every ten years, there is *Bordeaux et ses Vins*, better known as *Cocks & Feret*, its Bordeaux publishers. The latest (thirteenth) edition, 1982 has 1887 pages and costs 350 francs.

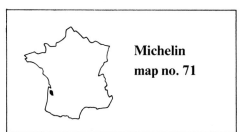

Michelin map no. 71

*Reproduced in David Peppercorn's *Bordeaux*, in Alexis Lichine's *Guide to the Wines and Vineyards of France* and in Peter Dominic's *Wine Mine* Summer 1964.

The official classification of the great growths of the Gironde: Classification of 1855

		ACRES	CASES
Premiers crus (first growths)			
Château Lafite	*Pauillac*	225	30,000
Château Latour	*Pauillac*	123	20,000
Château Mouton-Rothschild*	*Pauillac*	175	23,000
Château Margaux	*Margaux*	182	20,000
Château Haut-Brion	*Pessac, Graves*	108	12,500
Deuxièmes crus (second growths)			
Château Rausan-Ségla	*Margaux*	94	14,000
Château Rauzan-Gassies	*Margaux*	74	10,000
Château Léoville-Lascases	*St-Julien*	198	30,000
Château Léoville-Poyferré	*St-Julien*	131	23,000
Château Léoville-Barton	*St-Julien*	85	16,000
Château Durfort-Vivens	*Margaux*	50	6,000
Château Lascombes	*Margaux*	240	40,000
Château Gruaud-Larose	*St-Julien*	189	32,000
Château Brane-Cantenac	*Cantenac-Margaux*	211	29,000
Château Pichon-Longueville-Baron	*Pauillac*	77	11,000
Château Pichon-Lalande	*Pauillac*	150	18,000
Château Ducru-Beaucaillou	*St-Julien*	110	19,000
Château Cos-d'Estournel	*St-Estèphe*	140	20,000
Château Montrose	*St-Estèphe*	160	24,000
Troisièmes crus (third growths)			
Château Giscours	*Labarde-Margaux*	182	25,000
Château Kirwan	*Cantenac-Margaux*	86	12,000
Château d'Issan	*Cantenac-Margaux*	75	11.000
Château Lagrange	*St-Julien*	123	20,000
Château Langoa-Barton	*St-Julien*	49	8,000
Château Malescot-Saint-Exupéry	*Margaux*	74	12,000
Château Cantenac-Brown	*Cantenac-Margaux*	77	15,000
Château Palmer	*Cantenac-Margaux*	86	11,000
Château La Lagune	*Ludon*	137	25,000
Château Desmirail	*Margaux*	30	3,000
Château Calon-Segur	*St-Estèphe*	123	20,000
Château Ferrière	*Margaux*	10	1,000
Château Marquis-d'Alesme	*Margaux*	20	2,500
Château Boyd-Cantenac	*Margaux*	44	6,000
Quatrièmes crus (fourth growths)			
Château Saint-Pierre-Sevaistre	*St-Julien*	44	8,000
Château Branaire	*St-Julien*	118	20,000
Château Talbot	*St-Julien*	210	38,000
Château Duhart-Milon-Rothschild	*Pauillac*	98	15,000
Château Pouget	*Cantenac-Margaux*	20	3,500
Château La Tour-Carnet	*St-Laurent*	79	6,000
Château Lafon-Rochet	*St-Estèphe*	110	15,000

*Decreed a first growth in 1973

Château Beychevelle	*St-Julien*	170	30,000
Château Prieuré-Lichine	*Cantenac-Margaux*	143	28,000
Château Marquis-de-Terme	*Margaux*	77	11,000

Cinquièmes crus (fifth growths)

Château Pontet-Canet	*Pauillac*	182	35,000
Château Batailley	*Pauillac*	110	20,000
Château Grand-Puy-Lacoste	*Pauillac*	86	14,000
Château Grand-Puy-Ducasse	*Pauillac*	80	14,000
Château Haut-Batailley	*Pauillac*	49	6,000
Château Lynch-Bages	*Pauillac*	170	25,000
Château Lynch-Moussas	*Pauillac*	60	9,000
Château Dauzac-Lynch	*Labarde-Margaux*	77	15,000
Château Mouton-Baronne, Phillippe	*Pauillac*	125	15,000
Château du Tertre	*Arsac-Margaux*	110	14,000
Château Haut-Bages-Libéral	*Pauillac*	54	8,000
Château Pédesclaux	*Pauillac*	49	7,000
Château Belgrave	*St-Laurent*	107	25,000
Château Camensac	*St-Laurent*	149	20,000
Château Cos Labory	*St-Estèphe*	37	6,000
Château Clerc-Milon-Mondon	*Pauillac*	68	10,000
Château Croizet-Bages	*Pauillac*	52	8,000
Château Cantemerle	*Macau*	61	8,000

Sauternes and Barsac

The Sauternes vineyards were also officially classified in 1855. The cases are production of AOC Sauternes in a good year. Acres are those devoted to Sauternes.

Many châteaux also make dry white Graves, and one even a red Graves, from parts of their whole acreage.

Premier grand cru (first great growth)

	ACRES	CASES
Château d'Yquem	215	5,500

Premiers crus (first growths)

Château Guiraud	134	7,000
Château la Tour-Blanche	67	6,000
Château Lafaurie-Peyraguey	49	4,500
Château de Rayne-Vigneau	164	16,500
Château Sigalas-Rabaud	34	2,500
Château Rabaud-Pronis	74	3,750
Clos Haut-Peyraguey	37	3,000
Château Coutet	98	8,000
Château Climens	74	4,200
Château Suduiraut	173	11,600
Château Rieussec	136	7,000

Deuxième crus (second growth)

Château d'Arche	88	4,500
Château Filhot	148	11,000
Château Lamothe	20	2,000
Château Myrat*	—	—
Château Doisy-Védrines	52	3,000
Château Doisy-Daëne	34	3,500
Château Suau	16	1,500
Château Broustet	39	3,000
Château Caillou	37	4,000
Château Nairac	37	2,000
Château de Malle	55	5,000
Château Romer**	—	—

*Ceased production 1976   **Demolished for motorway

Graves: 1959 Official Classification

The vineyards of Graves were officially classified in 1953 and in 1959. Château Haut-Brion was also officially classified with the Médocs in 1855.

Classified red wines of Graves		ACRES	CASES
Château Haut-Brion	*Pessac*	108	12,000
Château Bouscaut	*Cadaujac*	75	10,000
Château Carbonnieux	*Léognan*	86	8,000
Domaine de Chevalier	*Léognan*	37	3,800
Château Fieuzal	*Léognan*	42	5,000
Château Haut-Bailly	*Léognan*	57	8,500
Château La Mission-Haut-Brion	*Pessac*	30	4,800
Château La Tour-Haut-Brion	*Talence*	20	2,300
Château La Tour-Martillac (Kressmann la Tour)	*Martillac*	47	7,500
Château Malartic-Lagravière	*Léognan*	25	4,000
Château Olivier	*Léognan*	45	7,000
Château Pape-Clément	*Pessac*	66	10,000
Château Smith-Haut-Lafitte	*Martillac*	111	20,000

Classified white wines of Graves			
Château Bouscaut	*Cadaujac*	15	1,500
Château Carbonnieux	*Léognan*	86	14,000
Domaine de Chevalier	*Léognan*	9	950
Château Couhins	*Villenave-d'Ornon*	17	3,000
Château la Tour-Martillac (Kressmann la Tour)	*Martillac*	—	—
Château Laville-Haut-Brion	*Talence*	12	2,000
Château Malartic-Lagravière	*Léognan*	17	800
Château Olivier	*Léognan*	37	9,000
Château Haut-Brion*	*Pessac*	10	1,500

Grand Crus Classés de St. Emilion

First classified officially in 1954, with revisions in 1958, 1969 and 1983, the St-Emilion classification has boldly established annual tastings by panels of three for every classified Château to maintain the region's reputation. Owners wanting Grand Cru classé and Premier Grand Cru classé have had to supply a Commission with financial information, their selling prices and samples. Starting with the 1984 vintage the following new classification is in force with no further revising until 1994. Château Berliquet has been promoted to, and Château Beausejour-Bécot relegated from, the premiers and six properties have lost their Grand Cru classé status.

Premiers Grands Crus classés

	ACRES	CASES
Ausone	17	2000
Cheval-Blanc	86	11.500
Beauséjour	11	3,300
Belair	28	4,000
Canon	44	8,000
Clos Fourtet	42	6,000
Figeac	85	12,500
La Gaffelière	40	8,000
Magdelaine	21	5,000
Pavie	86	16,000
Trottevieille	18	5,000

Grands Crus classés

	ACRES	CASES
L'Angélus	60	12,000
L'Arrosée	21	4,000

*Added 1960

Balestard-la-Tonnelle	21	3,500	La Clotte	12	2,000
Beauséjour-Bécot	16	9,000	La Clusière	7	900
Bellevue	14	2,000	La Dominique	40	6,500
Bergat	7	1,100	Laniote	11	2,500
Berliquet	23	4,000	Larcis-Ducasse	24	4,500
Cadet-Piola	17	3,000	La Marzelle	15	3,000
Canon-la-Gaffelière	45	10,500	Larmande	36	5,500
Cap de Mourlin	23	4,000	Laroze	70	12,000
Cap de Mourlin	20	2,600	La Serre	12	2,000
Chapelle-Madeleine	0.5	45	La Tour-de-Pin-Figeac	24	3,500
Chauvin	28	4,200	La Tour-du-Pin-Figeac	21	2,400
Corbin	28	5,800	La Tour Figeac	34	6,000
Corbin-Michotte	17	3,000	Le Prieuré	12	1,500
Couvent des Jacobins	17	3,000	Matras	23	3,500
Croque-Michotte	30	6,700	Mauvezin	10	1,000
Curé-Bon	11	1,600	Moulin-du-Cadet	12	2,000
Dassault	48	9,000	L'Oratoire	20	3,700
Faurie-de-Souchard	18	3,400	Pavie-Decesse	20	2,600
Fonplégade	42	9,000	Pavie-Macquin	25	2,300
Fonroque	42	9,000	Pavillon-Cadet	4	750
Franc-Mayne	17	2,000	Petit Faurie-de-Soutard	17	2,500
Gd-Barrail-Lamarzelle-Figeac	86	17,000	Ripeau	36	4,700
Gd-Corbin-Despagne	62	11,000	Sansonnet	7	3,000
Grand-Corbin	28	4,500	St-Georges-Côte-Pavie	12	2,000
Grand-Mayne	39	7,000	Soutard	48	7,000
Grand-Pontet	35	6,500	Tertre-Daugay	20	3,000
Guadet-St-Julien	11	1,600	Trimoulet	43	8,000
Haut-Corbin	11	2,500	Troplong-Mondot	70	13,500
Haut-Sarpe	26	6,000	Villemaurine	17	4,000
La Carte et Le Chatelet	11	2,000	Yon-Figeac	52	7,500

Pomerol: An Unofficial Classification

	ACRES	CASES			
Château Pétrus	27	3,800	Clos de l'Eglise-Clinet	11	1,500
Château La Conseillante	29	4,000	Château Lagrange	20	2,000
Château Gazin	56	7,800	Château La Pointe	52	6,750
Château Lafleur	6.5	1,350	Château Latour à Pomerol	18	1,500
Château Lafleur-Pétrus	18	2,100	Château La Croix	32	5,750
Château Petit-Village	27	3,750	Château La Croix-de-Gay	28	5,000
Château Trotanoy	27	3,300	Domaine du Clos l'Eglise	15	2,200
Château Vieux-Château-Certan	34	6,300	Château Feytit-Clinet	15	1,600
Château Certan de May	12	1,600	Château Gombaude-Guillot	17	1,700
Château L'Evangile	33	3,000	Château Rouget	31	3,000
Château Nénin	61	7,400	Château de Sales	116	16,000
Château Beauregard	32	4,100	Château L'Enclos	23	2,500
Château Certan-Giraud	17	1,850	Château La Fleur-Gazin	12	1,250

Classification of Bourgeois Wines of the Médoc and Haut-Médoc

The 1855 classification mentioned seven *crus exceptionnels* after the *crus classés*, to which a further six have been generally recognised since. Though unofficial they use the term on their labels.

Crus exceptionnels:

CHÂTEAUX	COMMUNE
Angludet,	Cantenac
Bel-Air Marquis D'Aligre	Soussans
La Couronne	Pauillac
Fonbadet	Pauillac
Gloria	St. Julien
Labégorce	Margaux
Labégorce-Zédé	Margaux
Lanessan	Cussac
Maucaillou	Moulis
De Pez	St-Estèphe
Siran	Labarde
La Tour de Mons	Soussans
Villegeorge	Avensan

Crus bourgeois:

Additionally, in 1932 the *cru bourgeois* proprietors of the Médoc formed a syndicate dividing their members into 18 *grand bourgeois exceptionnels*, 41 *grands bourgeois* and 58 *bourgeois*, revised in 1978 as printed below: A few names may be missing because their proprietors, seeking fame by other means, preferred not to join. Their 18 *grands bourgeois exceptionnels* are indicated by *.

Grand bourgeois

Château Agassac*	Ludon
Château Andron Blanquet*	St Estèphe
Château Beaumont	Cussac
Château Beausite*	St Estèphe
Château Bel-Orme*	St Seurin de Cadourne
Château Brillette	Moulis
Château Capbern*	St Estèphe
Château La Cardonne	Blaignan
Château Caronne Ste-Gemme*	St Laurent
Château Chasse-Spleen*	Moulis
Château Cissac*	Cissac
Château Citran	Avensan
Château Colombier Monpelou	Pauillac
Château Coufran	St Seurin de Cadourne
Château Coutelin-Merville	St Estèphe
Château Le Crock*	St Estèphe
Château Duplessis-Hauchecorne	Moulis
Château Dutruch-Grand Poujeaux*	Moulis
Château Fontesteau	St Sauveur
Château Fourcas Dupré*	Listrac
Château Fourcas Hosten*	Listrac
Château La Fleur Milon	Pauillac
Château Du Glana*	St Julien
Château Greyssac	Bégadan
Château Hanteillan	Cissac
Château Haut-Marbuzet*	St Estèphe
Château Lafon	Listrac
Château Lamarque	Lamarque
Château Lamothe	Cissac
Château Laujac	Bégadan
Château Liversan	St Sauveur
Château Loudenne	St Yzans
Château Mac-Carthy	St Estèphe
Château Malleret	Le Pian
Château Marbuzet*	St Estèphe
Château Meyney*	St Estèphe
Château Morin	St Estèphe
Château Moulin à Vent	Moulis
Château Le Meynieu	Vertheuil
Château Martinens	Margaux
Château Les Ormes Sorbet	Couquègues
Château Les Ormes de Pez	St Estèphe
Château Patache d'Aux	Bégadan
Château Paveil de Luze	Soussans
Château Peyrabon	St Sauveur
Château Phélan-Ségur*	St Estèphe
Château Pontoise-Cabarrus	St Seurin de Cadourne
Château Potensac	Adonnac
Château Poujeaux*	Moulis
Château La Rose Trintaudon	St Laurent
Château Reysson	Vertheuil
Château Ségur	Parempuyre
Château Sigognac	St Yzans
Château Sociando-Mallet	St Seurin de Cadourne
Château du Taillan	La Taillan
Château La Tour de By	Bégadan
Château La Tour de Haut Moulin	Cussac
Château Tronquoy Lalande	St Estèphe
Château Verdignan	St Seurin de Cadourne

Bourgeis

Château Aney	Cussac
Château Balac	St Laurent de Médoc
Château Bellerive	Valeyrac
Château Bellerose	Pauillac
Château La Becade	Listrac
Château Les Bertins	Valeyrac
Château Bonneau	St Seurin de Cadourne
Château Le Boscq	St Estèphe
Château Le Breuil	Cissac
Château La Bridane	St Julien
Château De By	Bégadan
Château Castera	St Germain d'Esteuil
Château Chambert	St Estèphe
Château Cap Leon Veyrin	Listrac
Château Carcannieux	Queyrac
Château La Clare	Bégadan
Château Clarke	Listrac
Château La Closerie	Moulis
Château Duplessis-Fabre	Moulis
Château Fonreaud	Listrac
Château Fonpiqueyre	St Sauveur
Château Fort Vauban	Cussac
Château La France	Blaignan
Château Gallais Bellevue	Potensac
Château Grand Duroc Milon	Pauillac
Château Grand Moulin	St Seurin de Cadourne
Château Haut-Bages Monpelou	Pauillac
Château Haut-Canteloup	Couquèques
Château Haut-Garin	Bégadan
Château Haut-Padarnac	Pauillac
Château Houbanon	Prignac
Château Hourtin-Ducasse	St Sauveur
Château de Labat	St Laurent
Château Lamothe Bergeron	Cussac
Château Landon	Bégadan

Château Lariviere	Blaignan
Crû Lassalle	Potensac
Château Lartigue de Brochon	St Seurin de Cadourne
Château Lavaliere	St Christoly
Château Le Landat	Cissac
Château Lestage	Listrac
Château Mac Carthy Moula	St Estèphe
Château Monthil	Bégadan
Château Moulin Rouge	Cussac
Château Panigon	Cibrac
Château Pibran	Pauillac
Château Plantey de la Croix	St Seurin de Cadourne
Château Pontet	Blaignan
Château Ramage la Batisse	St Sauveur
Château Romefort	Cussac
Château La Roque de By	Bégadan
Château Saint-Bonnet	St Christoly
Château de la Rose Marechale	St Seurin de Cadourne
Château Saransot	Listrac
Château Soudars	Avensan
Château Tayac	Soussans
Château La Tour Blanche	St Christoly
Château La Tour de Mirail	Cissac
Château La Tour Haut-Caussan	Blaignan
Château La Tour Saint-Bonnet	St Christoly
Château La Tour Saint-Joseph	Cissac
Château des Tourelles	Blaignan
Château Vernous	Lesparre
Château Vieux Robin	Bégadan

The Médoc (continued) With nothing to rival the vines and the châteaux except a few Romanesque churches in the villages, a journey through the Médoc becomes a pilgrimage to Bacchus. Every château has its temple called the *chai*, a cellar above ground where the oak casks containing the red wines of the last two vintages lie in orderly rows, as if they were pews on either side of a central aisle. Purple samples are drawn to be tasted, savoured and spat out on the earth floor.

Bottling takes place in another part of the *chai*. Nearly all Bordeaux fine wines are now château bottled and despatched by road. With so much exported, maturing and

51

bottling at the point of origin links the wine-maker more closely to the consumer and prevents fraud by third parties.

Margaux With 1500 inhabitants Margaux makes wines noted for their lightness and distinctive bouquet. Labarde-Margaux, where Château Giscours is a notable third growth, Arsac-Margaux (Châteaux du Terte and Dauzac-Lynch) and Cantenac-Margaux with seven 1855 *crus classés* all form part of this commune.

St-Julien St.Julien is little more than its post office, St-Julien-Beychevelle, so close to Pauillac that its wines are similar, if a shade lighter and more delicate. Châteaux Beychevelle, Branaire, Ducru-Beaucaillou, Léoville-Barton, and Léoville-Lascases are among its great names.

Pauillac Château Latour, its tower conspicuous in the middle of the vineyard, cannot be missed before entering Pauillac, the one wine town of the Médoc on the estuary. Nearly 7000 people live here but its rather primitive hotel and restaurants no longer rate an entry in the Michelin guide.
Châteaux Mouton-Rothschild and Lafite are conspicuous as the D2 road climbs up the slope to Cos d'Estournel and its commune St-Estèphe, the last of the Haut-Médoc, looking down on a really indecent case of exposure, the new petrol refinery by the estuary. To buy a case of Lafite 1983 requires about £450, which could buy five cases of Haut-Batailley or four of Cos d'Estournel. These 1983 wines are not yet bottled and will not be ready to drink for ten years at least.

St-Estèphe Calon Segur, Cos d'Estournel, Montrose, Cos Labory, Lafon-Rochet are the classed growths of this commune, which has nearly twenty *crus bourgeois* as well. Château de Pez, *Cru Exceptionnel* makes as fine and long-lived a wine as any.

Médoc AOC The northern half of the Médoc peninsula contributes many good though less distinguished wines. Château Loudenne for example is a *grand cru bourgeois*, particularly well known in Britain since the Gilbeys bought the property in 1875, building the largest *chai* in the entire Médoc in which to handle and house the wines they would buy throughout Bordeaux. Loudenne's neighbours Laujac owned by Cruse since 1852, Castéra and La Tour-de-By are also good.

Médoc white wines Only three Châteaux of this great red Bordeaux district make a little white wine in addition to their red. The wines are Château Loudenne Blanc, Caillou Blanc of Château Talbot and Pavillon Blanc of Château Margaux. Pleasant and dry without any pretension, Loudenne Blanc is sometimes available from British retailers. AOC of all three is Bordeaux Blanc.

The Bordeaux exporters
No survey of Bordeaux would be complete without mentioning the shipping firms whose annual turnover in 1979 was 4,400,000,000 francs, of which 40 per cent was from exports. Twenty out of two hundred firms do half the business. Much of it is in brands. Here are a few of the leaders.
Cordier Huge concern selling white wine to Germany where it is distilled into brandy. Owns Château Gruaud-Larose, Talbot and three others.

Barton & Guestier An Anglo-Irish/French firm founded about 1750. Ronald Barton still lives at St-Julien in Château Langoa-Barton though the firm now belongs to Seagram. The modern winery is at Blanquefort.

La Baronnie Formerly La Bergerie this company, based at Château Mouton-Rothschild, manages the Philippe Roths-child estates and markets the AOC Bordeaux brand Mouton-Cadet.

Calvet Extended to Bordeaux from the Rhône in 1870. Many minor Bordeaux Châteaux sold under distinctive Calvet labels. Recently merged with Whitbread.
CVBG (Consortium Vinicole de Bordeaux et de Gironde) A consortium of Dourthe, Kressman and other Bordeaux *négociants-éleveurs*, mainly exporting Bordeaux AOC wines.

Cruse et Fils Frères Founded in 1819 at 124 Quai de Chartrons, Cruse have never moved. For many years they owned Château Laujac, Pontet Canet, d'Issan, and others, until the family sold in 1980 to the *Société des vins de France*, the Pernod-Ricard group.

Ginestet Though forced to sell Château Margaux in 1976 this fine firm sells almost entirely Bordeaux wine. Châteaux Cos d'Estournel and Petit-Village remain in the family.

Louis Eschenauer Owned by John Holt of Liverpool since 1959 (now in the Lonhro Group); Châteaux Rausan-Sègla, Olivier, Smith-Haut-Lafitte and La Garde belong to the group.

Alexis Lichine & Co. Bought by Bass Charrington together with Château Lascombes in 1965.

De Luze Bought by Rémy Martin Cognac in 1981.

Gilbey de Loudenne Based at Château Loudenne sells its own brands La Cour Pavillon and La Bordelaise world-wide; acts also as agents for Châteaux Giscours, de Pez, Loudenne and Croix du Gay. Gilbeys and Peter Dominic are part of International Distillers & Vintners owned by Grand Metropolitan PLC.

Maison Sichel Originally German, the Bordeaux branch dates from 1883. Alan Sichel, author of *The Penguin Book of Wines**was a notable figure in the post-war London wine trade. Peter, his son, settling with the family at their Château d'Angludet *(cru exceptionel)* manages the Bordeaux company. Part-owners of Château Palmer, they export French wines exclusively.

Schröder & Schÿler Still a family firm exporting mainly to Sweden and Holland; due to celebrate its twenty-fifth anniversary in 1989.

Great years in Bordeaux
The International Wine and Food Society's Vintage Chart shows a 1 to 7 scale for nine sorts of wine, 7 being the best mark and 1 the worst. For claret 7 is awarded to five vintages since the Second World War and 6 to six others.
7: 1945, 1961, 1970, 1975, 1982
6: 1947, 1949, 1953, 1966, 1976, 1978.

*Replaced in 1984 by *The Penguin Wine Book* by Pamela Vandyke Price.

The sevens are the big slow developers, full of tannin which need keeping until they reach a state of unsurpassed excellence, remaining pleasant and interesting to drink for many years as they grow older gracefully. The sixes are placed second because, developing more quickly, they will not be quite so good or live so long.

This has always been the theory but modern methods of wine-making seem to be closing the gap. Experts now believe the right balance of fruit, acidity and tannin is what really counts. Moreover, the forecasters' highest quality does not necessarily give the greatest pleasure. High quality was expected from the 1952 clarets which failed to mellow with age, while in David Peppercorn's view (with which I, mouth still watering, agree) the 1953s gave more continuous pleasure than any previous vintage since the Second War until the 1961s were ready.

The 1961 yield was so small and prices therefore so high that the wine auctioneer, Michael Broadbent, hailing them as 'the gold dust of the wine world' advises keeping most of the first growths until the late '80s. 1961 was a vintage in which the few were largely drunk too soon by the few, or passed on at higher and higher prices from auction to auction with the rapidity of an oval ball moving from one Basque three-quarter to the next.

Fortunately it was followed by a large crop of light style wines. These 1962s, rated at 6 when they were reaching their best during the 1970s, not only gave comparable pleasure to the 1953s but lasted so well that your 1962 Château Latour – always the Grand Old Man of the Médoc – should still be in fine fettle in 2010. 1966, too, was a highly satisfactory year, with an average yield of big wines slower to mature than the 1962s. The *Crus classés* should now be perfect for drinking during the 1980s.

1970 was the next great year, with the highest yield since 1934, soon to be surpassed in 1973, 1976 and 1979. Sometimes, as in 1964 and 1971, St. Emilion and Pomerol are more successful than the Médoc but not in 1970, excellent in all districts.

Descriptions of great claret are apt to concentrate on the great wines and how magnificent they will become in time. But in fact good years are more like a classless society in which all excel, the juniors being delicious to drink first. For me this was well illustrated crossing to New York in the penultimate voyage of the liner *France* in 1974. In the tourist class dining room the cheapest 1970 clarets were two *Bordeaux supérieurs*, each 10 francs a bottle. Four years maturing had made them exceptionally good. On the last night we spent 15 francs on a *Cru Bourgeois*, wasting good money, for it proved to be as unready as Ethelred. To have celebrated with a 1970 *Grand Cru* at 45 francs would have been more foolish.

1975 and 1976: here is another 'big 'un and little 'un' pair (like 1952 and 1953, and 1961 and 1962). In 1975 a little rain after a hot dry summer brought forth an unexpectedly large yield of powerful wines, some lesser *crus* becoming ready within two years. The remainder are predicted to mature from 1985 onwards.

For Britain and for Bordeaux, 1976 was the summer of cloudless skies. The rains, coming in mid-September, ruined Britain's harvest and disrupted Bordeaux's. Nevertheless, the juniors, full of fruit and flavour, were excellent from 1978 onwards and their peers should give satisfaction and pleasure until the next century.

1978 was a miracle year in which hot weather from mid-August ripened the grapes in time for a late vintage that did not start until 9 October. The *crus bourgeois* should be ready from 1985. 1979 was a good rather than a great year worth recording for the largest crop since 1934. Light fruity wines to buy in 1985 for drinking until 1995. 1981 was a very good year slightly marred by rain. It may prove better value than 1982. 1982 has been already described as the perfect year, likely to be bought up rapidly during 1985.

M. Mitterand's France seems to have found favour in the sight of the Clerk of the Weather with a run of exceptional years. 'A year of steeplechasing over the obstacles of rain, drought and storms', said a Bordeaux spokesman of 1983. Then, from 17 September until November all was perfect, ending with only 14 per cent less than in 1982. Good white wines, dry and sweet, and big red wines. Yet another miracle! Followed by 1984, a poor year with normal yield cut by half, particularly in St-Emilion and Pomerol, by *coulure*.

Depending on a fine autumn, good years for Sauternes are not always the same as for claret. The best have been 1967, 1970, 1971, 1975, 1976, 1982, 1983.

The dog at Château Doisy-Daéne
Drinks Sauternes and scorns champagne;
But traitor curs from Côtes du Rhône
Will sup off nothing but a Beaune
> Michael Lipton, Haywards' Heath

The Loire

France's greatest rivers, the Loire (627 miles) and the Rhône (565 miles) each make wines of distinction over roughly the same distance: from Lyon to the Mediterranean and from Sancerre to the Atlantic, each being about 240 miles. Downstream from Sancerre the Loire changes course from north to west in the great bend south of Orléans heading for the sea through the *Pays de la Loire*, a countryside of ancient châteaux, spring flowers, summer fruits and enough sunshine to make a variety of light wines for summer revelry, leaving the Rhône's warming reds to take care of winter's needs.

Altogether I have counted seventy-two AOC and VDQS Loire wines, with a sigh of relief that there are no *vins de pays* as well. To meet them let us set forth from St-Nazaire, where sea-faring citizens and old wartime warriors may like to visit the great bizarre lock pen (the only one outside Germany that could dock the battleship *Tirpitz*) rammed by the British destroyer, *Campbeltown* on 19 March 1942, her bows filled with explosives that destroyed the gates.

Pays Nantais (Muscadet)

Crossing the fine two mile toll bridge to Paimboeuf on the left bank of the estuary, there is a fine close up of the last of the Loire as the first Muscadet vines begin to appear. Brittany's one and only wine, it will now be Muscadet and Gros Plant VDQS vines for most of the twenty five miles to Nantes.

Muscadet is both the Melon grape (re-named here when first introduced from Burgundy) and the fresh dry white wine it makes. The region, which has three

Location Nantes, Loire-Atlantique
Michelin Map 63
Land under Vines AOC 24,000 acres,
comprising: Muscadet Sèvre-et-Maine 19,200,
(Plain) Muscadet 2,000 acres and Coteaux de la
Loire 1,100 acres
Yields

Muscadet Sèvre et Maine	Maximum yield 40 hectolitres a hectare
Coteaux de la Loire	
Muscadet *Simple*	45 hectolitres a hectare

Annual Production

Muscadet Sèvre-et-Maine	3.2m cases
Muscadet *Simple*	322,000 cases
Muscadet Coteaux de la Loire	141,000 cases

Grapes Musk Melon
Growers About 6000
Wine strength Maximum 12° (Imposing
maximum safeguards against over-chap-
talisation, which would over-enrich rather than
over-sweeten)
Matured In concrete vats, never in wood.
Bottled Spring after vintage
Drunk Young 'Two months-two years' is the
local expression
Temperature Chilled
Years Less important than might be expected
so far north. Quality pretty consistent
Other wines of Region Gros Plant du Pays
Nantais. VDQS 6500 acres, Min. Strength 11°
1.5 million cases
Coteaux d'Ancenis VDQS Red and Rosé 98,000
cases, White 1,350 cases

Mouzillon and La Chapelle-Heulein, all barely a dozen miles from Nantes. The two rivers, each flowing north-west towards the city, meet at Saint Fiacre, one of the best wine communes, and the confluence continues to join the Loire at Nantes.

Coteaux de la Loire

Along the south bank the appellation will have become Muscadet Coteaux de la Loire, its wines a shade drier perhaps; and thus it remains until Brittany ends and Anjou begins, twenty miles nearer Angers.

The Admiral's Muscadet

Delightful with fish, great and small, these three Muscadet — Bon Breton, a wine box muscadet, and the château-bottled, Château de la Galissonnière, all three AOC Sèvre-et-Maine offer a choice. The name Galissonnière is that of the first owner of this walled vineyard at Le Pallet, Admiral de la Galissonnière, victorious opponent of the British Admiral Byng at Minorca in 1756. The present owners, Pierre Lusseaud and his son, have been very hospitable to groups from the Wine Mine Club.

Anjou-Saumur

> The valley of the Loire provides a fascinating field of discovery for the wine drinker.
>
> *Drinking Wine* - David Peppercorn, Brian Cooper,
> Elwyn Black

appellations for Muscadet even though their wines taste much the same, is the *Pays Nantais*. Although the appellations overlap, it is roughly bounded by an arc of a circle, centre Nantes and radius thirty miles, drawn clockwise from north-east, through south to the Loire west of the city. The best Muscadet comes from the south-east sector, roughly a 12 mile square. The Loire tributaries, Sèvre and Maine, give their names to the appellation, principal villages being Vallet, Clisson,

David Peppercorn M.W. made his first voyages of discovery in the mid-sixties when he was wine buyer for Peter Dominic and other International Distillers & Vintners' companies. Each year, in the first week of February, taking a different colleague for the experience, he would be off appraising the wines of the new vintage in bitterly cold cellars up and down the river

PLACES, GRAPES AND CASES — ANJOU

		CASES
Location	From Ingrandes to Montsoreau, Michelin Maps 63, 64 and 68	
Appellations	AOC	
RED		
Anjou	Cabernet Franc from many parts, similar to Saumur	650,000
Anjou	Gamay light young wines for early drinking	75,000
Saumur	Cabernet Franc from south-east of the town, similar to Anjou	100,000
Saumur	Champigny. Small enclave within Saumur, making province's best red wine	250,000
WHITE		
Anjou	Mostly Chenin Blanc medium dry or sweeter	740,000
Anjou	Coteaux de la Loire, Chenin Blanc both banks downstream from Savennières, high quality dry	15,000
Anjou	Coteaux de l'Aubance, Chenin Blanc, south bank opposite Angers, medium dry or sweeter	20,000
Coteaux du Layon	Chenin Blanc, high quality rich dessert wines of Layon valley	400,000
Coteaux du Layon Chaume	Chenin Blanc 1° stronger than the above (like 'Villages' in Beaujolais)	16,000
Bonnezeaux	Chenin Blanc, a *Grand Cru* village, with 250 acres of the Coteaux du Layon, Rich dessert	8,000
Quarts de Chaume	Chenin Blanc, *Grand Cru* hamlet with 112 acres of the Coteaux du Layon, Rich dessert	7,000
Saumur	Chenin Blanc, poor quality but good for making sparkling wine	300,000
Coteaux de Saumur	Chenin Blanc, poor quality, small production	1,000
Savennières	Chenin Blanc, village within Coteaux de la Loire, superb dry	11,000
ROSÉ		
Cabernet d'Anjou	The best rosé of the Loire, wholly Cabernet, pinker and drier	1.5 million
Rosé d'Anjou	The next best, paler and a little sweeter	2.0 million
Cabernet de Saumur	Wholly Cabernet, as for Cabernet d'Anjou above	
SPARKLING		
Saumur Mousseux	White 900,000 cases, Saumur Mousseux red 38,000 Both Méthode Champenoise	
Crémant de Loire	White 136,000, Crémant de Loire red 2700 Semi sparkling	
Appellations	VDQS	
Thouarsais (vin de) white		3,700
Thouarsais (vin de) red		2,000
Haut-Poitou (vin du) white		65,000
Haut-Poitou (vin du) red		95,000

from Touraine to the Pays Nantais. With him in 1969 I discovered that the fascination of the Loire as a whole was particularly true of Anjou, where there are rosés and reds from the Cabernet grape and white wines still and sparkling, sweet and dry, of high quality, from the Chenin Blanc.

Coteaux de la Loire At Château Roche-aux-Moines, the domaine of chatelaine Madame Joly comprises two vineyards: Coulée de Serrant and part of La Roche-aux-Moines. Their dry white wines, needing three to five years in bottle, can last for twenty years and are the pride of this

Loire-St. Nazaire-Anjou

Angers Castle

Anjou

Château le Plessis-Bourré

Muscadet

Château Durtal

Loir

N

W   E

S

D.C.Hoare

4 Angers

Baugé

4

Gennes

Ligné 3 Ancenis

5

St. Nazaire   1   Nantes

Chalonnes

9

Saumur

3

5   6

Vertou

4

Layon

8

Clisson

Vihiers

Bouaye

Bourgneuf

Cholet

Legé

Thouars

1 Muscadet Coteaux de la Loire
2 Muscadet de Sèvre et Maine
3 Coteaux d'Ancenis
4&7 Anjou et Saumur
5 Coteaux de la Loire
6 Coteaux du Layon
8 Coteaux de Saumur
9 Coteaux de L'Aubance

0   25

Scale in Kms.

Loire River Landscape

Loire Landscape

Château Serrant

St. Maurice Cathedral
Angers

seven mile stretch, appellation Coteaux de la Loire, along the north bank.

If these two wines are the most expensive, there are another forty named vineyards going downstream to Chalonnes, notably Château d'Epiré, Clos de Papillon, Châteaux de Bizolière and de Savennières.

A sweet and lovely appellation

Chalonnes is where the river Layon — little more than a ditch in summer — joins the Loire from the south-east. Road D125 leads up the valley to the hamlet called Chaume and its 120 acre slope, Quarts de Chaume. Here, Chenin Blanc grapes, afflicted with the *pourriture noble* — that rotten overripe state which makes a great sweet wine — are picked late in the autumn. The result is more flowery, if not so lush as in Sauternes by the Garonne further south, yet it can attain 14/15° quite naturally. Beaulieu, Faye, Rablay, Rochefort, St-Aubin, St-Lambert are all entitled to add their names to the sweet and lovely appellation that is Coteaux du Layon.

Lying to the North between these little hills and the Loire is the Coteaux de l'Aubance, a source of mainly light, white wines and rosés, named after yet another small tributary. Quite a few of them are exported by the Co-opérative at Brissac-Quincé.

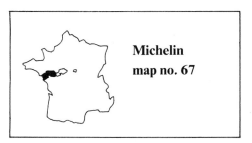

**Michelin
map no. 67**

Full of our subject

On the road to Angers just north of Brissac-Quincé, Michelin Map 64 has a windmill sign. This marks the cellars of Monsieur Daviau, whose family have been vignerons and millers for many generations. Wide variations in the Angevin soil make for interesting results and there are sweet Chenin wines of considerable age here as well as much younger and drier white wines from Chenin and Chardonnay, not to mention red and rosé wines from Cabernet, Gamay and Groslot.

Despite our own diligence in tasting from one village grower to another, it was the restaurants of Angers, such as the Vert d'Eau, that made us truly full of our subject. Nowhere else can there be such a selection of Angevin wines, many of them in half bottles the better to broaden the acquaintance.

A rosé route

From Angers to Saumur is still very much wine country, to a ten mile depth south of the river. The AOC here is Anjou-Saumur for white and red wines and Rosé d'Anjou for rosés from blends of Gamay, Groslot, Cabernet, Cot and Pineau d'Aunis. After Bordeaux, Burgundy and Côtes du Rhône, Loire wines come next in France's wine exports, three out of four cases from the Loire being sweet, cheap Rosé d'Anjou. Cabernet d'Anjou or Cabernet de Saumur indicate the better rosés, exclusively from this grape.

Saumur sparkling

The south-bank road taking in Cunault and Chênehutte-les-Tuffeaux, reaches Saumur through the suburbs of St-Hilaire-St-Florent, home of Ackerman-Laurence and Bouvet-Ladubay, two well-known sparkling wine firms. Keeping open house throughout the summer, they demonstrate the fascinating *méthode champenoise* (the process that makes the best sparkling wine) to all visitors seven days a week.

John Ackerman-Laurence, coming here in 1811 from Champagne, was, in fact, the pioneer of Saumur sparkling wine made from the Chenin Blanc grape. The still wines, white and rosé, of this region had been known in Britain and the Low Countries centuries before, largely because they could be shipped to the Atlantic and round by sea so easily.

Gratien et Meyer on D947, the south-bank road towards Chinon, is another old sparkling firm. They too are open to all comers, with free sampling all the year round at Château de Beaulieu, which has a fine view across the Loire. The *méthode champenoise* is still demonstrated by hand to visitors so that they can compare it with the latest fully automated production.

Saumur-Mousseux from the Chenin Blanc, with some black Cabernet grapes added, is the best fully sparkling wine after champagne. Alfred Gratien is associated with Gratien et Meyer, owns Bouvet-Ladubay and also makes champagne.

Crémant de Loire is a semi-sparkling or *pétillant* wine similarly made with the pressure in the bottle at least half that of Mousseux. By a decree of 1975 other regions can make Crémant, for example Crémant d'Alsace, Crémant de Bourgogne.

Anjou red wines

East of Saumur there is a vast blanket of vines (AOC Saumur) south of the river and a sign-posted *Circuit Touristique du Vin* winds over hill and dale from Saumur to Montsoreau where Anjou ends and Touraine begins. The *Cave Co-opérative*

des Vignerons de Saumur is in this blanket at St-Cyr-en-Bourg: an interesting place, open to visitors during working hours, the grapes are crushed at the top, the wine going through pipes to the bottom to emerge by road tanker some eighty feet below when needed.

Champigny, the next village northwards, has its own AOC, Saumur-Champigny for Anjou's one red wine (other than Anjou or Saumur Rouge). A lively, fruity Cabernet Franc, cousin of Chinon and Bourgueil, best drunk cool like Beaujolais, the 1982 in the Belle Vue hotel restaurant at Amboise so impressed me in 1984 that we tried to buy some next day in the region itself. There was no more 1982 but a dozen of 1983 from M. Berthelot at Parnay-par-Montsoreau has given much satisfaction, starting at the customs, where ten of my twelve bottles comprised the duty free allowance. Production seems to have doubled in the past few years to 250,000 cases a year.

Two VDQS

Vin de Thouarsais VDQS can be sweetly white, fruity red or lightly rosé from Thouars, 21 miles south of Saumur.

Vins de Haut-Poitou VDQS: Gamay, Sauvignon and Chardonnay, wines of growing repute, are produced by the *Cave Co-opérative du Haut-Poitou* at Neuville-de-Poitou north-west of Poitiers.

Touraine

Touraine, 'the garden of France', extends from the mouth of the Vienne almost to Blois. Viticulturally, however, its 60,000 acres making eleven million cases a year are widely scattered, embracing the pretty little Loir to the north and the valleys of its larger tributaries, the Vienne (already joined by the Creuse), the Indre and the Cher flowing in from the south.

Keeping to the Loire no map is needed to pinpoint Touraine's two wine towns, Bourgueil and Chinon, north and south of the big river respectively, some ten miles apart. A silver sphere (diameter 170 feet), part of the Nuclear Power Station at Avoine, gleams for miles around.

The Cabernet Franc cannot quite match its Bordeaux performance in this cooler corner of the land, yet Bourgueil and Chinon, costing less than a Bordeaux *cru classé*, make cool, pleasant drinking with rabbit, hare and partridge or those *rillettes de porc* that often precede any Loire main dish. North of the town, the *Cave Touristique de Bourgueil* (small entrance

PLACES, GRAPES AND CASES — TOURAINE

Location   From Montsoreau to Chambord, Michelin Map 6

Appellations	AOC	CASES
RED		
Bourgueil Cabernet Franc, north bank, north of Chinon		300,000
St Nicholas de Bourgueil Cabernet Franc, adjacent to Bourgueil, wine similar		190,000
Chinon Cabernet Franc, these three drink cool when young		335,000
Coteaux du Loir Pinot Noir and Gamay north of the big Loire; some rosé		3000
Touraine Pinot Noir and Gamay as named on label; some rosé		900,000
Touraine-Amboise Malbec, Gamay and Cabernet around this south-bank town		50,000
Touraine-Azay Le-Rideau, small area, rosé better than red		10,000
Touraine-Mesland Good reds, mainly Gamay, on north bank, west of Blois		70,000
WHITE (Chenin Blanc unless stated)		
Jasnières Village and best wine of the Coteaux du Loir, close NE of La Chartré		2500
Coteaux du Loire Small area around La Chartre-sur-le-Loire, 25 miles north of Tours		1700
Montlouis Vouvray's opposite number on south bank, dry, semi- and fully sweet		60,000
Touraine Chenin Blanc or Sauvignon Blanc as named on label		850,000
Touraine-Amboise Good quality, similar to Vouvray		25,000
Touraine-Azay-le-Rideaux Small area those from Saché rival Vouvray in great years		11,000
Touraine-Mesland Chenin and Sauvignon, fair quality		10,000
Vouvray High quality, dry semi- and fully sweet		370,000
SPARKLING		
Crémant de Loire Red		2500
Crémant de Loire White, high quality		140,000
Montlouis Mousseux		40,000
Vouvray Mousseux		250,000
Appellations	**VDQS**	
Cheverny Gamay red and rosé south of Blois		40,000
Local grape Romartin, dry white		40,000
Valencay Good wines dry white Chenin Blanc		24,000
Red Gamay		5000
Coteaux du Vendômois Red		27,000
White		5000
Around Vendôme on the little Loir		

fee, closed January) is open seven days a week.

Approaches to Tours
Going towards Tours along the south bank (D7) Azay-le-Rideau, barely a detour, is the first of three towns permitted to put its name after 'Touraine' to describe its above average, dry Chenin Blanc. The other two are Mesland and Amboise. Its other attraction — equally beloved of Balzac — lies hidden among a mass of trees in a bend of the river Indre. When reflected in calm water, this small Renaissance château is almost as pleasing as Chenonceaux.

Vouvray and Montlouis
The village of Vouvray also lies on this road, six miles beyond Tours. Visiting the cellars that burrow into the yellow chalk called 'Touraine Tufa', the vineyards that make a million gallons a year are nowhere to be seen. Climb up to the plateau from the main street and the mystery is solved by the hectare. Nearly all Vouvray is now made into dry but fruity white wine for export, or into *mousseux* or *crémant* in which — as in Saumur — the Chenin Blanc flavour is well preserved.

Vouvray's reputation, however, is not founded on these but on the sweet unblended dessert wines, only possible in exceptional summers; wines that can live up to fifty years — far longer than the finest Sauternes. M. Fouquet at 47, Rue Gambetta might find you a case - at a price; likewise the Foreau family firm at Clos Naudin or M. Gaston Huet, Mayor for many years. Montlouis, a relatively small region on the south bank, with a superb view of Vouvray and its vineyards, can do as well, but not in anything like the same quantity.

The wine of Onzain, where the wine co-operative sells most Touraine wines, is AOC Touraine-Mesland a few miles upstream from AOC Touraine-Amboise. The appellations cover red, white and a rosé from the Gamay grape, not quite so good here as in Beaujolais.

Chaumont Cheverny Chenonceaux
From modest cellars in the village of Huisseau-sur-Cosson, near Chambord, Aimé Boucher and his stepson, Claude Kistner, have supplied many delightful Touraine wines to Peter Dominic and received Wine Mine Club parties for at least twenty years. As a spectacle, Cheverny, ten miles south-west has more charm than the massive Chambord and what is more, its own VDQS wines, a fruity Gamay and a dry Chardonnay.

Eighteen miles south west across country leads to Montrichard on the Cher. The Bellevue (29 rooms) looks across the river and has been an overnight stop for the Wine Mine Club sampling the *mousseux* of *Armand Monmousseau*, still directing his old family firm now owned by Taittinger of Champagne. (Chenonceaux, the jewel of Touraine astride the Cher five miles downstream, now belongs to Meunier Chocolate, who deserves a bar of nutty for managing it well without compulsory guides.)

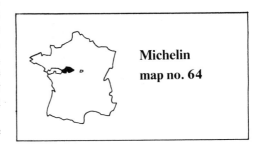

Michelin map no. 64

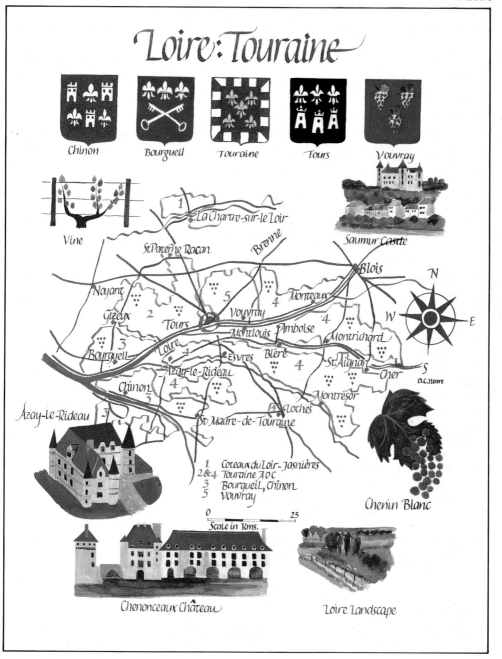

Loire: Touraine

Chinon

Bourgueil

Touraine

Tours

Vouvray

Vine

Saumur Castle

La Chartre-sur-le-Loir

St Paterne Racan

Brenne

Blois

Noyant

Monteaux

Gizeux

Vouvray

Tours

Montlouis

Amboise

Montrichard

Loire

Esvres

Bléré

St Aignan

Bourgueil

Azay-le-Rideau

Cher

Chinon

Montrésor

Azay-le-Rideau

St Maure-de-Touraine

Loches

D.C. Hoare

N
W E
S

Chenin Blanc

1 Coteaux du Loir - Jasnières
2 & 4 Touraine AOC
3 Bourgueil, Chinon
5 Vouvray

0 _____ 25
Scale in Kms.

Chenonceaux Château

Loire Landscape

PLACES, GRAPES AND CASES — UPPER LOIRE

		CASES
Location From Orléans to the Source. Michelin Maps 64, 65, 69, 73 and 76.		
Appellations AOC		
RED AND ROSÉ		
Sancerre Light Pinot Noir, popular locally, 3250 acres		115,000
Reuilly Light Pinot Noir		23,000
WHITE		
Sancerre Sauvignon, outstanding from the slopes of this little hill town		475,000
Pouilly-Fumé Sauvignon 1250 acres, similar to Sancerre from the lower, flatter valley		178,000
Blanc Fumé de Pouilly		
Pouilly-sur-Loire Chasselas, dry white, VDQS standard		17,000
Quincy Sauvignon 35 miles south-west of Sancerre, satisfactory substitution in good years		19,000
Reuilly Sauvignon		84,000
Appellations VDQS		
Orléannais *(Vin de l')* red, much of it made into vinegar		33,000
Orléannais *(Vin de l')* white, Chardonnay poor quality		1300
Coteaux du Giennois (red) Between Sancerre and Gien, Pinot Noir and Gamay		15,000
Coteaux du Giennois (white) Chenin Blanc and Sauvignon, poor		1000
Ménétou-Salon (red) A light Pinot Noir		12,000
Ménétou-Salon (white) Sauvignon Blanc, Sancerre second string		18,000
Château Meillant (red and rosé) South of Bourges, Pinot Noir and Gris, Gamay		6000
St Pourçain-sur-Sioule (red and rosé) 20 miles south of Moulins and close to Vichy, mostly Gamay		80,000
St Pourçain-sur-Sioule (dry white) Sauvignon, Chardonnay, Aligoté and local Tresallier in various proportions make this likeable wine		50,000
Côtes Roannaises (red) 50 miles south-west of Mâcon, Gamay grape, Beaujolais-style		16,000
Côtes d'Auvergne (red) Gamay, district around Clérmont-Ferrand		36,000
Côtes d'Auvergne (white) Chardonnay		21,000
Côtes du Forez (red and rosé) Co-operative at Chozieux, Beaujolais-style		20,000

Loir and Sarthe

Returning to England from any of the French channel ports with a day or two to spare, it is possible to explore these two delightful tributaries. A glance at Michelin Map 64 shows Vendôme, a good starting point, only forty miles to the north of Chenonceaux. From there the little Loir river road runs downstream to meet the Sarthe close to Angers. In Jasnières (just north of La Chartre) the little Loir has its own, dry white AOC wine.

Upper Loire

Sancerre (Michelin Map 65) The last stage of this journey begins and ends with plenty to see but nothing great to drink until we come to Sancerre in the Cher *département.* At Cosné after crossing the Loire from N7 to D955, the 1024 foot hill should appear

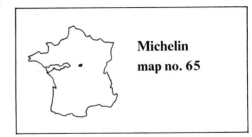

Michelin map no. 65

Loire: Sancerre, Pouilly-sur-Loire

Bourges Cathedral

Pouilly-sur-Loire

St. Etienne At Nevers

Pouilly-sur-Loire

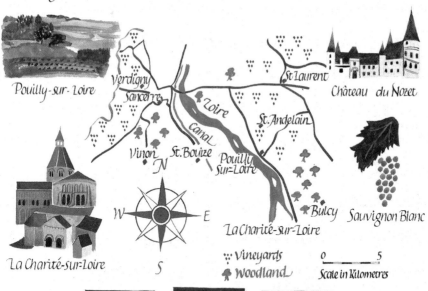

Verdigny

Sancerre

Loire

Canal

Vinon

St. Bouize

Pouilly
Sur-Loire

St. Laurent

St. Andelain

Bulcy

La Charité-sur-Loire

Château du Nozet

Sauvignon Blanc

La Charité-sur-Loire

N

W — E

S

Vineyards
Woodland

0   5

Scale in Kilometres

Sancerre

Quincy

Reuilly

five miles ahead. Its postal district includes two saintly villages on the river 440 feet below, St-Satur and St-Thibault, where the Hotel Etoile is right on the river and the bridge leads across to the Pouilly vineyards and the straggling town of Pouilly-sur-Loire five more miles upstream. Until 1860 the wines were all shipped by cargo boat down river from this point.

Sauvignon Blanc, a great grape

The chalky soil is said to be similar to our own along the Dorset hills; the grape is wholly Sauvignon (pride of Bordeaux when mixed with Semillon to make Sauternes), yet the difference can be detected in the flavour of these two white dry 'flinty' wines, Sancerre and Pouilly-Fumé, if tasted side by side. More important, their quality has caused growers elsewhere — in California, for example — to try their luck too with Sauvignon Blanc (Blanc-Fumé and Fumé-Blanc as it can be called) in the hope of achieving the same flavour and lovely fragrance, already fulfilled in the Napa Valley.

Sancerre

The little square of Sancerre is charming but in its cafés tourists sampling wine can be exploited. Better to call on Pellay Père et Fils, 12 Avenue Nationale or on M. René Laporte on the way down. Most leading growers are to be found in the commune villages below the top on the western side: Bannay, Bué, Crézancy, Menetou-Râtel, Ménétreol, Montigny, St-Satur, Ste-Gemme, Sury-en-Vaux, Thauvenay, Veaugues, Verdigny and Vinon. These, and additionally Chavignol, may be met on labels hyphenated to Sancerre.

Two to three times larger than Pouilly, Sancerre also has room to make an appreciable amount of red and rosé, beloved by 'the natives' as Vinho Verde people in Portugal love their own red wine. Fortunately for them nobody else covets it. At the top, from the Esplanade, there is one of the great views of France, a 24-mile 120° sweep from the forest of Cosné in the North, East to Auxerre and the hills of Burgundy, South along the Loire to La Charité.

Among the best Sancerre is the wine from the Clos du Chêne Marchand, a large vineyard where Bernard Bailly, Lucien Crochet and Lucien Picard are prominent wine-makers.

Pouilly-sur-Loire

This is the name of the town and the district, involving three names and two appellations. *Pouilly Fumé* or *Blanc Fumé de Pouilly* (Blanc Fumé being the local name for the Sauvignon grape) is the first, a fine wine made wholly from the Sauvignon, minimum strength 11°, *Fumé* derives from the smokey green bloom that appears on the grapes as they ripen. *Pouilly-sur-Loire* (quite unrelated to the Mâconnais village of Pouilly-Fuissé) is the second, covering the lesser white wine made from Chasselas grapes, minimum strength 9.5°. The district runs along the Loire right bank for about fifteen miles to a depth eastwards of about five, total acreage 1250. Communes are Pouilly-sur-Loire, Tracy-sur-Loire, St-Laurent, St-Martin-sur-Nohain, Garchy, Mesves-sur-Loire and St-Andelain, the last named being the principal wine town.

Sancerre's 600 families said to be in wine outnumber Pouilly's by three to one. But Pouilly can boast one ancestral home that makes a fine wine where visitors are welcome. Baron Patrick de Ladoucette, the owner, is usually away selling his Château du Nozet to Americans and Paris restaurants. Easy to find on N7 North of Pouilly-sur-Loire, why not telephone his Paris office 125 Avenue des Champs-Elysées, Tel: 720.66.62 for an appointment?

Less acid than Sancerre, Pouilly-Fumé only needs a year in bottle, whereas two, even three, can benefit Sancerre, but no longer. For restaurateurs with good wine lists these fine Loire white wines make good companions for good Beaujolais.

Quincy and Reuilly

Two more small Sauvignon Blanc AOC districts lie thirty six miles south-west of Sancerre. Production is small and a sunny summer is needed to realise their full potential, when they can taste as good as Sancerre and cost less. A M. Olivier Cromwell is one of the Reuilly growers offering a round-headed wine of course.

To the source.

After Nevers a series of roads takes us through Digoin, Roanne, Feurs to Le Puys, some 220 miles from Pouilly-sur-Loire. From Le Puys the Loire, gradually diminishing to one of many streams, curves east of N102 towards its source on the lower slopes of Gerbier du Jonc. After Solignac locate and follow these names on Michelin Map 76: St-Martin, Ussel, Arlempdes, Lac d'Issarles, La Palisse and finally Ste-Eulalie, the last village.

Marvellous walking, amid herbs and violets, the Manoir hotel at Arlempdes is a good base. Those who have dined and slept *en route*, chez *Frères Troisgros* at Roanne, now acclaimed as the best restaurant in France, may need the exercise.

Sir, behold them with our blessing
Once again assembled here;
A mixed dozen worth possessing
Pure and blameless — far from dear;
May we send them
To thy presence — anywhere?

Blessed be your hours of leisure
With our choisest Loire array;
Titillate your palate's pleasure
Help your drinking day by day;
May our Wine Mine
Draw you cheque book — right away!

Wine Mine Summer 1967 (*with penitent acknowledgement to Hymns A &M 576 and 577*)

Champagne

To the Mall and the Park
Where we love till 'tis dark,
Then Sparkling Champaign
Puts an end to their reign;
It quickly recovers
Poor languishing lovers.
Makes us frolic and gay,
   and drowns all sorrow;
But, alas, we relapse on the morrow.

She would if she could
Sir George Etherege (1635-1691)

Sparkling wines are made in all wine countries, many by the best *méthode champenoise,* evolved in Champagne; but even the Japanese are unable to imitate satisfactorily what in Europe by law can only be made in that old province, a hundred miles east of Paris, its capital Reims where from 496 AD all the Kings of France were crowned. Until the seventeenth century the festive coronation

Land under Vines   AOC demarcated 85,000 acres. Planted 60,000 divided between *Départements*: Marne 39,000, Aisne 2,000, Aube 4,000. Extension 12,500 acres 1984/1994. Rendement 95 hectolitres a hectare (38 hectolitres an acre)
Growers   15,000
Champagne Houses   120
Appellation   Champagne. Strength — about 12 per cent. Styles — De Luxe, Vintage, Non Vintage, Dry to Sweet:- Brut, Extra Dry Sec, Demi-Sec, Doux or Rich
Grapes permitted   Pinot Noir (black) Pinot Meunier (black) Chardonnay (white)
Bottles   Standard size 75 centilitres, Magnum = 2 bottles, Jeroboam = 4 bottles, Methuselah = 8 bottles, Salamanezah = 12 bottles. Also half and quarter bottles.
Pressure in any bottle = 6 kilogrammes per square centimetre (same as in a London bus tyre)
Ideal storage temperature   10-12.7°C (50-55°F)
Ideal drinking temperature   6-8°C (43-46°F)
General information   The Champagne Bureau, Crusader House, 14 Pall Mall, London SW1. Tel: 01-839 1461

wine would have been a still red, or rosé, from the Pinot grape imported by the Champenois from Burgundy.

Evolving the sparkle

Gradually it was found that by a quick, light pressing the wine remained white and that when the autumn became cold, fermentation ceased before all the sugar had been converted to alcohol. With warmer weather in the spring it started again — a secondary fermentation giving the wine a prickle that pleased the court of Louis XIV in the 1660s. In London the courtier St Evremond introduced it to Charles II and the Restoration dramatists, so that the verse above, hardly dated, is probably the first reference in English.

The famous Dom Pérignon, a monk aged 30, took over his duties as cellarer of the Bénédictine Abbey at Haut-Villers above Epernay in 1668, improving immeasurably the quality of the new white champagne by his blending experiments. By the time he died in 1715 there were stronger bottles to withstand the pressure of the secondary fermentation, while the new cork stoppers confined the carbonic gas it formed to a life sentence in them until brought to an end by the consumer. Thus, for the first time, a wholly natural, fully sparkling wine could be made.

Three districts but only one Appellation

For this sparkling wine there is only one Appellation d'Origine — Champagne — so celebrated that the decree of 22 July 1927 does not even require the customary words, *Appellation Contrôlée* to appear on the label. Within the EEC only sparkling wines from the permitted 85,000 acres may be called champagne. The wine field has four parts: the mountain of Reims planted with Pinot Noir on the plain south of the city; the valley of the Marne planted with Pinot Meunier along the northern bank of the river, chiefly downstream from Epernay; the *Côtes des Blancs* on the southern side of the Marne east and south of Epernay planted with the white grape, Chardonnay. These three, snaking along the hillsides, form an almost continuous strip, seventy miles long but only 300 to 2000 yards wide. This is the *Route du Champagne,* the three parts sign-posted Red, Blue and Green to tally with a map and guide, called 'The Champagne Road', free from the shippers, Syndicats d'Initiative and British wine merchants; very useful in a car, pottering through the charming vineyards and villages with their peculiar, faintly familiar names like Verzenay, Bouzy, Dizy and Ay.

THE TOP TEN (QUANTITIES IN BOTTLES OF MATURED WINE LEAVING CELLARS)

	1980	1981	1982	1983	1984
France	121,436,120	109,425,143	102,629,384	109,854,865	125,000,000
Great Britain	8,517,954	7,879,907	7,771,632	10,021,164	11,903,242
United States	7,905,480	7,885,155	7,082,964	9,718,538	12,820,067
West Germany	5,304,079	4,521,494	3,659,596	5,335,460	7,411,546
Belgium	5,888,436	3,812,340	3,676,304	4,107,562	4,932,763
Italy	8,634,410	6,657,977	4,525,041	3,754,667	4,800,482
Switzerland	3,515,192	3,779,913	3,285,762	3,681,856	5,326,059
Netherlands	1,261,419	834,655	752,155	1,202,381	1,385,771
Canada	1,018,689	1,198,106	1,099,363	993,048	1,561,814
Australia	689,663	752,118	758,677	827,712	1,803,445

HARVEST YIELDS OF CHAMPAGNE

	1980	1981	1982	1983	1984
The harvest yields calculated in bottles were:	106,666,667	92,189,047	295,199,926	302,033,326	196,000,000

The tiny fourth part, some seventy miles to the south in the Aube *département* around Bar-sur-Seine and Bar-sur-Aube, has been rather a Cinderella, whose champagne might make the village hop but not the May week ball. I went there once for interest, finding bottles of champagne and the much more esteemed, Pinot Noir rosé called Les Riceys, at the Post Office in that village. Now, however, the region's Pinot Blanc has been replaced with Pinot Noir, which Moët are glad to include in their Brut Imperial Non-Vintage.

Climate

Why should the Marne make a sparkling wine with a flavour more appreciated than that of other regions, the Loire for instance? There is no cut and dried answer; one can only point to a combination of a chalky sub-soil with perfect drainage in a continental climate tempered by ocean-borne warmer air coming from the Atlantic. This gives an average annual temperature of 10°C, only one degree above the lowest temperature for full ripening of the wine grapes, and a humidity suited both to its growth and to its wines which, coming from three different grapes and scores of villages, have to be made, blended and matured in the chalk cellars. These, begun in Roman times, now exceed a hundred miles of cool galleries, up to 150 feet below ground, mainly underneath Reims and Epernay.

The vintage

Out of doors the year's routine is typical of the calendar on page 9. The young vines fruit after five years bearing well until they are thirty years old. Maintaining them involves twenty-five different operations a year — ploughing, pruning, spraying, etc. — mechanised where possible. Flowering — when the lilies come out too — lasts four or

PRINCIPAL CHAMPAGNE EXPORTERS

Ay	*Charles Heidsieck
*Bollinger	*Lanson
	*Krug
Epernay	*G H Mumm
*Moët & Chandon	*Pommery & Greno
*Perrier-Jouët	*Louis Roederer
*Pol Roger	Taittinger
Canard-Duchêne	*Veuve-Clicquot-
	Ponsardin
Reims	
*Heidsieck Monopole	**Tours-sur-Marne**
	Laurent-Perrier

*Member of Champagne Academy holding annual course for members of British wine trade.

five days at the end of May or early June. With good weather the vintage will begin a hundred days later, men and women coming to help the Champenois from many parts of France. For making white wine, grapes must be perfect and uncrushed. Sorters discarding as necessary, the whole job is completed without mechanical harvesters in about twelve days.

In Champagne the presses, operated principally by co-operatives and the big houses owning vineyards, are designed to press lightly 4000 kilos (4 tons) of grapes at a time, the juice descending quickly to the *cuves débourbage* below for a short time, before passing into oak casks or stainless steel vats to become wine after fermentation at 20°C.

For those selling their grapes the price is fixed annually in advance by the trade's controlling body, the *Comité Inter-professionnel du Vin de Champagne (CIVC)*. 150 kilos (330 lbs) of grapes are required to yield one hectolitre (22 imperial gallons) of juice. In practice each 4 ton press will produce 2666 litres (585 imperial gallons) but only the first pressing

of 2050 litres (450 imperial gallons) is good enough for the *cuvée* making champagne. The two subsequent pressings, *premiére* and *deuxiéme tailles,* completing the 2666 litres can be used for local drinking and distilling *marc de champagne.*

The cuvée

Each spring the experts of each champagne house start to make a new non-vintage wine that matches its predecessor. First they will blend one *cru* in different proportions with its neighbours, then others, tasting and comparing all the time. Paul Krug, for example, composes his Brut Reserve from nearly fifty different *crus*. After reducing them to eight different village wines he will blend each pair, 1 and 2, 3 and 4 etc. in different proportions, demonstrating even to a visitor how these two wine blends taste better than any of the eight. The four he will then blend into two and the two into one, each step creating an improvement. This is the great characteristic of champagne: the blend far excels the wines of single vineyards composing it.

The standard *cuvée* is roughly two parts of Pinot Noir to one of Chardonnay with a little older wine from reserves added. This is what gives champagne its consistent, mellow, subtle bouquet and flavour.

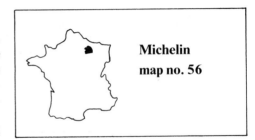

**Michelin
map no. 56**

Champagne-The Wine Region

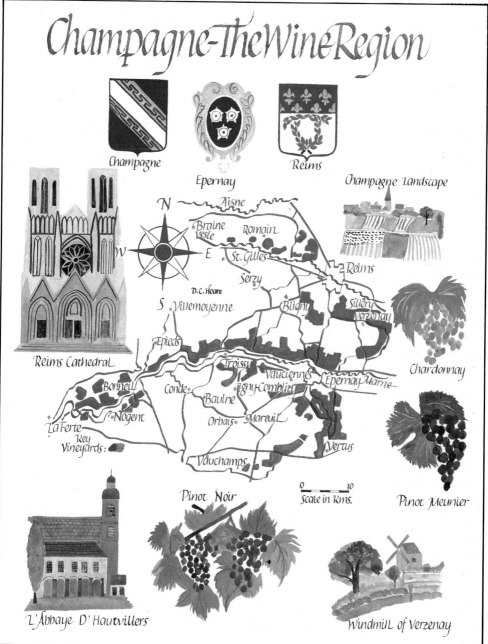

Champagne

Epernay

Reims

Champagne Landscape

Reims Cathedral

Chardonnay

Pinot Meunier

Pinot Noir

Scale in Kms.

L'Abbaye D'Hautvillers

Windmill of Verzenay

Méthode champenoise

Bottling operations begin early in April; the blended wines forming the *cuvée* are pumped to a huge vat, where the *liqueur de tirage* — a little yeast, sugar and champagne — is added. The bottles, usually sealed nowadays with a (temporary) crown cork as in a tonic water bottle, are stacked horizontally. The secondary fermentation, which can take from ten to a hundred days, starts immediately. When complete, that added sugar will have been converted to alcohol, raising the strength from 10° to 11° and the bottle will contain carbonic gas and an oily-looking brown sediment.

Two to five years of ageing are likely to elapse before the preparation for shipment begins, although the legal minimum is only one year for non-vintage and three for vintage champagne after the secondary fermentation.

Now comes the most interesting part of the *méthode champenoise,* fascinating visitors, who are warmly welcomed by all the big houses.

Remuage

The bottles, still horizontal, are placed in *pupitres* for *remuage,* a process of rotating, oscillating and tilting each by hand at intervals, causing the sediment to slide down to the cork in six to twelve weeks. The bottles will then be upside down and vertical. The French, recognising that a *remueur* handling up to 30,000 bottles a day could go as mad as Charlie Chaplin on the car production line with his brace of spanners, in 'Modern Times', take the precaution of making a *remueur,* who has a three-year training, the highest paid man in the cellars.

At least one firm however, has replaced its thirty-five *remueurs* with some two hundred gyro-palettes controlled by a computer, which being as efficient as mechanical harvesters relieve *homo sapiens* of a monotonous, uncreative job. Likewise *dégorgement* can now be done by machine.

Dégorgement

The *dégorgeur* who removes the sediment can uncork 1500 bottles a day. Still upside down, they reach him on the automated line; their necks have passed through a freezing mixture for seven minutes, so that the sediment is now encased in an ice pellet, which sticks to the side of the glass. When the *dégorgeur* puts a bottle upright and removes the temporary cork, out shoots the pellet. A little champagne, also lost, is replaced by a *dosage* of fine sugar dissolved in old champagne, the *liqueur d'expédition.* The size of this dosage varies: the minimum quantity makes *Brut,* the driest style: the maximum *Doux,* the sweetest; extra dry, dry or *sec, demi-sec* are the intermediaries in rising order of sweetness. The permanent cork, the dressing of the bottle and, ideally, a further rest period of several months, complete this preparation.

From sweet to dry

The evolution from sweet to dry occurred only a hundred years ago. Greater knowledge in the nineteenth century led to many improvements. Stronger bottles reduced the number bursting from internal pressure during the secondary fermentation, from 10 per cent to one quarter per cent. From 1850 to 1900 exports grew steadily from five to twenty-five million bottles a year and although the French themselves were left short, there was quite enough wine for champagne salesmen to go forth and sell wherever there was money.

But champagne prospered because

determined shippers believed that if the public would accept a dry wine it would then be drunk more at table, increasing sales immeasurably. Gradually they succeeded, reducing the dosage, I suspect, little by little until at last the label 'Very Dry' and its taste found favour with an Oxford undergraduate — Edward, Prince of Wales. Victory for the 'dry bobs' was assured by the 1874 vintage, the first ever to be shipped Brut or really dry.

Thus champagne became the wine for all occasions: from the royal shooting party where Edward, whether Gallic prince or Francophile monarch, would keep the sales rolling with his shouts of a bottle from 'the Boy', to the Grand Ball itself, kept rolling far into the night by 'the Bubbly'.

Grandes marques

Of some twenty-seven houses comprising the *Syndicat de Grandes Marques,* fifteen have appreciable sales in Britain. Among them, Bollinger and Krug stand out as the perfectionists, always aiming at and indeed achieving the highest quality. Since 1970, they have both been linked with Roederer and Veuve Clicquot-Ponsardin in a 'group of common economic interest'. Moët & Chandon; with their satellites Mercier and Ruinart, form part of the huge Moët-Hennessy-Dior combine and are the biggest producers. Heidsieck Monopole, Mumm and Perrier-Jouët operate under the banner of the Canadian House of Seagram, while Pommery and Lanson are part of a French food-processing group. Making and marketing globally a wine that must mature in bottle for several years requires increasing capital, which in times of inflation means mergers. Altogether there are 150 of these *négociants-manipulants,* some of the smaller firms

making very good, less expensive champagnes, Ayala, George Goulet, Giesler, Alfred Gratien, Jacquesson and Lambert being well known in Britain.

Buyers' Own Brands

Others supply British wholesale and retail outlets with champagne for their House brands. Known as BOBs in the trade, the buyer can change his supplier, should he wish without changing the name of his brand.

Styles and varieties

The following on the label indicate the flavour: *Brut* — very dry *Extra Dry* — dry *Sec* — slightly sweet *Demi-Sec* — sweet *Doux* or *Rich* — very sweet.

87 per cent of production is *Brut* and *Extra Dry.* 11% is *Sec* and 2% *Demi Sec* and *Doux.*

De Luxe Many of the Grandes Marques houses now ship a *De Luxe cuvée* in limited quantities. Moët & Chandon's Dom Pérignon and Bollinger R.D. are among the best known. Dom Pérignon was the first and has had twenty-one *cuvées* since 1921. 1979 and 1982 are the most recent. At £20 to £25 a bottle they should be two to three times better than non-vintage champagnes; rather a lot to expect.

Rosé or Pink Usually made by adding red wine from one of the best Pinot vineyards to the *cuvée,* pink champagne undoubtedly has an air of colour and gaiety. It has to be made with immense care lest the taste becomes too dry from the tannin in the skins of red grapes.

Blanc de Blancs A style of delicacy and charm made from the white grapes only, thus tending to cost a little more. Dom Ruinart *Blanc de Blancs* 1969 was much admired and Taittinger is nearly always vintage *Blanc de Blancs.* Most wines of the style are non-vintage. However, my personal favourite — acclaimed by the wine-writers — has been the Lambert *Blanc de Blancs* 1979, shipped in 1984 with a silver label to celebrate the Wine Mine Club's 25th anniversary, price £7.49.

Blanc de Noirs A white champagne made from black grapes. Relatively top-heavy, rarely met.

Doux or Rich A fully sweet style achieved by increasing the liqueuring or dosage to about 4 per cent as opposed to a half to three-quarters per cent for *Brut* and *Demi-Sec.*

Vintage and Non-vintage There is usually little actual difference in quality between vintage and non-vintage wines from the same shipper: the difference lies in their respective flavours. The vintage wines, because they are made only in the best years, are usually fuller than · the non-vintage, which are normally blended from the wines of several years. Only about 15 per cent of champagne is 'vintage'. As with port, the shipper declares a vintage. 1970, 1976, 1982 and 1983 are great years. Vintage and non-vintage will mellow in bottle, vintage for five to ten years, non-vintage up to three years. After that they slowly acquire a burnt *(maderisé)* flavour but can still be drunk.

Coteaux champenois This appellation covers *Vin natur de la champagne* or, in short, 'still champagne'. Bollinger, Laurent-Perrier and Moët & Chandon (Saran natur) make excellent examples.

Bouzy This still red wine of the region and also the sparkling Rosé des Riceys are entitled to the appellation *Coteaux champenois.*

Crémant A semi-sparkling champagne, see below.

Other sparkling wines

Every wine country uses some of its grapes to make sparkling wines — dry and sweet, red, white, rosé but mostly white. Many are less costly substitutes for champagne and just 'as effective at getting guests at parties 'gassing away' too in no time. In the EEC sparkling wines must be made from fresh grapes, grape must or still wine, their carbon dioxide gas being wholly derived from fermentation. French, German and Italian terms agreed in the EEC are:

Sparkling Pressure not less than three atmospheres at 20°C in closed container, Mousseux, Schaumwein, Spumante.

Semi-Sparkling Pressure between 1.5 and 3 atmospheres, Petillant, Spritzig, Frizzante.

Aerated wines Greatly inferior, these are wines just impregnated with carbon dioxide gas in the same way as mineral waters.

Crémant Attaining a little over three atmospheres, Crémant falls between sparkling and semi-sparkling. The name implies a creamy or foaming wine along the Loire, in Burgundy and even outside France. Crémant d'Alsace however is *fully* sparkling, possibly in keeping with the Alsatians' fit-to-burst appetite.

Méthode champenoise Secondary fermentation in the bottle makes the best quality. The two words, taken for granted in Champagne, will be found where appropriate on all EEC sparkling wine labels (and, one hopes, on California's).

Transvasage After secondary fermentation in bottles, the wine is transferred to tanks, where the deposit, sinking to the bottom, allows the clarified wine to be bottled under pressure from the tank. Germany's Kupfer-berg Gold is a good example.

Cuve close Also called *Charmat* after its inventor, closed tanks replace bottles. In the first tank the wine is aged by heating and cooling, in the second tank fermented and in the third tank clarified by refrigeration. *Autoclave* in Italian, Cuve close is said to be best for preserving the muscat fragrance in Asti spumante.

Alsace

Those who say they want to learn all about wine had better begin with Alsace lest they find the complexities of Bordeaux and Burgundy too discouraging. Alsace wines are 95 per cent white, wholly made from the grape by which they are named, written large on the label. As in Champagne one *Appellation d'Origine* — Alsace — covers them all, including the uninteresting 5 per cent red and rosés and the little sparkling Crémant d'Alsace that is made.

Protected by the Vosges mountains to the west, with the Rhine forming the Franco-German frontier to the east, Alsace is a dry, fertile, sunny plain with the perfect climate for growing fruits of many kinds. The vineyards, facing east on the lower slopes of the Vosges, are ideally placed. But even before Bismarck made Alsace a German province, from 1872 to 1918, the wines were of poor quality, and with the phylloxera present the Alsatian growers were glad to have a market in Germany.

It was not until after 1945 when the vineyards and villages had been devastated in the course of liberation that the growers started replanting with the declared aim of quality thenceforward. And in 1951 F.E. Hugel & Fils, who had in fact first introduced London to Alsace wines in 1936, gained their first British post-war customer — the Savoy Hotel.

Peaceful progress
Forty years of peace have enabled over 9000 growers to achieve a renaissance with a selection of very fine white wines indeed. For every hundred bottles of white AOC wine drunk in France, forty-five now come from Alsace; and 30 per cent of all Alsace AOC wine in 1983 was sold abroad. Though their language and their grapes are largely Germanic, the Alsatians' social habits are French. The Germans are beer drinking gobblers, who like to sip their own excellent light wines before or after meals. The Alsatians are gastronome-gobblers, who make wines to go with their food. For evidence turn to the *bonnes tables* map in the Michelin Guide, the stars are as numerous around Strasbourg as they are from Dijon to Chagny.

Land under vines   AOC 12,300 hectares (30,393 acres)
Permitted yield   100 hectolitres per hectare + 20 − 30 per cent
Production 1983   940,000 hectolitres (125 million bottles)
Fillings   White wines 96 per cent. Red and rosé 3 per cent. Crémant 1 per cent
Producers   9200; wine villages 120; employed in wine 30,000
Appellations   Alsace, Alsace Grand Cru, Crémant d'Alsace (sparkling)
Grapes permitted   Chasselas, Gewürztraminer, Muscat, Pinot Blanc, Pinot Gris, Pinot Noir, Riesling, Sylvaner
Qualities   Réserve, Réserve Personelle, Vendange Tardive, Selection de Grains Nobles
Home market   20 per cent of French consumption of AOC white wines is Alsace. Out of five bottles of Alsace AOC wines, one will be made and sold by small growers, two by merchant-producers and two by co-operatives, that at Eguisheim being the largest
Exports (1984)   277,000 hectolitres 40 million bottles (record)

Best customers
1   Germany
2   Netherlands
3   Belgium
4   Great Britain
5   USA
6   Canada
7   Denmark
8   Switzerland
9   Japan

Great years   1982, 1983

Chaptalisation

German and Alsace wines each benefit from chaptalisation to make them palatable. In the German regions, at least a hundred miles further north, too much acidity requires soluble sugar to be added before fermentation to increase alcoholic strength. After fermentation it can only be added legally in the form of grape must. In Alsace dry sugar is added to the juice before fermentation, which then converts all the sugar present into alcohol. AOC decrees require musts with at least enough sugar to make a wine of 8.5 per cent alcohol; the addition then gives a dry white wine of 11 per cent, a suitable strength for the palate. The German scientist Oechsle (1774-1852) gave his name to the scale used for measuring specific gravity and therefore the sweetness of grape must. 1° Oechsle indicates a litre of grape juice heavier by 1 gram than a litre of water. 100° Oechsle indicates that 1 litre of must contains 100 grams of sugar (including other substances). Dividing the Oeschle figure by 8 gives the approximate potential alcohol strength of the wine when all the sugar has been fermented.

Improving the quality

Fragmented ownership, in which only 300 out of the 9200 growers own a plot over five hectares ($12\frac{1}{2}$ acres) − and for 90 per cent their one or two hectare plots provide only a partial living − has not prevented the leading firms, notable F.E. Hugel et Fils, Trimbach, Dopff 'Au Moulin' and Dopff & Irion, from increasing exports by improving quality. For Riesling and Gewürztraminer there are now three grades, with these Oeschle figures.

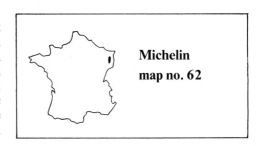

**Michelin
map no. 62**

Alsace: The Wine Region

Barr

Gertwiller

Wintzenheim

Gewürztraminer

Obernai

Andlau

Riquewihr

Mittelbergheim

Strasbourg
Nordheim
Molsheim · Braune Ittkirch
· Dotlsheim · Plobsheim
Lutzelhouse · Obernai
Schirmeck Barr
St. Blaise Epfig Stotzheim
Saasenheim
Chatenois · Sélestat
Bergheim
· Ostheim
Lapoutroie
Wintzenheim Colmar
Enguisheim
Longemer Munster · Hattstatt
· Rouffach
Fecht
Ensisheim
Thur · Cernay
St. Maurice Thann
Sewen
Soppe-
Le Bas
Rhine

0   10   20
Scale in Kms

N

W   E

S

D.C. Hoare

Riquewihr

Riquewihr

	Standard	Réserve	Réserve Personnelle
Riesling	70°— 75°	76°—85°	80° — 95°
Gewürz-traminer	85°	85°—95°	95°—105°

And to be thoroughly French, avoiding confusion with Germany, Alsace Spätlese and Beerenauslese wines are respectively *vendange tardive* and *sélection de grains nobles* with the following minimum Oeschle figures.

	Riesling	Muscat	Gewürz-traminer	Pinot Gris
Vendange tardive	95°	95°	105°	105°
Sélection de grains nobles	110°	110°	120°	120°

These late-picked grapes must not be gathered before an agreed date. Chaptalisation is not permitted and tasting by a panel is obligatory.

The additional appellation Alsace *grand cru* for white wines has been approved but is not much used at present. The yield per hectare is reduced to 70 hectolitres from the normal 100 but the alcoholic strength remains at the standard minimum of 10° for Riesling and Muscat, 11° for Gewürz-traminer and Pinot Gris. Site names may be used in conjunction with *Grand Cru* and a list of those so honoured is expected soon.

All Alsace AOC wines must be bottled in the region, preferably in the traditional green flute bottles.

The Grapes

The Alsace appellation drafted in 1945 became law in 1962. The grapes permitted, with proportions grown at present, are as follows:

Gewürztraminer (20 · 4 per cent) For most people this is love-at-first-sniff, so enticing is its spicy, fruity, pungent bouquet. Grown too in the Palatinate and Yugoslavia, no other region does it quite as well as Alsace. And no other wine holds a candle to it as a partner for smoked salmon and comparable foods strongly flavoured themselves such as Strasbourg's *pâté de foie gras.*

Riesling (19 · 6 per cent) Distinguished, elegant, medium dry, regarded as their best wine, as in Germany, but much fuller with a minimum strength of 10°. For the late Jean Hugel, Riesling was always first choice with *pâté d'Alsace, foie gras, truite au bleu, coq au vin* and other specialities of the region.

Muscat (3 · 5 per cent) This grape is generally associated with the sweet, rather cloying dessert wines met in Italy and the Mediterranean. In Alsace, however, it is luscious on the nose, dry on the mouth and some experts prefer it to Gewürztraminer.

Pinot Gris (Rulander) (4 · 6 per cent) The alternative name Tokay, said to be the grape imported from Hungary in 1550, has been disallowed by EEC regulations since 30 June 1984. I regarded the wine as a light sort of Riesling until I read in Hugh Johnson's *Wine Companion:* 'Dense, stiff and intriguing smell . . . rich deep-bosomed'. Quite a hot bottle! For laying down?

Pinot Blanc (Clevner) (17 · 6 per cent) The popular, straight-forward beverage wine of Alsace, slowly replacing the Sylvaner.

Pinot Noir (5 · 9 per cent) If and when we meet any red or rosé Alsatian wine, this will be the grape and the name on the label.

Sylvaner (20 · 7 per cent) The popular wine of Alsace, softer and cheaper than Riesling, refreshing and good value, yet plantings are being reduced.

Chasselas (3.3 per cent) (Gutedel in Germany, Fendant in Switzerland) is one of the eight *cépages nobles* but plantings decrease and the wine, which does not keep, is less esteemed nowadays.

Edelzwicker This term means a blend of the *cépages nobles* described above. Zwicker was disallowed in 1972. High consumption of Edelzwicker makes Germany the best customer.

The region

Fifty-four miles long and only one or two wide, the vine-growing region is divided between the *départements* of Haut-Rhin and Bas-Rhin. It begins in the former at Thann, a dozen miles north west of Mulhouse and ends in the latter at Wolxheim a dozen miles west of Strasbourg. Colmar and Sélestat divide it into three parts: one south of Sélestat, which includes Ribeauville and the quaint old half-timbered town of Riquewihr, having the highest reputation, while Colmar is the centre of the trade.

The grower-merchants

The astonishing feature of Alsace wine is how the ancient family firms have survived invasions forcing the inhabitants, some possibly still living, to change nationality five times. Hugel, one leading firm, has passed from father to son since 1637. The Trimbachs, Dopffs, Beckers have all been in business for three centuries. Used to change, they have certainly applied it to their trade since the Second World War.

Visitors

There is a well-posted *route des vins* through, or close to, the wine villages along which *caves de dégustation* are so numerous that an abstaining reserve driver in the car would be a help. The firms named above welcome visitors by appointment made through their London agents. Hugel & Fils at Riquewihr also welcome those without notice.

Crémant d'Alsace

Any of the Alsatian grapes are permissible for this sparkling appellation of 1976. The wine is fully sparkling, production has risen to a million bottles (still less than 1 per cent of the total) four-fifths drunk by the Alsatians themselves.

Alsace vintages

In general Alsace wines are drunk young and chilled. But in good years the best will certainly improve in bottle for at least four years. Being exceptionally good, 1982 and 1983 wines can be put away until the next century. (At a Hugel family wedding in 1921 a Pinot Gris 1862 was by far the best-loved guest.) Great years are 1961, 1966, 1969, 1971, 1976, 1982, 1983.

I went to Strasburg, where I got drunk
With that most learn'd Professor Brunk:
I went to Wortz, where I got drunken
With that more learn'd Professor Ruhnken.
Richard Porson (1759—1808)

Burgundy

Two hundred miles south-east of Paris on the routes, by road or rail, to Switzerland and the Mediterranean, the red and white wines of the thirty-mile golden slope between Dijon and Santenay, south of Beaune, have long been famous. A little sweeter than claret when young, the two red wines grow more alike as they age. Asked one afternoon if he had ever mistaken claret for burgundy, Harry Waugh, as good an expert as any, replied, 'No, not since lunch', which should by now have earned him a permanent place in *Familiar Quotations*.

That red wines as great as Bordeaux clarets can be made at all as far north as Dijon and Beaune is due to a continental climate, drier and hotter in summer and autumn than is southern England, where our vineyards have been limited to white wines. The slope also helps considerably by facing south-east.

Many of the other villages along the wine road N74 at the foot of the slope have double-barrelled names like Gevrey-Chambertin because in the last century the vineyard (Chambertin) was world famous but the villages were not, so they made the change to put themselves in the picture.

Rank and file

The quality classification of these Côte d'Or (and Chablis) wines smacks of the feudal system with the Lords, the *Grand Crus,* coming first, the Knights the *Premiers*

Land under vines	(acres)		
Département	**Total**	**AOC**	**Non-AOC**
Yonne	8,200	6,002	2,198
Côte d'Or	21,500	19,052	2,448
Saône et Loire	26,845	22,877	3,968
Rhône	52,822	49,675	3,147
Totals	109,367	97,606	11,761

Thus 90 per cent of the acreage is AOC and 10 per cent VDQS, Vin de Pays and Vin de Table

Number of Vineyards   18,650 of which 9717 produce AOC wines only, average size being about 10 acres

Production

Annual Average   1978 − 82 inclusive 807,000 hectolitres or 9 million cases.

1982 new record 1,287,000 hectolitres or 14.3 million cases

1983 936,000 hectolitres or 10.4 million cases

Fillings   1983 white 50.07 per cent; red 49.93 per cent. Production of white − 30 per cent up on 1982 − exceeded red for first time

Exports   75 per cent of average harvest, 80 to 90 per cent of wines exported leave the region in bottles

Reserves   On 31 August 1984, 1,212,000 hectolitres lay in the region. This figure is a 12 per cent decrease from 1983 but an 8.7 per cent increase on the previous five years and a 15 per cent increase on the last fifteen

Employed in wine   42 percent of vineyard owners are over 55 years old; they control 31 per cent of the area under vines

Best customers
1   USA
2   Belgium/Luxembourg
3   Great Britain
4   Switzerland
5   West Germany
6   Netherlands
7   Canada

ANNUAL OUTPUT – COTE D'OR

		Cases
Red Grand Cru, Premier Cru		103,000
White Grand Cru, Premier Cru		27,000
	TOTAL	130,000
Red Villages		1,385,000
White Villages		390,000
	TOTAL	1,775,000

Crus, next and the village names last. The thirty *Grands Crus* with their own AOC and no further address announce themselves as Le Montrachet, Richebourg, Romanée-Conti, Le Musigny etc., whereas the *Premiers Crus* are preceded by the village name, for example, Pommard Les Epenots, Meursault Perrières, Beaune Clos des Mouches. Other examples of village names are Nuits-St-Georges, Vougeot, Chassagne-Montrachet and Puligny-Montrachet.

Supply and demand
But viticultural Burgundy also includes Auxerre and Chablis north of the Côte d'Or and the Côte Chalonnaise, Mâcon and Beaujolais to the south of it. Add the lowest appellation Bourgogne and the total annual output, red and white, is about twenty million cases (12 bottles each), against about forty-two million cases for Bordeaux. Of those twenty million cases about 70 per cent will be Chablis, Mâcon, Beaujolais and Bourgogne AC, leaving from the Côte d'Or itself less than two million cases, white and red, or one bottle in ten.

Being far from sea transport, Burgundy's best customers have always been her nearest neighbours, Switzerland, Germany and Benelux. Over half the twenty million cases are exported to countries including Britain and the USA. Switzerland and the USA pay high prices for the finest wines, particularly the white.

These figures emphasise how demand exceeding supply has been a growing problem for Burgundy, possibly ever since Professor George Saintsbury in 1886 pronounced his Romanée-Conti 1858 as 'absolute perfection . . . unequalled for the combination of intensity and delicacy in bouquet and flavour, for body, colour and every good quality in wine'. (Today, whatever its merits, the price of the 1966 at £3700 a case, is also unequalled even by Château Pétrus.)

Vineyards reclaimed
To combat the problem fine red burgundies between the wars were vatted to mature much sooner. The trend has continued. During the 1970s the Chablis region, which supplied Paris before the coming of railways allowed the Midi to capture the market, has been extended from 1000 to 4000 acres. There has been a planting renaissance too in the Côte Chalonnais, and in the Hautes Côtes, the higher slopes westward of the classical Côte d'Or vineyards.

Chaptalisation
As already explained on page 76, Dr Chaptal's invention means adding sugar to the must (never the wine) to increase its strength. The cooler the summer the more necessary it becomes. In Italy, California and other hot countries it is illegal. The addition of sugar increases the alcoholic volume and improves the taste of young wines, making them easier to sell. Adding too much sugar gives a false impression, so in Burgundy the quantity added must not increase the strength of the wine by more than 2°. In practice, 1° to 1 · 5° is more usual

and in great years chaptalisation may not even be necessary.

Grape varieties

Red The Pinot Noir is the only permissible grape for Côte de Nuits, Côte de Beaune and Côte Chalonnaise. The Gamay is the only permissible grape for Beaujolais, and Mâcon Rouge. Passe-tout-Grains is an appellation made of two-thirds Gamay and one third Pinot Noir crushed together.

White The Chardonnay is the principal grape making Chablis, Côte de Beaune, Côte Chalonnaise and Mâconnais white burgundies. Bourgogne Aligoté is an appellation permitting white burgundy to be made from Aligoté, a secondary grape. Aligoté wines are light, pleasantly perfumed, good in carafe and relatively cheap. Maximum yield 50 hectolitres per hectare. Minimum strength $9 \cdot 5°$.

The 'Climat'

The classic vineyards of Burgundy were originally large domaines created by the Bénédictines and other religious orders. During the French Revolution they were split into allotments of a few acres; later the Napoleonic laws of inheritance dividing property equally between children, increased the number of owners. Consequently every *climat* — as these vineyards are called — is split up, Clos de Vougeot's 125 acres, divided between some seventy owners, being typical. Ironically, the one term left 'domaine-bottled' usually applies to a domaine only capable of making about two *pièces*, a *pièce* being a hogshead of 228 litres or twenty-five cases (each of 12 bottles).

Too little owned by too many

Romanée-Conti, the smallest *climat* is only $4\frac{1}{2}$ acres; Nuits-St-Georges, Clos de la Maréchale, the largest one under single ownership, only 24 acres. If every owner elected to bottle his own wine, apart from the cost of the equipment, fermenting in dribs and drabs would make quality control impossible. In practice, the village wines (for example, AOC Gevrey Chambertin, Nuits-St-Georges, Aloxe-Corton, Beaune, Pommard, Meursault) are made by the *négociants-éleveurs* (for example, Boisset, Bouchard Père et Fils, Clair-Daü, Drouhin) buying the grapes or the wine, as is also done in Champagne. These firms then blend the wines, marketing them under the appropriate AOC village label.

But in view of past irregularities, the French like to buy at source. Serena Sutcliffe's *Wines of the World* estimates that 40 per cent of burgundy is domaine-bottled and sold direct to the public by growers, who display their notices 'vente directe' from Easter onwards, taking the *négociants'* share of the profit without necessarily possessing their wine-making skills. This is more serious for the wine than the *négociants*; for if the proprietors are constantly pouring out samples for visitors during the summer instead of superintending work in their vineyards and cellars the quality could easily suffer. On the other hand, domaine-bottling is desirable for the *Grands Crus* and the best *Premiers Crus*, lest they find their way into the *négociants'* blending vats.

Enforcing the laws

This is a complex question; those wishing to understand it fully should read pages 40—54 of Anthony Hanson's *Burgundy*. He concludes that legislation of 1935 and 1974 has greatly improved the authenticity of Côte d'Or red burgundy, though a system, acceptable to the growers, ensuring that each wine is of the quality expected of its particular AOC, has still to be found. At present any surplus over the maximum yield (declared for each AOC each year) must only be sold for distilling or for vinegar, unless submitted and given its AOC certificate by a panel after analysis and tasting. In practice there are too many wines and not enough unbiased, knowledgeable tasters.

These rules prevent growers from blending burgundy from their own properties with that from other owners. Whenever wines are sold, *congé* (a small tax) must be paid to the local authority who issues an *acquit* (transport certificate) without which no wine can be moved to its destination. The procedure is somewhat simplified for cash sales to tourists or when exported commercially.

Labels
The following terms indicate clearly that a wine is domaine-bottled.
Mise en bouteilles par le propriétaire, Mise à la proprieté, Mise en bouteilles au domaine, Mise au domaine. The name of the grower followed by the word: *Propriétaire, Propré-taire-récoltant*, Viticuleur,* or *Vigneron**.*

The following terms are misleading.
Mise en bouteilles dans nos caves (Not clear whether the bottler is the owner of the vineyard; should not be considered as domaine-bottled.)

---

* Récolte. Harvest or crop.
** Vigneron. Vine-grower or vineyard worker, but can be an absentee owner with a crop-sharing agreement with a winemaker on the job.

Mise en bouteilles au château (Unless the château has some obvious connection with the name of the wine, this wine should not be considered as domaine-bottled.)

Making the wine
Except for points of detail, Côte d'Or red burgundy is made in much the same way as red Bordeaux. Maturing rather more quickly, the *Grand Crus* of great years like 1976 and 1978 will last for decades like their Bordeaux counterparts.

While cold fermentation before a short maturing in steel or concrete vats (as described for white Bordeaux) is usual for Chablis and Mâcon, the classic Côte de Beaune white burgundies remain in the small oak barrels, in which they are fermented for a further six months before bottling. The Montrachets, Meursault *Grand Crus* and Corton-Charlemagne then need a good five years fully to develop the grandeur that allows them to last as long as comparable red burgundies and clarets; up to sixty years perhaps if the cork, best renewed after twenty-five, remains sound.

Hazards of hail
The great enemy in the Côte d'Or is hail. Hardly a summer passes without an English newspaper headline, 'Hail wrecks Burgundy vintage'. Fortunately the storms are extremely local; in fact the vineyards are called *climats* because the crop of one small vineyard may be destroyed by hail while its neighbour remains untouched. Complete disaster seldom descends upon one village or on one person, because most proprietors own one plot here and another there.

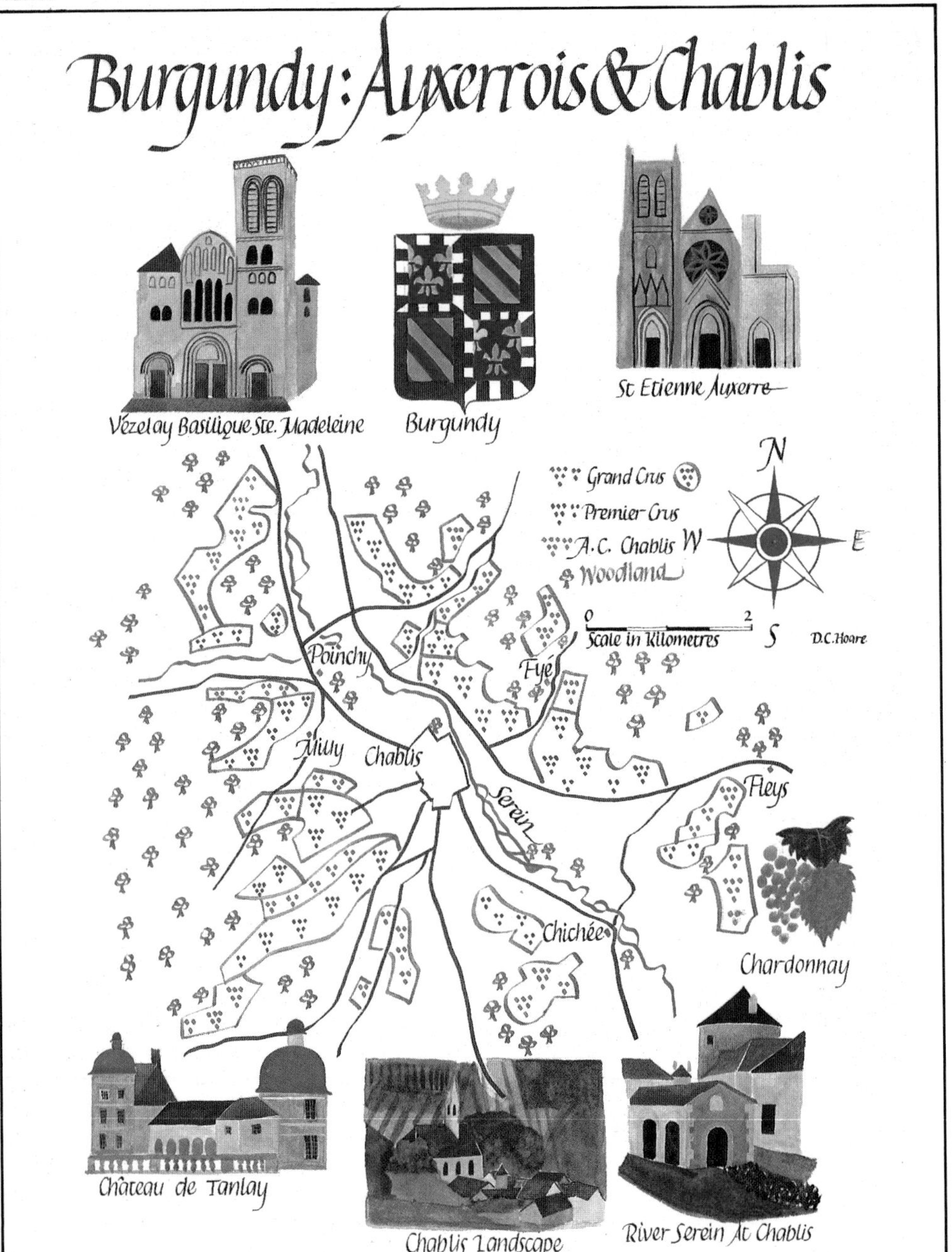

Burgundy: Auxerrois & Chablis

Vézelay Basilique Ste. Madeleine

Burgundy

St Etienne Auxerre

Grand Crus
Premier Crus
A.C. Chablis
Woodland

N
W E
S

0   2
Scale in Kilometres   D.C. Hoare

Poinchy

Fyé

Milly   Chablis

Serein

Fleys

Chichée

Chardonnay

Château de Tanlay

Chablis Landscape

River Serein At Chablis

DISTRICTS AND APPELLATIONS

Auxerrois Going south on motorway A6 or the main road N5, this district comprises six communes that include Irancy, Coulanges-la Vineuse and St Bris astride the river Yonne, less than ten miles west of Chablis and south of Auxerre. It is making a comeback, trying to provide red and white burgundies at reasonable prices.

In the Yonne district only, red wines made from local grapes, César and Tressot, qualify for the appellation which is Bourgogne. Maximum crop is 50 hectolitres per hectare. Minimum strength 10° red; 10.5° white.

Chablis

Driest of all the white burgundies, the seven Chablis *Grands Crus* and the dozen *Premiers Crus* are grown above the sleepy little town and its reedy river Serein on a bald south-west facing hump, where the chalky Kimmeridge bobs up again after crossing the Channel from Hampshire and Dorset. The combination of Chardonnay grape (called Beaunois here) and Kimme ridge soil leads to a light yellow wine with a touch of green, a subtle bouquet and a crisp, full flavour. To drink these *Grands* and *Premiers Crus* of a great vintage, such as 1978 or 1979, before they have had five years in bottle is a crime against their traditional companions — the oysters.

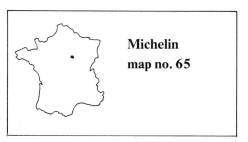

Michelin map no. 65

This restraint, however, need not be applied to the two lesser appellations, Petit Chablis and Chablis, which are ready to drink when bottled. Likely to come from the less calcareous plain, they are comparable to Mâcon Blanc and Mâcon Viré.

Being a hundred miles north of Dijon, spring frosts have frequently wrecked a year's prospects in spite of stoves being lit and tended in the vineyards all night. Recently water sprays have proved more effective, increasing the yield and encouraging more planting.

Grands Crus Blanchots, Bougros, Les Clos, Grenouilles, Les Preuses, Valmur and Vaudésir. (La Moutonne is part of the last two.) Maximum acreage: 250.

Premiers Crus Fourchaume, Montée de Tonnerre, Monts de Milieu, Vaucoupin, Les Fourneaux, Beauroy, Côte de Lechet, Mélinots, Montmains, Vaillons, Vaudevey and Vosgros. Maximum acreage 1084 with a further 770 permissible. On labels some other names may appear in conjunction with these *Premiers Crus.*

Some winemakers Bacheroy-Josselin, René Dauvissat, Jean Durup, William Fèvre, Henri Laroche, Long-Depaquit, Louis Michel, J. Moreau, Caves Coopérative La Chablisienne.

Before Christmas 1984 at least three of these *Premiers Crus* cost under £6 a bottle, quite the best value in fine white burgundies obtainable. Good value too even at £14 · 95 is *The Wines of Chablis* by Rosemary George, published by Sotheby in 1984. This is the first book of consequence in English on Chablis and the Yonne vineyards.

Byrrh
Is a bit too dyrrh:
So unhablis
Is Chablis.
(Kenneth L. Lewis, Bristol).
Wine Mine, Summer 1970.

Côte de Nuits
(Fixin to Nuits-St-Georges)

Virtually all red wines, the northern half of the Côte d'Or runs from Marsannay, five miles south of Dijon for about twelve miles southwards to the village of Corgoloin beyond Nuits-St-Georges. Marsannay makes notable red and white wines and a Pinot Noir rosé that is superb.

Fixin (5 miles from Dijon), first of the villages, has 51 acres for its nine *Premiers Crus* in a total of 316 acres. In Les Hervelets, one of the nine, Tim Marshall, a young Yorkshireman who succeeded in becoming the only British *courtier* in Burgundy, owns a plot, as avid *Wine Mine* readers may remember from his 1970 and 1971 vintages.

Gevrey-Chambertin (6 miles from Dijon) is renowned world-wide for its galaxy of eight *Grands Crus*, all Chambertins headed by Chambertin and Chambertin Clos de Bèze only five hundred yards up the slope from the main road N74. These two are rated by Alexis Lichine as the third-best *climats* in Burgundy, placed after Romanée-Conti and La Tache. Others, more fanciful, have likened them to Beethoven's 9th, the choral symphony. Their lesser, hyphenated relations Latricières-Chambertin and others he places from twelfth to fifteenth. The names of the twenty-six *Premiers Crus* are less familiar; they are small and apt to go to long-standing customers in France or Switzerland.

Morey-St-Denis (8 miles from Dijon) In the days when wine-writers waxed lyrical, Chambertin was always the King and Musigny the Queen of burgundies. Sandwiched between them Morey-St-Denis, certainly a Prince of the Royal House, is seldom recognised. It has five *Grands Crus* — Bonnes Mares (in part), Clos de Lambrays, Clos de Tart, Clos de la Roche and Clos-St-Denis. 'All the wines of Morey are worth study, for authenticity and a chance of a bargain', declares Hugh Johnson in his *Wine Companion,* so I'm proud to say that one or other of these four has rarely been absent from any Dominic list these past thirty years.

Chambolle-Musigny (9 miles from Dijon) Only two *Grands Crus* here but of what quality! Lichine puts Musigny (28 acres) fifth and Bonnes Mares (larger part 33 acres) seventh in his all-Burgundy table of merit. A further 150 acres are occupied by fifteen *Premiers Crus* that include those pretty names Les Amoureuses and Les Charmes beloved of Britain's best burgundy imbibers.

Vougeot (9 miles from Dijon) Famous for its Clos, 125 acres enclosed by a great thirteenth-century wall with a massive Renaissance château at the top, both were built by the monks of Citeaux. The sloping

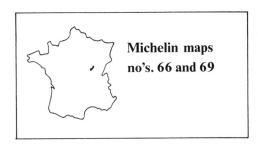

Michelin maps
no's. 66 and 69

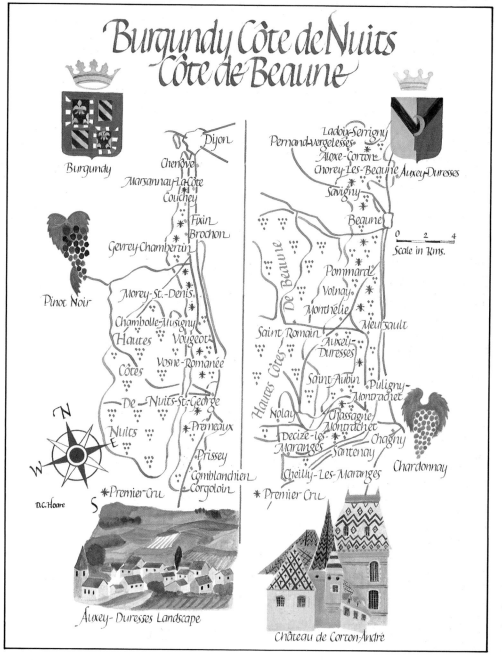

Burgundy Côte de Nuits Côte de Beaune

Burgundy

Pinot Noir

Dijon
Chenôve
Marsannay-La-Côte
Couchey
Fixin
Brochon
Gevrey-Chambertin
Morey-St.-Denis
Chambolle-Musigny
Hautes
Côtes
Vougeot
Vosne-Romanée
De Nuits-St-George
Nuits
Premeaux
Prissey
Comblanchien
Corgoloin

*Premier Cru
D.C.Hoare

N W S E

Ladoix-Serrigny
Pernand-Vergelesses
Aloxe-Corton
Chorey-Les-Beaune Auxey-Duresses
Savigny
Beaune

0 2 4
Scale in Kms.

De Beaune

Pommard
Volnay
Monthélie
Meursault
Saint Romain
Auxey-Duresses
Hautes Côtes
Saint Aubin
Puligny-Montrachet
Nolay
Chassagne-Montrachet
Decize-les-Maranges
Chagny
Santenay
Cheilly-Les-Maranges

* Premier Cru

Chardonnay

Auxey-Duresses Landscape

Château de Corton-André

87

vineyard divided into 107 plots with seventy-five owners produces many different Clos de Vougeot, the best coming from the part alongside the wall south-south-east of the château. Though they can't tell us this on their labels, you will find the names on the plan of the Clos, pages 201/202 of Anthony Hanson's Faber book *Burgundy.*

This Château is a national monument, owned since 1944 by that vigorous, vinous brotherhood the Confrèrie des Chevaliers du Tastevin, which holds jovial banquets in the course of promoting the wines of Burgundy to the world. I joined a guided tour one Sunday evening in April 1983, which finished with a free glass and a film. It is open daily all the year except from 20 December to 25 January.

Vosne-Romanée (12 miles from Dijon) The greatest galaxy in the red burgundy heaven comprises almost fifty acres owned by the Domaine de la Romanée-Conti, associated with Mme. Bize-Leroy and M. Aubert de Villaine, who are active on the marketing side.

Romanée-St-Vivant is rented from Domaine Marey-Monge. The Domaine also has a 1.66 acre stake (200 cases) in Le Montrachet. These are the only red burgundies that feature regularly in London auctions. In 1984, prices per case of the very fine 1969 and 1971 vintages were around £360 for Grands-Echézeaux, £650 for Richebourg, £800 for La Tache and £1200 for Romanée-Conti 1971.

Nuits-St-George (14 miles from Dijon). A small town rather than a village, with two good restaurants and a hotel, the name everybody knows has no *Grand Cru,* making up for the omission with thirty-nine *Premiers Crus.* The nine are a contribution

ACREAGE AND ANNUAL PRODUCTION
DOMAINE DE LA ROMANÉE–CONTI

	Acres	Cases
La Romaneé-Conti	4.45	600
La Tache	14.80	2000
Richebourg	8.60	1200
Grands-Echézeaux	8.70	1200
Echézeaux	11.50	1500

from Prémeaux, the village down the road and part of the appellation. Familiar names may be Les-St-Georges, Les Vaucrains, Les Cailles, Les Porrets.

Côtes de Nuits Villages Wines of Prissey, Comblanchien and Corgoloin, the last three communes of the Côtes de Nuits are sold under this appellation, to which Fixin and Brochon further north are also entitled.

Some Wine-makers The grower-merchants based in the Côtes de Nuits number nearly two hundred. Here are some names of the best known exporters, preceded by the towns in which they are based; the plots they own are spread about the region.

Marsannay: Clair-Daü
Gevrey-Chambertin: Armand
    Rousseau, Louis Trapet, Domaine
    des Varoilles
Morey St-Denis: Héritiers Cosson,
    Domaine Dujac, Robert Groffier
Chambolle-Musigny: Clerget, Grivelet,
    Hudelot-Noëllet, Comte de Vogue
Vougeot: Bertagna
Vosne-Romanée: Henry Lamarche,
    Liger-Belair, Mugneret, Noëllat,
    Marey-Monge
Nuits-St-Georges: Boisset, Bruck,
    F. Chauvenet, Faiveley, Geisweiler,
    Henri Gouges, Lupé-Cholet, Tim
    Marshall
Prémeaux: Charles Viénot

Côte de Beaune (Aloxe Corton to Santenay)
The Côte de Beaune begins with a red and a white burgundy, as famous as any met so far, in its first commune Aloxe (pronounced Aloss) -Corton. From Beaune through Pommard and Volnay the vineyards are again all Pinot Noir until we reach Meursault and the Montrachets, at the tail end where the white Chardonnay reigns supreme.

Aloxe-Corton (25 miles from Dijon). These vineyards, lying below and around the conspicious wooded hill with a flat top on our right passing Ladoix-Serrigny, go back to 858 AD, possibly earlier since Charlemagne in 775 gave land for vines hereabouts to the monks of Saulieu.

The appellations are simplified by remembering that Corton, either alone or with another vineyard name hyphened to it, indicates a *Grand Cru;* whereas Aloxe-Corton refers to a *Premier Cru* or a village wine and is second best. As elsewhere the vineyards are split among different proprietors, the appellation Corton entitling them to grow Pinot Noir *or* Chardonnay. The red Le Corton, however, is considered good enough to rank with a Chambertin; its hyphenated neighbours include Bressandes, Clos du Roi, Perrières and Maréchaudes.

The *Grand Cru* appellation for the white wine is Corton-Charlemagne. Besides the actual 42 acre vineyard of this name, a few smaller *climats* are entitled to it. Corton-Charlemagne often needs as much as seven years in bottle to show why it is so esteemed. Among the proprietors is the Maison Louis Latour with headquarters at Château Corton-Grancey in the village and a stake in many of the vineyards here and elsewhere in the Côte d'Or. Other proprietor-merchants offering Corton *Grands Crus* include Bouchard Père et Fils, Drouhin, Jadot, La Reine Pédauque and Pierre Ponnelle.

Savigny-les-Beaune Bounded by Aloxe-Corton to the east, N74 to the south and the Autoroute A6 to the west, these vineyards lie on either side, climbing the two miles up the little Rhoin river valley, to the small town Savigny-les-Beaune, source of good sound red burgundies from some twenty *Premiers Crus* and as many growers.

Beaune (28 miles from Dijon). Capital of the Côte d'Or *département* and certainly capital of Burgundy's wines, Beaune is a delightful old town of churches, walls, cellars and sights, worth walking round with Robert Speaight's *Companion Guide to Burgundy* in hand. The vineyards lie along the familiar slope north-west of the town, so close that M. Claude Bouchard has only a 15-minute walk from his office in the old Château de Beaune to inspect a wayward tendril in Clos de la Mousse, an $8\frac{1}{2}$ acre vineyard that belongs wholly to his firm which began in 1731.

Altogether Bouchard Père et Fils vinify 3000 pièces (75,000 cases) a year, many from their domaines which now total 209 acres, 180 of them being *Grand* and *Premiers Crus*. In summer a multi-lingual hostess takes visitors round the cellars under the Château which hold six million bottles and, given notice, they will provide a tasting for those with appointments.

Beaune's thirty-four *Premiers Crus* covering 854 acres include: Grèves, Clos des Mouches, Cent Vignes, Cras, Epenottes, Marconnets, Clos-de-la-Mousse, Teurons and Vignes-Franches.

Some wine-makers Bouchard Père et Fils, Chanson Père et Fils, Joseph Drouhin, Hospices de Beaune, Louis Jadot, Louis Latour, Don Jacques Prieur, Pierre Ponnelle, La Reine Pedauque, Ropiteau Frères, Roland Thévenin.

The Hospices de Beaune The famous hospital in Beaune with the yellow, green and black polychrome roof was an alms house founded in 1443 by Nicolas Rolin, tax collecting Chancellor of Burgundy. Having made so many people poor they said it would be wise for him to appease the Almighty by providing for some of them. After being the first to give vineyards to endow it, Rolin and his wife have been followed over the centuries by others, making up thirty-two *cuvées* altogether from about 140 acres.

Amid celebrations that include two dinners and a luncheon that lasts till dinner, wine buyers from home and abroad assemble in Beaune for the public auction of these *cuvées*, held in the market hall near the Hospice on the third Sunday each November when the wines, being only a few weeks old, are difficult to judge. However, it is all in aid of charity and *restaurateurs* like a Hospice wine or two on their lists, so high prices are paid.

Though there is now a modern hospital across the road, the original Gothic Hôtel-Dieu, open to the public and not to be missed, still houses some old people and orphans.

The three festivities known as Les Trois Glorieuses begin on Saturday with a Chevaliers du Tastevin dinner in the Château de Clos de Vougeot; on Sunday there is the Diner aux chandelles in the Bastion cellars near the Hospices and on Monday the luncheon is La Paulée* de Meursault. Old wines however are too scarce to lavish on these huge parties, which are really for the vignerons and their guests.

Pommard and Volnay After Beaune the *Route des Vins* branches through the villages of Pommard and Volnay, the former so well known that bottles can conceal almost anything except burgundy from its twenty-six *Premiers Crus*. Les Rugiens and Les Epenots are the best known.

In Volnay pride of place goes to Caillerets; the 1889 vintage inspired Maurice Healy, who wrote *Stay me with Flagons*, to instruct his readers on preparing themselves to drink a great bottle. It appears that one should combine the reverence of a Deacon about to be ordained with the concentration of Jack Nicklaus about to hole a twenty yard putt. From Volnay N73, the vineyard road, climbs past Monthélie, with an old world charm greater that that of its wines, to Auxey Duresses yet another commune where the white wines are better that some Meursault and good reds cost less than those of Volnay and Pommard.

Meursault White burgundies are made from grapes fully ripe so that all the sugar is converted into alcohol during fermentation to give a dry, full-bodied, velvety white wine. This commune makes the most and indeed some of the best, which come from Perrières, Poruzots, Charmes, and Genevrières, the four top sites in a total of sixteen. The village of Blagny at the southern end also makes a distinguished contribution to the Meursault appellation.

Wines can be bought at retail prices in the

---

* Local name for a siesta.

Château de Meursault, now owned by Patriarche, an old company with progressive ideas, as well as in the *Cave de l'Hôpital* operated by the well-known firm of Ropiteau Frères based in the town.

Meursault also has a small acreage of Pinot Noir, making red burgundies sold as Volnay.

Puligny-Montrachet. In this commune the magical word is Montrachet, derived from Mont-Rachet, 'the hill without a tree' and pronounced 'Mon-rash-ay'. The celebrated vineyard, making the finest white burgundy of all, runs across the boundary between the communes of Puligny with ten acres and Chassagne with nine, and in 1879 they appended the great name.

These nineteen acres are split among a dozen owners, who succeed in making 2500 cases all told in a good year. The Marquis de Laguiche with four acres contributes some 650 cases, distributed by Joseph Drouhin of Beaune. Baron Thénard (distributors: Remoissenet) should provide another and Bouchard Père et Fils about 300. Another 300 should come from the domaines of Jacques Prieur of Meursault, Romanée-Conti and Comtes Lafon. These names are the best known. Please remember that to drink Montrachet before it is seven to ten years old is a terrible waste of your money and the wine-makers' skill.

Fortunately the four surrounding vineyards, Chevalier-Montrachet (1650 cases), Bâtard-Montrachet (3850 cases), Bienvenues-Bâtard-Montrachet (1100 cases) and Criots-Batard-Montrachet (800 cases) make, with Le Montrachet, a *Grand Cru* entity, unlikely to be rivalled even though the Chardonnay grape now makes fine wines in Australia and California.

Entirely given to white burgundies,

Puligny's best value lies in its eleven *Premiers Crus* and, its own village appellation, Puligny-Montrachet.

Some wine-makers Domaine Robert Ampeau at Meursault; Domaine Leflaive at Puligny-Montrachet; Louis Jadot at Beaune.

Chassagne-Montrachet The name of this next commune makes it as closely associated with fine white burgundies as Puligny. But, apart from a third of Montrachet, a third of Batard-Montrachet and all four acres of Criots, it concentrates mostly on red burgundies, six out of eight *Premier Crus* having a red or white appellation. Red Chassagne-Montrachet can be a very good buy.

Santenay Franco-Scot, Paul Dauthieu thought that this sanitary sort of name put British people off the lighter red burgundies made in this southern commune of the Côte d'Or. True, the place does have some salty waters said to flush away gout and the rheumatics, but to Hugh Johnson, raising a glass and crying 'Bonne Santé(nay)!', the waters are a sign of good health. Santenay gives us 90,000 red cases and 1200 white most years.

Hautes Côtes de Nuits and Hautes Côtes de Beaune

I frankly confess that when I noticed 'Hautes Côtes de Nuits Cuvée Bevy FB 1978 Geisweiler' in a 1983 list neither of these appellations meant anything to me. Anthony Hanson (in *Burgundy*) explains that in the hills beyond the communes along the wine road N74, there were once thriving Pinot Noir vineyards — with some Chardonnay and Aligoté — sadly diminished

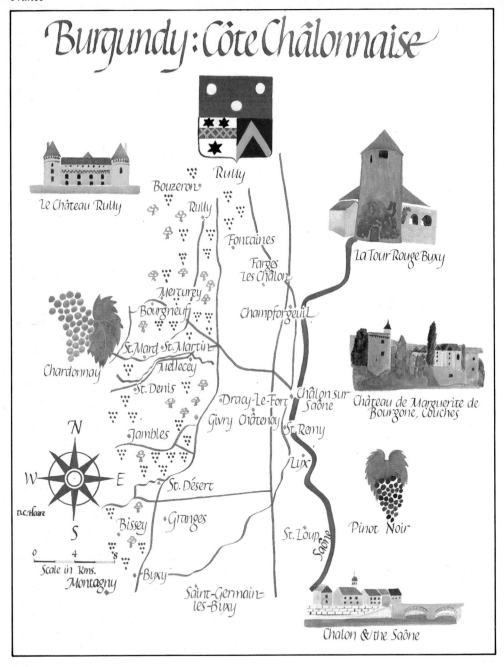

Burgundy : Côte Châlonnaise

Le Château Rully

La Tour Rouge Buxy

Château de Marguerite de Bourgone, Couches

Pinot Noir

Chalon & the Saône

Rully
Bouzeron
Rully
Fontaines
Farges Les Châlon
Champforgeuil
Merturey
Bourgneuf
Chardonnay
St. Mard St. Martin
Mellecey
St. Denis
Dracy-Le-Fort
Châlon sur Saône
Givry Châtenoy
St. Remy
Jambles
Lux
St. Désert
Bissey
Granges
St. Loup
Saône
Byxy
Montagny
Saint-Germain-les-Buxy

N
W E
S

D.C. Hoare

0   4   8
Scale in Kms.

by mildew and finally finished by First World War casualties.

By degrees since 1961 they have been replanted in a manner suitable for mechanisation. In the van was Geisweiler, *négociants* since 1804, with seventy hectares at Bevy, near Nuits-St-Georges. This has now led to their *Cuvées 18éme siècle,* old style wines at an old-fashioned price. Bouchard Père et Fils also bought a property called Château de Mandelot. At Orches, five miles west of Meursault, there is now a modern co-operative largely serving the Swiss.

The appellation of these *Hautes Côtes* is just Bourgogne but judging by a case of Bourgogne St-Christophe 1978 costing 36 francs from Bernard Roy of Auxey-Duresses when last I was there, plain Bourgogne can be very good indeed at four years old.

Côte Chalonnaise

Stretching a dozen miles south of Chagny, four village appellations, Rully, Mercurey, Givry and Montagny (white wine only) comprise the Côte Chalonnaise. John Arlott and Christopher Fielden's *Burgundy Vines and Wines* was the first English book to describe how the 'wine explosion' of the 1960's had brought capital to revive these vineyards, which died of disease and neglect after 1918 when so many of its men lay dead in Flanders fields.

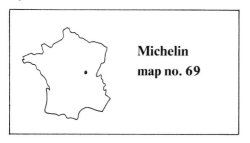

**Michelin
map no. 69**

After the Second World War Rully's Chardonnay grapes made sparkling wine, including the excellent Cristal Dry, which at wedding receptions launched many a bride. One of them married a Midshipman, inspiring a *Pinafore* parody in *Peter Dominic's Wineyard* years ago.

For he holds that Cristal Dry
That wine from Burgundy
A matrimonious harmonious
   tone implants:
And so do his sisters and his cousins and his
   aunts!
His sisters and his cousins —
They just order it in dozens —
And his aunts!

About 1970 the supplier, Meulien-Pigneret, was bought by the son of a Rully grower, trained in oenology at Dijon University. His name was Jean-François Delorme and when he came to London, David Peppercorn (at that time buyer for International Distillers & Vintners) told me he would go far. This indeed proved correct. Serena Sutcliffe, tells in *Great Vineyards and Winemakers* how his Domaine de la Renarde has achieved in twenty years no less than 140 acres spread over the four communes, making wines of high quality. A man with red, white and sparkling fingers, Jean-François had led a great recovery for Chalonnais burgundies, apt to cost half the price of their northern neighbours.

Rully's white burgundies have a marked bouquet and flavour. Hanson regards Delorme's 'as not far removed from Meursault'. His red Rullys are ready earlier and finer than Mercureys, he declares. Nevertheless, Mercurey's production of these charming, less full-bodied burgundies makes it the most important of the communes. Givry Rouge, becoming

Burgundy: Mâcon & Beaujolais

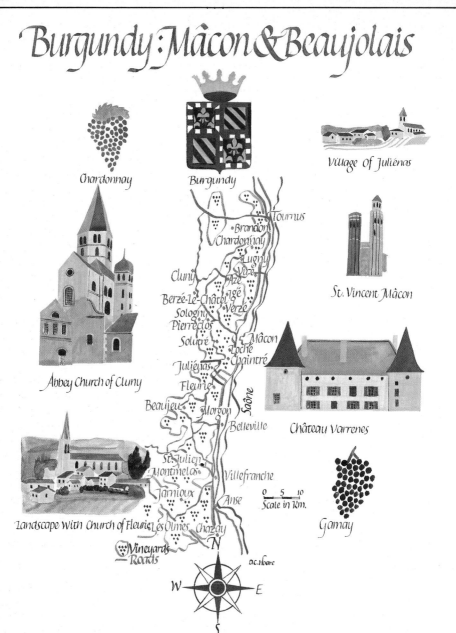

Chardonnay

Burgundy

Village Of Juliénas

Abbey Church of Cluny

St. Vincent Mâcon

Tournus
Brandon
Chardonnay
Lugny
Cluny
Viré
Azé
Igé
Berzé-Le-Châtel
Verzé
Sologny
Pierreclos
Mâcon
Solutré
Loché
Chaintré
Juliénas
Fleurie
Beaujeu
Morgon
Saône
Belleville

Château Varrenes

St. Julien
Montmelas
Villefranche
Jarnioux
Anse

0   5   10
Scale in Km.

Landscape With Church of Fleurie
Les Olmes
Chazay

Gamay

Vineyards Roads

D.C.Hoare

N
W   E
S

ANNUAL PRODUCTION IN CASES — CÔTE CHALONNAISE

Districts and appellations	Rouge	Blanc	Crémant
Rully	33,000	33,000	170,000 from the whole region
Mercurey	162,000	18,000	
Givry	39,600	4,400	
Montagny	—	40,000	
Bourgogne Aligoté			Aligoté appellation granted in
de Bouzeron		11,000	1979 to this village only

familiar in Britain, needs a good year like 1982 to be at its best. Its Clos Saloman, still in the family, supplied the Pope in 1375 and used to be kept in cask for three years not two. Montagny's appellation is for Chardonnay, which may be labelled *Premiers Crus* if strengths exceed 11.5°. The local reds are just AOC Bourgogne or Passe-Tout-Grains. There are good co-operatives at Montagny and at Buxy.

Route de Vin N481 from Chagny to Cluny is a pleasingly rural route passing the charming village of Mercurey where a stop might be made for a *dégustation* or for lunch at the flowered Hostellerie du Val d'Or.

Some wine-makers François Protheau et Fils, Domaine Thénard, Caves des Vignerons du Buxy-Saint-Gengoux.

Mâconnais
As we see annually in the Beaujolais Nouveau race, Mâcon wines reach London

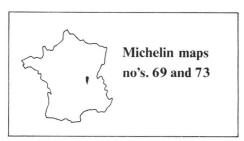

**Michelin maps
no's. 69 and 73**

or Paris in a matter of hours. And not only by air — a new railway line and a new autoroute bring Paris within three or four hours of Lyon. Before 1854, when the railway arrived, transport was twice yearly: in October before the winter ice froze the Saône, the Loire or the Canal du Centre, and in Spring, quantity being less a *tonneau* or two, necessary for the morale of the boatmen.

Mâcon The white wines, being from Chardonnay grapes, are true white burgundies. For red wines the Pinot Noir does not grow well enough on the chalky soil to merit more than AOC Bourgogne. The Gamay does better and, using *macération carbonique,* red wines more like AOC Beaujolais are made. But with Beaujolais on granite and Mâcon on chalk their wines should always be different.

Appellations with minimum strengths
White: Mâcon Blanc 10°, Mâcon Supérieur 11°, Mâcon-Villages 11°. (43 villages, best-known Clessè, Prissé, Lugny, Viré.)
Red: Mâcon Rouge 10°, Mâcon Supérieur 11°

With seventeen co-operatives (membership 2700), other growers and a score of merchants, bottlings under these Mâcon labels must come to about 1¾ million cases a year.

Appellation	
Pouilly-Fuissé 11°	373,000
St Véran 11°	133,000
Pouilly-Loché,	
Pouilly-Vinzelles, and	
Pouilly with other village	
names permitted to hyphen 11°	55,000
TOTAL	561,000

Pouilly-Fuissé Not to be confused with Pouilly-Fumé from Pouilly-sur-Loire, these Chardonnay wines are the best of the Mâconnais. Coming south from Cluny the rocky lumps of Solutré and Vergisson rise out of the Saône valley, the sleepy wine villages unseen at their feet.

Beaujolais

After the complexities of white burgundy and the Mâconnais, it is a relief to reach a region where there is one grape and one wine, most of it ready to be drunk very soon after the vintage. Beaujolais, lying immediately to the west of N6, the Paris-Mâcon-Lyon road, is five to ten miles wide and thirty-five miles long. Hilly at first for fifteen miles going south through the chief wine villages, it widens out into a farming countryside of woodland and woodpeckers, hills and hoopoes, meadows, streams and of course vineyards.

These were not planted until after the Revolution and by guess or by God they chose the Gamay grape, which excelled itself on the poor sandy soil as never before or since. Consequently, the region is said to contain six thousand jolly wine farmers, most of them selling their grapes to the region's co-operatives and quaffing their fair share of the five or six million cases made each year. Another two hundred merchant firms look after the rest of France and the world.

Macération carbonique (page 20) is the modern method of making red wines that require no ageing in wood and can be bottled, sold and drunk soon after the vintage. Beaujolais, fruity and fresh, has always been a wine to drink young, much of it consumed locally in good condition from casks topped up as fast as it was drunk.

Nowadays the grapes are gathered in bunches, stalks and all. In the press house the plastic tubs from the vineyards are emptied, ideally into small, sixty-hectolitre vats. The weight of the top layers suffices to crush and produce juice from the lower layers, which start to ferment naturally. The carbon dioxide thus produced seals the uncrushed upper layers from the air, enabling the enzymes within each of these grapes to ferment them in an atmosphere of carbon dioxide. After only five or six days a sixty-hectolitre vat will contain thirty litres of must, which is then pressed to extract the rest of the juice.

Appellations

Appellations, with minimum strengths and approximate annual production in 1983, an exceptionally good year:

Beaujolais 9° (6 · 25 million cases). This is the traditional 'purple-stained mouth' wine made mainly in the southern farming land, south and west of Villefranche and available annually from 15 November after the vintage. *Supérieur,* seldom used, is 10°.

Beaujolais-Villages 10° (4 · 1 million cases). Covers villages in the northern part of the region other than the nine *cru* villages below.

Beaujolais Crus 10° (3 · 4 million cases). From north to south these nine *crus* are:

St-Amour, Juliénas, Chénas, Moulin-à-Vent, Fleurie, Chiroubles, Morgon, Brouilly and Côtes de Brouilly. These wines, not bottled before March after the vintage, are at their best from one to four years after it. In Morgon, Chénas and Moulin-à-Vent they do lay down some bottles for longer, to show — not very convincingly — how the Gamays can keep up with the Pinots.

Merchant-shippers Out of some twenty firms those best known in Britain are Georges Duboeuf, Loron & Fils, Mommessin of Mâcon (who welcome visitors with appointments from their agents), Pasquier-Desvignes and Piat, who needed new premises outside Mâcon in 1980.

Piat et Cie Founded in 1849 the Piat family firm developed a close relationship with International Distillers and Vintners (Peter Dominic's parent company) during the 1960s until in 1974 when Charles Piat retired IDV bought the business. The *crus* are always well represented in retailers' wine lists by top properties with which Piat have long had exclusive arrangements. These include the Princess de Lieven's Morgon, Château de Bellevue, Julienas, Domaine de Beauverney and the Château de St-Amour, where the Siraudin family have lived since 1478. Buying Beaujolais from such a company, based not in Beaune but on the spot in Mâcon has obvious advantages and Piat's traditional 'pot' bottle is now known world-wide.

Beaujolais terms explained
Vin de l'année (wine of the year) describes all Beaujolais of the last vintage until the next. *Beaujolais Nouveau*, the 'new'

Beaujolais, means the same.

Beaujolais Primeur (the first Beaujolais) is the youngest possible Beaujolais, a *cuvée* hurriedly made for immediate drinking before the main stream is ready to take its place in the spring onwards. *Primeur* must not be bottled before 7 November and is released for sale from 0000 hours on 15 November*; hence the mad-dash races, with attendant publicity, to be first with the new wine in Paris or London. Bottlings and releases of *Primeur* must cease by 10 December when it should be labelled '*Nouveau*' or Beaujolais 1986, or whatever the year may be, until the next vintage.

There is no legal restriction on selling any type of *vin de l'année* indefinitely, but being intended for early drinking *Primeur* and *Nouveau* lose their freshness and should be consumed by Easter. Given a good year like 1983, these deep pink Beaujolais are fun in mid-winter. *Primeur* is not cheap because removing the sediment in a matter of weeks by frequent rackings is labour-intensive. Those prepared to wait will get better value from the *Villages* and the *Crus*, particularly the latter, at their best when one to four years old.

Hanson suggests there are so many village names, the one to go for is the cheapest, St-Véran, a recent appellation embracing villages with names unknown at the northern end of Beaujolais.

AOC Coteaux du Lyonnais
This VDQS region was promoted to AOC on 11 May 1984. The appellation is for red, white and rosé wines made south of

---

*Starting in 1985 annual release will be (from 0001) on the third Thursday in November.

Beaujolais as far as Lyon. 95 per cent are red from Gamay grapes. The few white wines are from Chardonnay, Aligoté and the Melon de Bourgogne. Annual production is 110,000 cases.

Burgundy vintages
Red 7: 1945, 1959, 1978, 1982, 1983

6: 1947, 1949, 1953, 1961, 1962, 1964, 1969, 1976, 1979
White 7: 1962, 1971, 1976, 1978, 1982, 1983
6: 1945, 1949, 1952, 1953, 1961, 1964,1966, 1967, 1969, 1973, 1975, 1979, 1981

Explanation 1 to 7 scale, page 53.

The Jura

Only eighty miles east of Burgundy, where the foothills of the Alps begin, the Jura hills are dwarfed by the great mountains across the border in Switzerland, and its wines over-shadowed by the fame of their western neighbours. Nevertheless though the vineyards are small, there is a variety of red, white, pink and — most original — yellow wines.

Their town is Arbois, childhood home of Pasteur (1822–1895) where he returned to make his greatest discovery — that fermentation was not, as believed, a chemical reaction, but a live process caused by living organisms in the air. Though pasteurization was to prove more useful for preserving milk, his research benefited the vintners by clarifying the process of wine-making.

Jura wines were known to the Romans, to Rabelais, to Rousseau and to Brillat-Saverin, a native of Belley near by. *La famille Maire* has been making them since 1632. But, as elsewhere in France, the inheritance laws, bequeathing property to all sons equally, subdivided them excessively and quality fell away. Their return to favour is largely due to Henri Maire, who put Arbois back on the wine map and his sparkling *Vin Fou* advertisements all over

Land under vines 2800 acres
Annual production About 500,000 cases
Appellations Red, white, rosé or gris, sparkling, *vin de paille*; Côtes du Jura
Growers 1000
Grapes permitted Red: Ploussard (or Poulsard), Trousseau, Gros Noirien (Pinot Noir) White: Savagnin (Alsace Traminer) Melon d'Arbois (Chardonnay)
Wine and strengths Red: 12° Rosé: 11.5° White: 12° Vin jaune: 14°
Producers Henri Maire, Château d'Arlay, Caves Jean Bourdy, Hubert Clavelin
Caves Co-opératives Arbois, Château-Chalon

France. A visit to Les Tonneaux, the company's reception centre by the Town Hall in Arbois with tours of the cellars, vineyards by minibus, films and tastings requires no advance notice and is well worth while.

Red, white and gris
Poulsard and Trousseau grapes, with a little Pinot Noir, make red and rosé wines. By itself the former can achieve fruity light rosés, but the three together give more colour and body. Their pale skins can be left with the juice for days, making fuller rosés than their pale pink colour may indicate.

Vins gris is the local term for rosés;

Cendre de Novembre is a popular Henri Maire brand. The name *gris* (grey) derives from an ashy hue at the edge when the glass is tilted. A shorter maceration causes the paler colour.

White wines from (locally named) Melon d'Arbois or Gamay Blanc, both said to be Chardonnay, are mostly made into sparkling by the *méthode champenoise.*

The *vin jaune* or yellow wine is made from a Savagnin grape, slow to ripen with a small yield. After fermentation, it is left in oak barrels, on ullage (i.e. not quite full) for six years. A flor yeast believed to come from the wood of these casks, only used for *vin jaune,* soon spreads across the surface, sealing it from the air. After six years undisturbed it has been transformed into a very good dry aperitif, Jerez or Madeira being more like its spiritual home, but quantities are so small that very little leaves France.

Vin jaune is said to be France's longest-lived wine, an honour that otherwise would go to Château Latour of Pauillac. The best *vin jaune* is Château-Chalon, a commune not a castle. It is in fact an interesting freak, scarce and expensive, particularly as its traditional *clavelin* bottle only holds 0 · 64 litres. *Vin de paille,* the straw wine, is no relation. The white grapes are put on *pailles* (mats) in the sun to concentrate the sweetness, a practice for making dessert wines in many Mediterranean lands.

Savoie

A *département* that includes the ever snow-capped Mont Blanc, the lakes of Annecy and Bourget, the rivers Rhône, Ain and Isère, besides making a celebrated mineral water at Evian on the French shore of Lac Léman, could be better known for its water than its wine. Being close to the mountains the climate is cooler and the rainfall lighter than for example in Beaujolais lying to the west, resulting in poor red wines but quite good white wines prone to acidity. Otherwise Savoie, its waters providing *Ecrevisses* and the pike for *Quenelles de brochet Nantua,* its cows content to chew the rich pasture that gives us Vacherin and Reblochon cheeses, is gastronomically *très agréable.*

The general AOC *vin de Savoie* and the fifteen commune names that can follow it are not important, though I remember one, Aprémont with satisfaction. The following each have an AOC of their own.

Appellations

Crèpy, on the French (southern) shore of Lac Léman, between Geneva and Evian, has 250 acres planted with Chasselas (called Fendant in Switzerland and Bon Blanc in Savoie) yielding about 40,000 cases a year of this fresh, dry white wine.

Roussette-de-Savoie. The Roussette grape is grown on the slopes above the Lac de Bourget, France's largest lake located north of Chambery, and also in the Rhône Valley above and below Seyssel. Like Vouvray, these white wines can be dry, sweet or sparkling; consumption is local.

Seyssel. Varichon & Clerc of the Château des Séchallets in the middle of this small town on the Rhône have been making their sparkling *méthode champenoise Blanc de*

Blancs since 1901. Offered by Justerini & Brooks, The Wine Society and Peter Dominic over the years, it seems to have become so popular that the local production from Roussette, Molette and Chasselas grapes has to be augmented by others bought outside the appellation, which is no longer Seyssel but *vin Mousseux*

Blanc de Blancs. There is no reason why the quality should deteriorate.

Bugey VDQS. This village lies downstream from Seyssel towards Lyon. Its good red, white and sparkling wines are all VDQS, recent plantings of Chardonnay making the best still white wines.

Côtes du Rhône

Between Lyon and Avignon, the Rhône must be Western Europe's oldest and hottest fine wine valley. Pliny the Elder c. 23–79 AD describes the wines of the Côte Rotie as tasting of wood-tar, popular locally but nowhere else. The heat produced sweet wines which the Romans liked to be mellowed and improved with resin as was the Greeks' practice. The crafty growers of Vienne however persuaded them that along the Rhône the flavour was entirely natural.

For centuries now the main red wine grape has been the Syrah, which has numerous other names, though nobody knows whether it might be the Shiraz from Persia or the Sérine from Syracuse. Whatever its origin the Syrah has long made the classical hill wines, Côte Rôtie and Hermitage and looks like doing as well in parts of Australia, California and South Africa.

At Ampuis, twenty miles south of Lyon where the Côtes du Rhône appellation begins, that other great wine river, the Loire, is about the same distance to the west flowing slowly north to a cooler clime mainly suited to white wines. The racing Rhône speeding south in a warmer, more consistent climate achieves both red and white wines of high quality, rounding them

off with an exceptional rosé at Tavel. All these table wines are dry.

Full and robust, the best of its red wines (and even some of the whites) have needed ten years and more to reach their best, nowadays an unacceptable wait commercially. Current methods of vinification are directed at making them good to drink in a matter of months not years to reduce costs and please the majority. Yet it is to be hoped that the old style, long-maturing Côte Rôtie, Hermitage and Châteauneuf red wines will not die out altogether. Some friends of mine in West Sussex, who hold tasting-lunches in their homes from time to time, recently unearthed a Châteauneuf-du-Pape 1918 and found it superb.

Summer heat makes winter wines

The vines (particularly at Châteauneuf-du-Pape where stones the size of boulders reflect the heat) get a proper baking, with very suitable results for drinking in a cold climate. If you don't happen to be 'old and grey and full of sleep' already, a bottle of Châteauneuf with the Sunday joint should induce the W. B. Yeats comatose syndrome in no time.

There are now eighteen *Appellations Controlées*, some of recent date. Until the

PLACES GRAPES AND CASES − CÔTES DU RHÔNE

Groupe Septentrional (northern)

DEPT	WINE	GRAPES	CASES (12 BOTTLES)
Rhône	Côte Rôtie	Syrah 80% min, Viognier 20% max	46,000 red
Rhône	Condrieu	Viognier	3500 white
Rhône	Château Grillet	Viognier	830 white
Drôme	Hermitage	Syrah	33,000 red
Drôme	Hermitage	Marsanne & Roussanne	11,500 white
Drôme	Crozes-Hermitage	Syrah	285,000 red
Drôme	Crozes-Hermitage	Marsanne & Roussanne	18,500 white
Ardèche	St Joseph	Syrah	95,000 red
Ardèche	St Joseph	Marsanne & Roussanne	5000 white
Ardèche	Cornas	Syrah	20,000 red
Ardèche	St Péray	Marsanne & Roussanne	15,000 white sparkling
Drôme	Clairette de Die	Clairette & Muscat (white semi-sparkling Brut and Tradition)	500,000 white semi-sparkling
Drôme	Chatillon-en-Diois	(AOC 1974; formerly VDQS) Gamay, Syrah, Pinot Noir	27,000 red
Drôme	Chatillon-en-Diois	Aligoté & Chardonnay	3000 white
Ardéche	Côtes du Vivarais	VDQS, Grenache, Cinsault, Carignan, Syrah, Gamay	60,000 red
Ardèche	Coteaux de l'Ardèche	Vin de Pays, Gamay	6000 red

Groupe Méridional (southern)

DEPT	WINE	GRAPES	CASES (12 BOTTLES)
Vaucluse	Rasteau	Vins Doux Naturels, Grenache 90% min. Other Rhône 10% max.	25,000 VDN
Vaucluse	Beaumes-de-Venise	Vins Doux Naturels, Muscat de Frontignan	60,000 VDN
Vaucluse	Gigondas	Grenache, Cinsault, Mourvèdre, Clairette	33,000 red and rosé
Vaucluse	Coteaux de Tricastin	Grenache, Cinsault, Mourvèdre	750,000 red and rosé
Vaucluse	Côtes de Ventoux	Grenache, Cinsault, Mourvèdre	2,000,000 red and rosé
Vaucluse	Châteauneuf-du-Pape	Grenache, Syrah, Mourvèdre and others	1,000,000 red 15,500 white
Gard	Tavel Rosé	Grenache, Clairette, Cinsault, Picpoul, Bourboulenc	330,000 rosé
Gard	Lirac	Grenache, Clairette, Syrah, Cinsault, Mourvèdre	250,000 red and rosé
	Côtes du Rhône Villages	red 12.5% white 12%	1,600,000 red 27,000 white
Gard	Côtes du Rhône		1,490,000 red
Gard	Côtes du Rhône		85,000 white

101

late 1960s you would have been likely to find in merchants' lists only Châteauneuf-du-Pape, Hermitage and possibly Côte Rôtie, where production leaves little for export. Côtes du Rhône (the equivalent of AOC Bordeaux or Bourgogne) is the basic appellation, covering parts that are not qualified for anything better. Côtes du Rhône Villages covers seventeen villages, five of Drôme, the tributary flowing in above Montelimar, nine of Vaucluse and three of Gard. Their names are on page 107.

The Northern Rhône
In the early 1960s most of these vineyards could be seen in one day in novel fashion. Every Sunday in summer the shallow draught, diesel-driven *Frédéric Mistral* (named after the Provençal poet not the abominable wind) left Lyon before dawn, reaching Avignon at 7.30p.m. after a 160 mile journey downstream. Neither Rhône water nor wine was the main attraction; with M. Nandron, Lyon's leading restaurateur in charge of the catering, that distinction went to the Dimanche déjeuner. Let us make the trip briefly.

Côte Rôtie
After twenty miles the 'roasted hill' rises up from Ampuis on the right bank as steeply as any Mosel vineyard to its humps at the top, the Côte Blonde and the Côte Brune. Though there is a legend about a blonde and brunette, the names reflect chalk and clay, the finest wines being blends from a handful of plot-holders. Best of the Rhône reds they needed three years in cask and were long lived. Recently the appellation has been extended to include 750 acres on the flat ground behind the hill and the new techniques provide lighter wines ready sooner.

Condrieu and Château Grillet
Three miles downstream on the same side, the seventeen steep acres of Condrieu are planted with the white Viognier grape. Yielding only 150 gallons an acre gives the world three thousand cases of Condrieu a year, so to taste this remarkably fine dry white wine we have to spend a lot of money staying at the Beau Rivage hotel, beautifully sited on a bend of the river.

Château Grillet, the 6-acre jewel in the Condrieu crown, is rightly proud of its smallest appellation in France. To drink one bottle from the 200 to 600 cases made annually we could try the famous Pyramide in Vienne, a restaurant where the meal alone will be around £35 a head. Better to have been in London in 1815 when Château Grillet 1811 was being sold at Christie's auction for 110 shillings a dozen.

Hermitage and Crozes-Hermitage
About thirty miles on, this huge hill with a chapel on the top has been growing vines since Caesar conquered Gaul. It is on the left bank, with Tain l'Hermitage, the town, at its foot. There are about 320 acres of steep terraced vineyards facing south, planted with 85 per cent Syrah for the red wine and 15 per cent Marsanne and Roussanne for the white.

Crozes-Hermitage comprises 1500 acres on the lower slopes facing north,

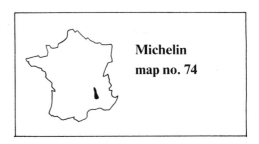

Michelin map no. 74

Côtes du Rhône-North

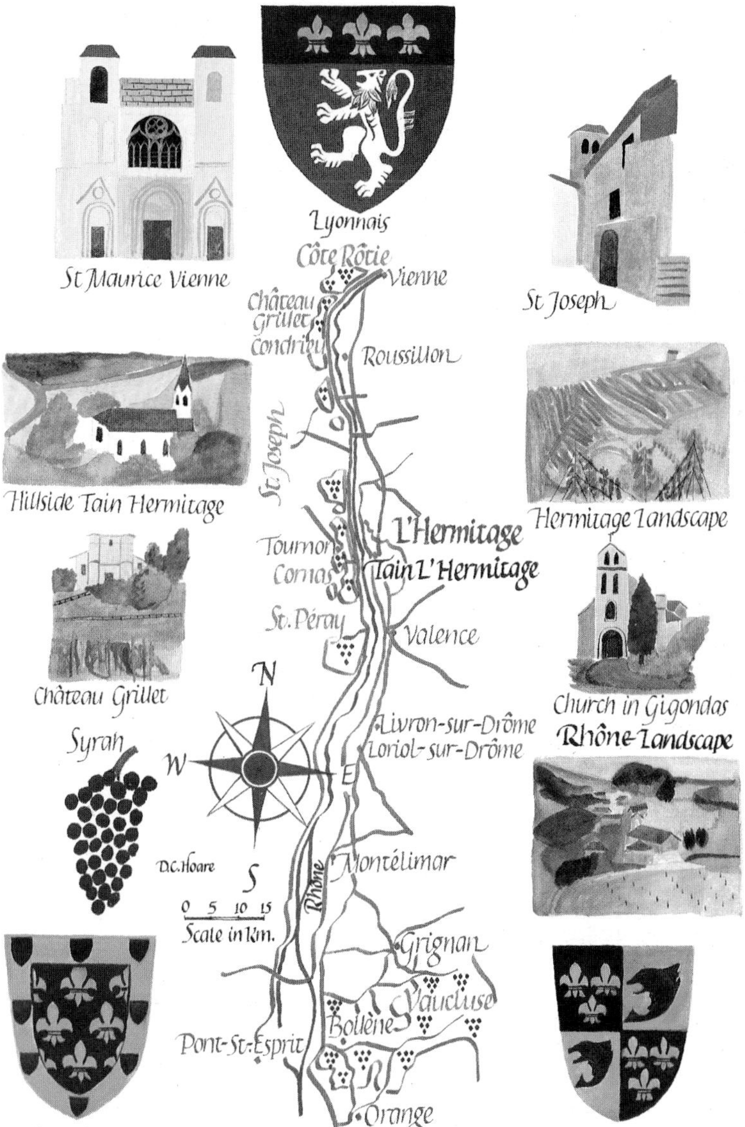

St Maurice Vienne

Lyonnais

Côte Rôtie
Vienne
Château
Grillet
Condrieu
Roussillon

St Joseph

Hillside Tain Hermitage

St Joseph

Hermitage Landscape

Château Grillet

Tournon
Cornas
St. Péray

L'Hermitage
Tain L'Hermitage
Valence

Church in Gigondas
Rhône Landscape

Syrah

N
W   E
S

D.C.Hoare

0   5   10 15
Scale in Km.

Livron-sur-Drôme
Loriol-sur-Drôme

Rhône
Montélimar

Rhône Landscape

Grignan
Vaucluse
Bollène
Pont-St-Esprit

Orange

Vivarais

Dauphine

making wines less good and less costly. The biggest owners, on the hill as their boards proclaim, are the négociants Paul Jaboulet Aîné, Chapoutier, Vidal-Fleury and Delas. The first ships La Chapelle, the second Chante-Alouette.

St-Joseph

Tain is linked by a bridge across the river to Tournon, where St-Joseph, a new appellation, was created in 1956, Mauves being the best known of its seven villages. Relatively unknown and maturing sooner, St-Joseph can be better value than its august neighbour. Jaboulet makes a fine St-Joseph called Le Grand Pompée; in relation to the Pompey we know in Britain, Le Grand Gosport would be a geographically more accurate name.

Cornas and St-Peray

Nine miles on from Tournon, I do not recall drinking Cornas but by all accounts it is a slow *Syrah* developer being transformed from purple ink to red plush velvet in a decade or so. St-Peray's appellation is for a white Marsanne wine made mainly by the *méthode champenoise* into full rich sparkling, St-Peray Mousseux.

After these sixty miles from Lyon we are now abreast the city of Valence where the northern part (the Groupe Septentrional) of the Côtes du Rhône ends, giving us a break for M. Nandron's *Dimanche déjeuner* and even a siesta before reaching Orange, fifty miles on, where the southern part (the Groupe Méridional) begins. But first there are three 'fringe' wines.

Clairette de Die

Die is a small town on the Drôme forty miles south-east of Valence. Its yellowish-gold AOC wine, from twenty-five parishes and Clairette and Muscat de Frontignan grapes, is made semi-sparkling by a secondary fermentation in the bottle as in Champagne or by an old traditional méthode Dioise. This involves a slow alcoholic fermentation adding sulphur dioxide to slow down the yeasts followed by a re-fermentation of unresolved sugar in tightly closed casks. The result should be a sparkling Muscat wine, strength 10.5°, 'generally considered an acquired taste' says Lichine's Encyclopedia. With six million litres emerging from Die each year, somebody must have acquired it! Another 1974 appellation permitted the local co-operative to make Châtillon-en-Dioise red and a little white, formerly VDQS and far better left as such.

Côtes du Vivarais and Coteaux de l'Ardèche

The former is a red VDQS of Côtes du Rhône style, made in the Ardèche *département* of gorges, grottoes and the delightful canoe-lovers' river. The latter is a *vin de pays*, sometimes labelled Gamay de l'Ardèche. Good Syrah and Cabernet Sauvignon are expected.

The Southern Rhône (group méridional)

A deviation eastwards near Orange would take the *Frédéric Mistral* up the Aygues river into Vaucluse, where Mont Ventoux,

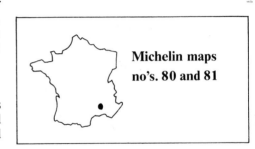

Michelin maps no's. 80 and 81

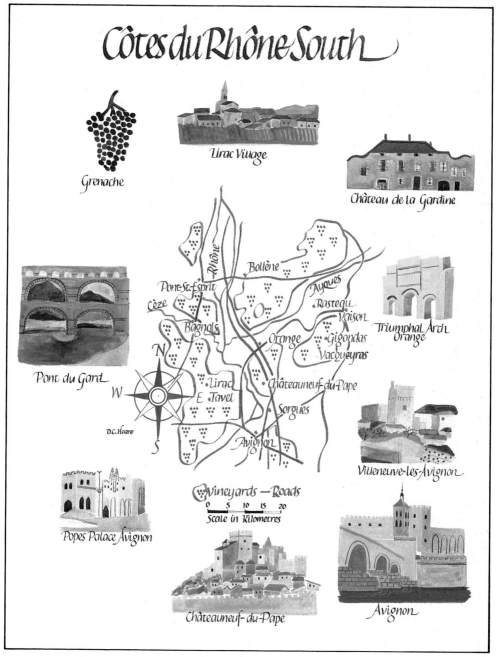

Côtes du Rhône South

Grenache

Lirac Village

Château de la Gardine

Pont du Gard

Rhône
Bollène
Pont-St-Esprit
Cèze
Bagnols
Ayques
Rastean
Vaison
Orange
Gigondas
Vacqueyras
Triumphal Arch
Orange

N
W · E
S
D.C.Hoare

Lirac
Tavel
Châteauneuf-du-Pape
Sorgues
Avignon

Villeneuve-les-Avignon

Popes Palace Avignon

Vineyards — Roads
0 5 10 15 20
Scale in Kilometres

Châteauneuf-du-Pape

Avignon

often snow-capped, dominates the country-side. Rasteau and Beaumes-de-Venise, two of the Côtes du Rhône villages, have become better known for their 14° dessert wines (vins doux naturels).

Gigondas
In the days when nobody knew this name, its wine was being sold to blend with Châteauneuf-du-Pape only a dozen miles away. Since the Second World War Gabriel Meffre's fifteen acres, cleared with American surplus equipment and planted with Syrah, Cinsault, Mourvèdre and Clairette have become nearer three thousand making sound red wine, *Appellation Contrôlée* since 1971.

Coteaux du Tricastin
South-east of Châteauneuf-du-Pape with the Ouveze, another Rhône tributary between them, these slopes were planted in the Meffre manner during the 1960s by former Algerian settlers with the black grapes above. *Appellation Contrôlée* was awarded in 1974.

Côtes du Ventoux
Another appellation awarded in 1974 to a large area east of Avignon and Gigondas. Concentration is on fresh light reds and rosés for early drinking. One of the wine towns is Sourgues, — only seven miles out of Avignon — where Jean Astier is based, shipping two Vaucluse Vins de Pays, red and white, popular in litre bottles.

Châteauneuf-du-Pape
Back on the Rhône we pass our last and most famous region, the town's towers in sight to our left, with seven miles to go to Avignon. The Papacy was there from 1307 to 1378 when Franco-Roman relations were strained, the first Pope being Pope Clément V, who had already planted his own Graves vineyard in Bordeaux. His successor, John XXII planted vines and built a fortified summer residence on the cool high ground for his retirement. Being on chalky soil the place and its wine were called 'Châteauneuf-Calcernier' until the growers effected an advantageous change. Then in 1923, for their own protection, they made a set of rules that became the basis of the national *Appellation d'Origine* in 1936.

Over-keen marketing men claim that thirteen grapes go to make the famous red wine but in fact only some are used from a permissible list of Rhône regulars. For red wines they are Grenache, Syrah, Mourvèdre, Cinsault, Terret Noir, Muscardin, Vaccarèse, Counoise. For white wines they are Clairette, Bourboulenc, Roussanne, Picpoul, Picardin. In practice for the red wine, 50-70 per cent will be Grenache, with some or all of the next three and perhaps a 'seasoner' or two.

The 1918 wine mentioned would have been fermented for a month or more and aged for five years in wood. Nowadays using various forms of *macération carbonique,* wines are on sale within fifteen months of the vintage. Costs must be kept down, particularly because the huge stones in these vineyards can play havoc with machinery. Between these extremes of very old and very new there are still some domaine-bottled wines of great years like 1978 and 1979 worth laying down for up to fifteen years from the vintage. Robin Yapp of Mere, Wiltshire and Simon Loftus of Adnams, Southwold Brewery Suffolk specialise in this field.

Leading domaines include Château Rayas, Domaine de Mont-Redon, La Nerte, Domaine de Cabrières, Beaucastel,

Les Clefs d'Or, Clos de l'Oratoire des Papes and Vieux Télégraphe.

Tavel and Lirac

These two villages, each with its own appellation, lie on the right bank of the Rhône less than eight miles south-west of Châteauneuf-du-Pape. Growing the same grapes on the same sort of arid, stony chalky soil, in a large hollow, Tavel's dry, full-bodied 11-12° wine is really a Châteauneuf rosé from a different spot. The 1900-acre vineyard averages around 330,000 cases a year. It takes a two-day maceration for the grape skins to impart their pink colouring to the juice, then comes a light pressing, a fermentation away from the skins, followed by bottling in the spring when the wine is fresh, fruity and ready for those who take their rosés seriously.

Lirac makes a similar rosé, perhaps the better value for being less famous than Tavel; and some good red wines too come from ex-Algeria settlers. Of the commune's 8750 permissible acres, only 1250 are AOC Lirac; the rest are either unplanted or AOC Côtes du Rhône.

Côtes du Rhône Villages

The villages are:
Drome: St-Maurice-sur-Eygues, Rousset-les-Vignes, Rochegude, St-Pantaléon-les-Vignes, Vinsobres
Vaucluse: Cairanne, Vacqueyras, Rasteau, Valréas, Visan, Roaix, Sablet, Beaumes-de-Venise, Séguret
Gard: Chusclan, Laudun, St-Gervais
Côtes du Rhône: This basic appellation, strength red 12.5°, white & rosé 12°, covers about 140 communes.

Vintages and négociants

The weather is more variable in the northern Rhône, where great years have been 1961, 1962, 1966, 1967, 1969, 1970, 1976, 1978, 1979, 1982, 1983.

Négociants in the north: E. Guigal, Ampuis; J.L.Chave, Tournon; Delas Frères, Tournon; M. Chapoutier, Tain l'Hermitage; Paul Jaboulet Aîné, Tain l'Hermitage; Georges Vernay, Condrieu; J. Vidal-Fleury, Ampuis.

Négociants in the south: Bellicard d'Avignon; Gabriel Meffre, Gigondas. Père Anselme, Château Fortia, Louis Mousset, Domaine de la Nerte, Château Rayas, Noel Sabon, all at Châteauneuf-du-Pape. Domaine du Vieux Télégraphe at Bedarrides.

Provence

All wines will travel if well enough made and the reds, whites and rosés of Provence are no exception. But psychology plays a part in wine appreciation. You are unlikely to find that the 'little beaut rosé' as your Australian girl friend with the *Club Méditerranée* called it, is quite such a little 'beaut' at home with the wife on a wet Wednesday in Worksop after a hard day at the office. Exported, these Provence wines have to compete with those of the Rhône and the Midi. Some of them — AOC and VDQS — usually do; thus sufficient knowledge to recognise Provençal wines on the shelf when wine shopping can lead to enjoyable bottles at low cost.

> **Land under vines**   About 26,000 hectares (65,000 acres) AOC and VDQS
> **Annual Production**   700,000 hectolitres (about 8 million cases) 60% co-operatives, 40% private wine-makers
> **Regional appellation**   AOC Côtes de Provence
> **Separate appellations within the region**   AOC Aix-en-Provence, AOC Bandol, AOC Bellet, AOC La Palette
> **Grapes**   Carignan, Grenache, Cinsault, Mourvèdre, Syrah, Cabernet Sauvignon
> **Styles**   Rosé, 60 per cent; red 35 per cent; white 5 per cent

Provence comprises five *départements*, three maritime and two inland. Bouches-du-Rhône (Aix, Marseille, Cassis), Var (Draguignan, Bandol, St-Raphael) and Alpes Maritimes (Cannes, Nice, Menton) are maritime. Vaucluse, and Basses-Alpes, east of Avignon and north of Aix, are inland. The wines of Vaucluse being similar and adjacent to Châteauneuf-du-Pape are described under Côtes du Rhône, page 106.

AOC Wines of Provence
Coteaux d'Aix-en-Provence AOC
Promoted AOC on 11 May 1984 the Coteaux cover an area north of Aix, eastwards to Rians, where a fine but expensive Cabernet Sauvignon, Château Vignelaure (111 acres) is made. Costing less are Château de Fonscolombe (235 acres) and Domaine de la Crèmade (160 acres), the two red wines from the Marquis de Saporta estates at Le Puy-Ste-Reparade, ten miles north of Aix, in the family since 1720.

Coteaux des Baux-de-Provence AOC
Also promoted AOC on 11 May 1984, these red, dry white and rosé wines from St-Remy-de-Provence, Fontvieille and Les Bauxs-de-Provence are similar to those of the Coteaux described above.

Cassis AOC
Many visitors to Provence must share my own happy memories of fried red mullet and pink or white Mas Calendal at the hotel Liautaud on the quay in the charming little port of Cassis, only fourteen miles from Marseille. Of the three colours, Cassis white comes first, preferably from Domaine de la Ferme Blanche, Domaine du Paternel or Clos Ste-Magdelaine, considered the three best estates.

Bandol AOC
Red, white and rosé, the vineyards are five miles inland from Bandol around Le Castellet and La Cadière d'Azur, where the co-operative makes 55,000 cases a year. Domaine Tempier and Château des Vannières are reputedly among the leaders; the Bunan brothers, with seventy-five acres at Le Castellet, export some of their excellent Clos du Moulin des Costes and Mas de la Rouvière. The red wines of Bandol are certainly the best along the whole of this coast from Marseille to Menton.

AOC Bellet
White, red and rosé from the slopes inland from Nice; after supplying the restaurants there, little remains.

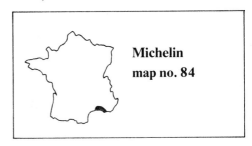

Michelin map no. 84

Provence

Notre Dame Fréjus

Sospel

Vines

Moustiers St. Marie

Cinsault

Aix-en-Provence

Bouches Du Rhône

Argens

Draguignan

Fréjus

St. Raphaël

Aille

Var

Marseille

Cassis

Bandol

Toulon

St. Tropez

Côte D'Azur Varoise

Castle at la Napoule

N

W   E

S

Vineyards
Roads

D.C.Hoare

0   10   20
Scale in Kms.

Saintes-Maries-De-La-Mer

Old Church at Comps

Villefranche Landscape

Bargemon

Provence

AOC Côtes de Provence

A promotion from VDQS to AOC in 1977 made this the general appellation of Provence for regions other than those named already. The properties that qualify are scattered about an area shaped like a half moon between Toulon and St-Raphael, some close to the coast, others inland as far as Draguignan in places close to N7 and the motorway A8, such as Vidauban, Les Arcs and Taradeau. Most of the production of Provence is consumed there.

Best of the exports

The following are among the best wines that are exported: Château Montaud-Pierrefeu on the D14 road east of Pierrefeu, Château Minuty at Gassin near St-Tropez, Domaine de St-Martin between Taradeau and Les Arcs and Domaine des Féraud near Vidauban.

Cháteau Clos Mireille at Brégancon, west of Cape Bénat, Château de Selle at Taradeau and Château Rommassan at Le Castellet, Bandol all belong to Domaines Ott based at Antibes, whose London distributors Mentzendorff & Co., Asphalte House, Palace Street, London SW1E 5HG, arrange visits on request.

Pradel Rosé, a popular brand, is made half-way between Nice and Cannes at Villeneuve-Loubet, birthplace of Escoffier, the chef who created Pêche Melba. The house is now a museum.

Promotion list

Vins d'Argens from the valley of this name near Draguignan; Mont Caume, from twelve communes around Bandol; Coteaux Varois, from forty-six communes around Brignoles are all *vins de pays* expecting promotion to VDQS in 1985.

Languedoc-Roussillon

In French, *midi,* being midday when the sun is due south, the name is singularly apt for this vast, sweltering southern part of France between the Rhône delta south of Avignon and the Spanish frontier beyond Perpignan. Going in that direction, viticulturally it is all Languedoc with various patches of AOC, VDQS and *Vin de Pays,* red, white, rosé, dry and semi-sweet, until Roussillon begins fifteen miles from Perpignan.

This, the oldest wine region of France, started by the Romans, is six times the size of the Bordeaux region and makes three times as much wine, largely coarse purple *vin ordinaire* to provide French families' daily litres: formerly wine so bad that

Mendes-France when *Premier* after the Second World War tried — quite unsuccessfully of course — to persuade France to drink milk instead.

Plain plonk and its problems

A century ago good wine was being made from the foot-hills on the Massif Centrale, but the demoralised growers, their vineyards destroyed by the phylloxera, planted inferior species in the plains. In Bordeaux one vine is permitted to make no more than one bottle; here they make six, resulting in a huge surplus equivalent to 55/110 million cases a year. This surplus the government buys, distilling it into

Land under vines   430,000 hectares (1,075,000 acres), six times the size of Bordeaux, approximating to 35 per cent of French acreage under vine
Annual production   370 million cases (three times Bordeaux but quality not comparable)
Grapes permitted   Red/rosé: Carignan, Cinsault, Grenache, Mourvèdre. White: Clairette and others. Sparkling: Mauzac (same as Blanquette)
Appellations   AOC and VDQS are about 5 per cent of the annual production, *Vin de Pays* about 15 per cent, leaving *Vin de Table* 80 per cent
AOC* White: Clairette du Languedoc. Sweet: Muscat Frontignan, Mireval, St Jean de Minervois, Rivesaltes, Banyuls, Collioure, Maury. Sparkling: Blanquette de Limoux
VDQS* Red/Rosé, Costières du Gard, Quatouze, La Clape, Corbières, Coteaux du Languedoc, Minervois, Fougères, St Chinian
Vin de Pays* 15 per cent of annual production, yield 80/100 hectolitres/hectare *Vin de Pays du Gard* − Growers of 223 communes in the *département* of Gard are eligible. *Vin de Pays de l'Hérault* − Growers of at least 240 communes are eligible. *Vin de Pays de l'Aude* − Growers of at least 280 communes are eligible. *Vin de Pays Catalan* and *Vin de Pays Pyrénées-Orientale* − Growers of at least 30 communes are eligible for one of these two *Vin de Pays*.

sugar (in the form of grape juice concentrated by boiling it first) is added to increase it. Convinced that the government will continue to buy any surplus lest riots with fatal casualties should result as in 1976, 'plonk' is far more profitable for a grower than making AOC or VDQS wines. Moreover, the purveyors of cheap brands in Paris want only cheap wines by the tanker, strength 10 or 11 degrees; nobody who counts is interested in changing things for the better. No wonder Alexis Lichine in his *Guide to the Wines and Vineyards of France* declares Languedoc-Roussillon as being to wine what the Middle East is to oil! Nine out of every ten of its bottles are this sort of 'plonk'. It was better, in fact, when blended with the big wines from Algeria, which France refused to import after 1965 when President Boumediére confiscated new oil wells in the Sahara. The Russians were pleased to import them instead. Nowadays, blending Algerian or other non-EEC wines with French wines is forbidden and Sicily and Puglia have become the suppliers.

industrial alcohol in order to maintain the price of the wine.

Being *vin ordinaire* there are few controls and no places of origin need appear on the labels. In France it is sold in bulk by the degree hectolitre and its strength 10°, 11°, 12° is conspicuous on labels in the shops.

Quantity reduces strength, so in practice

A solution easier said than found
The remedy lies in replanting the slopes with 'noble' grape varieties to produce less wine of higher quality. A little enlightened self-interest on the part of the brand owners and shippers could fund the project, improving their profits in time. The viticultural knowledge is on the spot in the famous *Ecole Nationale Supérieure Agronomique,* part of France's oldest university, Montpellier. Only the workers may be missing. Margharita Laski and her husband J.E. Howard, who owned a small property in the Hautes-Corbiéres, described in a Wine Mine Club Newsletter how the younger generation have all left the

---

* It is as well to emphasise that all three of these appellations are guarantees of origin not quality. With no grape specified, the *vin de pays* system must depend upon reliable, incorruptible local tasting panels on a scale difficult to achieve where the number of communes is so great.

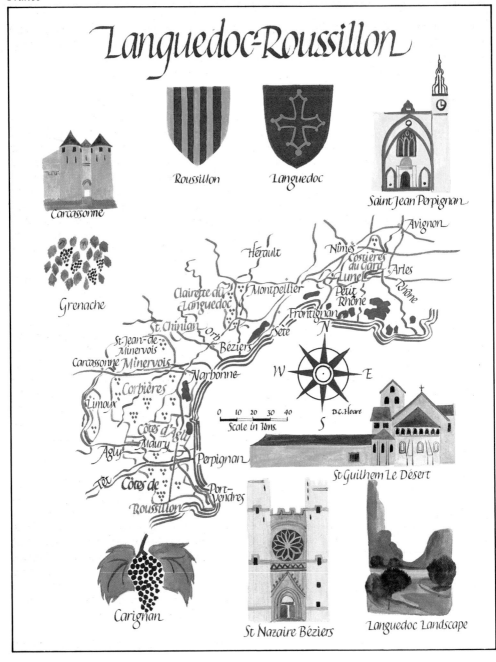

Languedoc-Roussillon

Carcassonne

Roussillon

Languedoc

Saint Jean Perpignan

Grenache

Hérault

Nîmes

Avignon

Costières du Gard

Arles

Lunel

Rhône

Clairette du Languedoc

Montpellier

Petit Rhône

St. Chinian

Frontignan

Orb

Sète

N

St. Jean-de-Minervois

Béziers

Carcassonne Minervois

Narbonne

W

E

Corbières

Limoux

0 10 20 30 40

Scale in Kms.

D.C. Hoare

S

Côtes d'Agly

Maury

Agly

Perpignan

St Guilhem Le Désert

Tet

Côtes de

Roussillon

Port-Vendres

Carignan

St Nazaire Béziers

Languedoc Landscape

wine villages for white collar jobs, because the peasant holdings are too small and too awkwardly sited to compete with the 'plonk' of the plains.*

However, since the 1960s when many French vignerons from Algeria, Tunisia and Morocco — some dedicated and highly knowledgeable — resettled here, progress has been made. Those with capital have dug up the old Aramon and Alicante varieties replanting with those prescribed for this region. *Macération carbonique* has given the former heavy, 'heady' red wines a fruity touch of the light fantastic, while Côtes du Roussillon, made AOC in 1977, is doing particularly well with *vins doux naturels,* although the good Côtes du Roussillon wines really offer a more secure future. Credit is also due to the co-operatives for a marked improvement in quality since the noble grapes were planted.

Languedoc (Nimes to Narbonne)

The explanation of this unusual name (Languedoc) is that by the thirteenth century elsewhere throughout France the word for 'yes' was *oil,* which became *oui.* Here they said *oc* for 'yes', so it became the province whose *langue* (tongue or language) was *oc.*

A survey of districts and appellations as

---

*Change and decay in the Hautes-Corbiéres, December 1982.

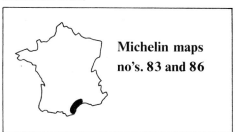

**Michelin maps
no's. 83 and 86**

seen or passed going through the region on Autoroute 9 from Nimes may as well begin with *Vins de Sable,* none the worse for being unqualified.

Domaine Viticoles des Salins du Midi, Listel A century ago this old salt company began planting vines around the Gulf of Lions in the sand where the phylloxera is unable to survive. This allowed 'noble vines' to be planted without grafting on to American root-stocks. From 4200 acres they now produce annually $1\frac{1}{2}$ million cases of claret-style reds, perfumed whites and pleasing rosés under the brand name Listel, which visitors can sample at their interesting Aigues-Mortes winery. Groups should first contact head office at 68 Cours Gambetta, 34000 Montpellier.

Costières du Gard VDQS This district, fifteen miles by ten, runs from just south of Nimes towards Aigues-Mortes in the Camargue. Good reds and rosés, similar to Côtes du Rhône, go down locally with *saucisson d'Arles* and *salades de crudités.*

Being on the 'No Popery' side of the Rhône, prices are lower, a point in favour of Vin de Pays Coteaux du Salavés and Vin de Pays du Gard Rouge (3 litre wine box).

Clairette de Languedoc AOC Stretching some fifteen miles north-east from Pézenas along the right bank of the Hérault river, Clairette de Languedoc gets its AOC for a dry white wine from the Clairette grape; but few people think it is deserved. Its red wines rate merely as Coteaux du Languedoc VDQS below; among the best are those from the co-operative at St-Saturnin just outside this demarcated area.

Coteaux du Languedoc AOC Promoted

AOC on 11 May 1984, as many as thirteen districts are permitted to add their names to this one, and name dropping could be tedious. Faugères, a small blob on the wine map in the Cevenne foothills, eighteen miles north of Beziers, and St-Chinian, a much larger one the same distance north-west, each make attractive (macerated) red wines. The appellation is for red and rosé, which must be at least half Carignan and the other half Cinsault, Grenache, Counoise, Mourvèdre, Syrah or Terret Noir; minimum strength 11°.

In Britain one successful *vin de pays* has been Domaine de Parc from M. Henri Epine's 105-acre vineyard near Pézenas. Only two private estates surrounded by a high wall over four miles long now exist in France. His is one; Château de Chambord in Touraine the other.

Picpoul de Pinet, almost on the Autoroute between Pézenas and the lake Bassin de Thau, makes a VDQS dry wine.

Between Nimes and Beziers the strong, sweet *vins doux naturels,* which the French like to drink as aperitifs, or with *petit fours* biscuits instead of afternoon tea, are made from Muscat grapes principally at Lunel, Frontignan, Mireval, and St-Jean de Minervois. The first three are AOC their co-operatives being the chief producers of these brown sticky wines lacking the fresh charm of Beaumes-de-Venise.

Narbonne to Spain
Corbières, Corbières Supérieurs, VDQS
Drawing a line fifty miles long from Narbonne to Carcassone, and two more forty miles long, one from each of these towns, south-west at right angles to the Pyrenees, creates a colossal square, which forms the biggest VDQS region in France. Within this large and lovely landscape of

hills, valleys, dried up rivers and (in late autumn) a glorious patchwork quilt of red, orange, yellow and gold from vines of many species, there are a dozen good wine villages and at least five co-operatives.

Typical perhaps of some of the growers is M. Villeneuve, a retired architect, who specialised in designing wine co-operatives. His 160-acre vineyard at St-Martin de Toques is ten miles south-west of Narbonne, where he lives during the winter, coming to his vineyard house in the summer. He is one of many who replanted with Carignan (55 per cent), Cinsault (25 per cent), Grenache (10 per cent), and divers species making up the hundred. The percentages planted by other growers will of course vary. From his own 160 acres the laws (at 40 hectolitres a hectare) should mean 6400 hectolites (70,000 cases) a year of red VDQS Corbières. Many people think the region should be upgraded to AOC, which of course would give M. Villeneuve a higher price. On the other hand he might not sell all his wine.

Out of forty-five *Vins de Pays* made in Languedoc-Roussillon the Corbières co-operatives contribute six: Val de Orbieu, L'Aude, Coteaux Cathares, Vallée de Paradis, Coteaux du Littoral Audeis and Cucugnan. In the interests of quality, *Vins de Pays* are restricted to 45 hectolitre per hectare and their strength must be 9°/10°. Their contribution to the wines of Languedoc-Roussillon is 15 per cent.

Fitou A.C. A village on the coastal Etang de Leucate, though part of Corbières has an AOC for its mainly Carignan red wines, which must spend nine months in cask before bottling.

La Clape VDQS On the coast south-east

of Narbonne, this is another small Carignan area making good red wine.

Minervois AOC Due to become wholly AOC in July 1985, this is another red, mainly Carignan, region where the vineyards are on the foot-hills of the Massif Centrale north of a forty-mile stretch of the river Aude seen on the right driving from Narbonne to Carcassonne along N113. This road keeps to the plain through Lézignan-Corbières, the commercial wine town of these parts. Some good wines are made, though the proportion of vineyards replanted with 'noble' grapes is low. The little walled town of Minerve lies in a setting of vine, cypress and olive that only Tuscany and Greece can surpass.

Blanquette de Limoux AOC From a source in the Pyrenees the Aude flows north to Carcassonne before making a sharp turn east for the Mediterranean. Its first towns are Quillan and Limoux, seventeen miles apart, where this very good *méthode champenoise* and very dry sparkler is made from vineyards between them, a strip never more than seven miles wide. The Romans first made a white wine here and at Gaillac (Tarn) from the Mauzac grape, also called Blanquette. Nowadays, some Clairette, Chenin Blanc and Chardonnay are grown too. Annual production may be 750,000 cases from 4000 acres, the efficient modern co-operative making 80 per cent.

Roussillon

Squeezed into the southern corner between the Pyrenees and the Mediterranean, Roussillon begins about fifteen miles north of Perpignan. New appellations were decreed in 1977.

Côtes du Roussillon AOC This covers the region except for the villages below. Mainly red and rosé, at least one dry but fruity Côtes du Roussillon Blanc does exist. Château Corneilla, a dozen miles down the road towards Spain from Perpignan, makes a charming 11° claret-style wine, and there are two *Vin de Pays — Catalan* and *Pyrénées-Orientale. Les Quatres Côteaux,* as the name implies, is a blend involving four co-operatives and whenever James Long, the buyer, pays a visit he meets all four Presidents simultaneously over lunch.

Côtes du Roussillon Villages AOC These villages mainly lie about twenty miles east of Perpignan between the rivers l'Agly and Tet. Their names are, Estagel, Latour du France, Planézes, Caramany, Montner and Montalba, where there is a very modern co-operative. They are making a reputation for light red wines from the usual grapes — Carignan, Cinsault, Grenache and Mourvédre.

Sweet wines Rivesaltes, Maury and Banyuls each have an AOC for *vin doux naturel* made from Grenache and one or two obscure grapes besides Muscat. *Vins doux naturels* are required to reach at least 14° strength naturally, without any addition. Brandy, from 5 to 10 per cent of the volume, may then be added. This makes the name unnaturally misleading. Aged in wood they acquire the burnt flavour known as *maderisé* or *rancio.*

My 1965 booklet from Perpignan says of Banyuls 'It becomes, when mellow, a red wine whose colour is enhanced by those very purple and golden lights found in illuminated mediaeval texts'. Holy Moses! That should be worth *Private Eye's* Pseuds' corner?

The south-west

Widening interest in table wines during the past twenty, inflationary years has sent trade buyers forth into barely known districts, searching for tolerable wines, preferably from Bordeaux, Burgundy and Rhône grapes, to offer at lower prices than those of these regions. Fortunately, where there are rivers there are usually wines; those of Bordeaux along the Garonne, main artery of the south-west we have already met. But each of its big tributaries has at least one notable wine and there are many Côtes and Coteaux with assortments of AOC, VDQS and *Vin de Pays* between them.

This survey can start at Bergerac, the country town on the Dordogne sixty miles east of Bordeaux, yet only thirty from St-Emilion, already known for its sweet Monbazillac, a dessert wine which in times past competed with the finest Sauternes. Now the demand is for red wine and in 1983, for the first time, red production beat white by 208,000 hectolitres to 176,000. At present prices, Bergerac reds are very good value and Pécharmant, the best of them, with only 200 hectares planted out of a possible 500, could expand.

Monbazillac AOC

This village, four miles south of Bergerac lies in a sea of vineyards stretching westwards for a dozen miles to Ste-Foy-la-Grande on N113. The grapes, Sauvignon, Sémillon and Muscadelle, are late-picked with noble rot as in Sauternes, which this sweet white wine resembles, though lighter in flavour and in price. The vineyards covering 10,000 acres make 750,000 cases. Other village names entitled to the AOC are Pomport,

Rouffignac, Colombier and St-Laurent-des-Vignes. A choice rarity from a single vineyard is Château la Brie.

Prominent on this hill at St-Laurent-des-Vignes is the Château de Monbazillac, bought and restored by (UNIDOR) *the Union des Coopératives Vinicoles de la Dordogne* whose nine Bergerac co-operatives make over 40 per cent of AOC Bergerac wines. These can be tasted at the château, their showplace open to the public daily, with a restaurant also open in the summer.

Bergerac AOC

For table wines, red, white and rosé the appellation is AOC Bergerac — and 1° stronger — Côtes de Bergerac. Accorded individual AOC's are Pécharmant, north of the town, making a good claret-style worth laying down for up to five years; Côtes de Saussignac making a light sort of Monbazillac; and Montravel twenty-five miles away towards Bordeaux for some dry and some slightly sweet white wines. Bergerac red wines are about 50% Merlot with the other half from Cabernet Franc, Cabernet Sauvignon and Malbec.

Côtes du Duras AOC

Duras is a small town south-west of

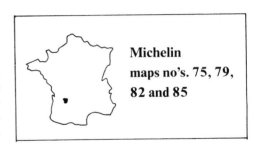

Michelin maps no's. 75, 79, 82 and 85

116

SouthWest

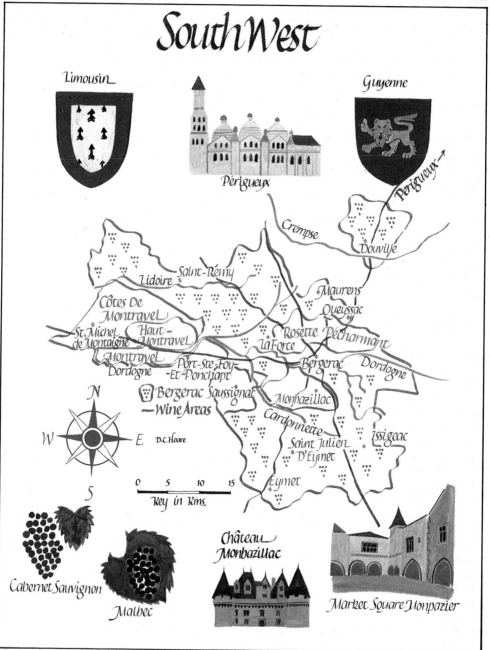

Limousin

Périgueux

Guyenne

Périgueux →

Crempse

Douville

Saint-Rémy

Maurens

Lidoire

Queyssac

Côtes De
Montravel

Haut-
Montravel

Rosette Pécharmant

St. Michel
de Montaigne

La Force

Montravel
Dordogne

Port-Ste-Foy-
Et-Ponchapt

Bergerac

Dordogne

🏠 Bergerac Saussignac
— Wine Areas

Monbazillac

N

W   E   *D.C.Hoare*

Cardonnette

Issigeac

Saint Julien
D'Eynet

S

Eymet

0   5   10   15
Key in Kms.

Cabernet Sauvignon

Malbec

Château
Monbazillac

Market Square Monpazier

Bergerac and thirteen miles south of Ste Foy-le-Grande. 2500 acres make 400,000 cases a year, two white to one of red. The Sauvignon Blanc is outstanding.

Côtes du Buzet AOC
On the Garonne thirty-six miles south-south-east of Duras, Buzet received its appellation in 1973 and nobody knows quite why. Virtually an extension eastwards of Entre-Deux-Mers, annual production is about 250,000 cases, mostly claret of VDQS standard.

Côtes du Marmandais VDQS
Replanted with Bordeaux's best vines of late, the two co-operatives — one at Cocumont just off Autoroute 62, Bordeaux to Toulouse, and the other in the town of Marmande — are now making 300,000 cases a year. A light claret develops in four years and the white wine is equivalent to sound Bordeaux from Graves or Entre-Deux-Mers.

Cahors AOC
Those, who like me, cannot abide the strong black wine of this otherwise lovely old town on the loop of the Lot need reassurance: the black wine has, literally, been reformed. It *was* almost wholly made from Bordeaux's Malbec grape, called Auxerrois here — little used in classic claret now — which, planted on the local limestone and given a prolonged fermentation, sired this black monster.

Since the early 1960s the vineyards have been replanted on more suitable gravelly land with a mixture of Merlot, Syrah, Gamay and a pair of local vines all contributing a mellowing 30 per cent to Malbec's dark satanic 70. This reformation has achieved a light red wine, ready in two to three years, best drunk cool like Beaujolais and rated good enough to have been awarded AOC in 1971. Production is 800,000 cases and if we do not meet any in Britain, there is *La Taverne* in the town of Cahors with its Michelin star, where a bottle with the pigeon would be a fine prelude to a final *verre dégustation* of one of the many old Armagnacs, another great speciality of this old family restaurant.

Gaillac AOC
Dordogne, Lot, Tarn . . . *Three Rivers of France,* Freda White's 1952 book, reprinted yet again in paperback in 1984 and still worth having on this journey now reaching Gaillac, on the Tarn fourteen miles west of Albi, first introduced many of my generation to the attractions of south-west France.

Gaillac is among the oldest of French wines, the Romans moving northwards from the Midi following the course of the Tarn. And, in the Middle Ages, Gaillac wines reached Britain via the Tarn, which flows into the Garonne at Moissac. Today almost the entire production of 625,000 cases is made by four co-operatives, which have co-operated in planting Merlot and Sauvignon, Gamay and Syrah to give the mellow touch to the old traditional grapes.

Principal exporter is the *Cave Co-opérative de Vinification des Coteaux de Gaillac et du Pays Cordais* at Labastide-de-Levis near Albi, which supplies Gaillac Blanc to Peter Dominic. The largest of the four founded in 1949 has 680 members with 5000 acres making 600,000 cases a year, red, white and sparkling, including the popular *Vin de Pays du Tarn Blanc.*

South-west of Gaillac at Rabastens another co-operative founded in 1956 has 540 members and 4500 acres. Its Gaillac

Rouge is now about 60 per cent Syrah to 50 per cent Gamay with Négrette, the old local grape being phased out.

Côtes du Fronton AOC

Meeting this name for the first time soon after having a picnic lunch by the Dordogne at Fronsac, I thought it might be a misprint. Far from it, Fronton (Michelin Map 82) 17.5 miles almost due north of Toulouse and 20 miles west of Gaillac was awarded its appellation in 1975. The local Négrette, the Tannat of Madiran (q.v.), the Malbec of Bordeaux (alias Auxerrois in Cahors) — let it be recorded solely for the benefit of keen ampelographers — these all combine to make annually 300,000 cases of fruity red wine.

Madiran AOC

For many years I remember Madiran as just a name that appeared on a wine map of France in the red Michelin; now a renaissance has expanded these vineyards in the Adour valley, twenty-five miles north-east of Pau, to 2000 acres. A claret like red wine is being made from Tannat and Cabernet grapes. The dry white Pacherenc du Vic Bilh can be sweet if the grapes are left for late-picking.

AOC Béarn

Salies-de-Béarn, between the Adour and its tributary Gave d'Oloron, is about thirty-five miles north-west of Pau and a little less from Bayonne. Its appellation is for red, rosé and white wines, mainly vinified and sold by two co-operatives, *Union des Producteurs Plaimont* at Riscle, north of Madiran and the *Cave Coopérative Tursan,* a hamlet in the wilds near Geaune, half-way between Pau and Mont de Massan.

AOC Jurançon

A late-harvested golden white wine, the vineyards are on precipitous slopes south of Jurançon, now a southern suburb of Pau. The rich, sweet wine spends four years in wood before bottling and has a unique perfume. Production is only 24,000 cases.

AOC Irouléguy

Another Basque wine is made around St-Jean-Pied-de-Port and St-Etienne-de-Baigorry at the foot of the Roncevalles pass. The red — 33,000 cases from 460 acres — is light, similar to Madiran. Supplied solely by the co-operative at St-Etienne-de-Baigorry, I enjoy it there at my favourite hotel Arcé, where the Nive rolls by below the bedroom windows.

AOC vin de Corse

High strength (12.5°) makes Corsican wines better suited to improving weak blends than to titillating the human palate. Provision, however, has been made for a *vin de pays l'Isle du Beauté,* a description that may flatter what is a sound rosé.

Germany

Land under vines   98,386 hectares (243,000 acres)
Growers   90,000
Regions 11   Sub-divisions: Bereich 34; Grosslage 152; Einzellagen 2600
Production   1983: 13,300,000 hectolitres (about 147,788,000 cases). 1982 (record): 15,776,000 hectolitres (about 175,289,000 cases)
Classes   1983: Qualitätswein 62%. Qualitätswein mit Pradikat 33%. Deutscher Tafelwein and Deutscher Landwein 5%
Grape varieties   88% white — Müller-Thurgau 26%, Riesling 19%, Silvaner 9% (Traditional varieties). Kerner 6.5%,   Scheurebe 4.4%, Bacchus 3.5% (New crossings).
12% red — Spätburgunder 4% (Pinot Noir), Portugeiser 3%,   Trollinger 2%
Awards and seals   The DLG (German Agricultural Society founded 1885) awards seals to wines, submitted voluntarily to a blind tasting, which receive a higher number of points than the minimum required for the obligatory AP number. A red seal may be used for all wines and usually denotes a mild or slightly sweet wine. A yellow seal is used for *trocken*, very dry wine. A green seal is used for *halbtrocken*, semi-dry wine.
Best customers 1983
   UK
   USA
   Netherlands
   Denmark
   Canada
General Information   German Wine Information Service, 121 Gloucester Place, London N1. Tel: 01-935 8164

As explained in earlier chapters, making fine wine in our northern clime, though difficult, does bring the satisfaction of achievement. The Germans, unable to make red wine in any quantity, except in Baden and Württemberg, where they drink it all, concentrate on white wines of varying sweetness, at which they excel, particularly when the true (Rhine) Riesling grape is planted in their soil.

By adding unfermented grape juice, (Süssreserve) to fully fermented dry wine before bottling, modern practice achieves the right balance between acidity, alcohol and fruity sweetness. Quality with Müller-Thurgau, Riesling and Silvaner does not depend on restricting the yield to, say, 40 hectolitres a hectare as applied to Bordeaux châteaux. Here, in order to achieve satisfactory wines of normal strength (7°-9°) it can be as high as 30 to 100 hectolitres a hectare. Yields have been increased fourfold, helping to establish Germany's wines firmly in Britain, the USA and the Netherlands.

The growers

The State Domaine is the largest vineyard owner, the Church has many fine sites and there are great properties in private hands, yet the average holding is under one hectare

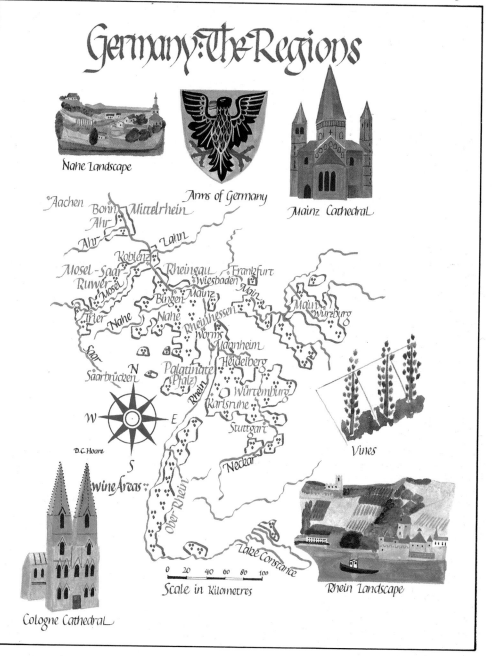

Germany: The Regions

Nahe Landscape

Arms of Germany

Mainz Cathedral

Aachen
Bonn · Mittelrhein
Ahr
Ahr
Lahn
Koblenz
Mosel-Saar-Ruwer
Mosel
Rheingau · Frankfurt
Wiesbaden
Trier
Bingen · Mainz
Nahe
Nahe
Main
Würzburg
Rheinhessen
Worms
Mannheim
Heidelberg
Saar
N
Saarbrücken
Palatinate
(Pfalz)
Würtemburg
Rhein
Karlsruhe
W
E
Stuttgart
D.C.Hoare
S
Neckar
Wine Areas
Vines
Ober-Rhein
Lake Constance
0 20 40 60 80 100
Scale in Kilometres
Rhein Landscape

Cologne Cathedral

121

(2.47 acres) and the co-operatives, with about 60,000 grower-members, are now responsible for over one third of total production. The majority sell their grapes to their local co-operative, but those making their own wine can sell it direct to the public; 39 per cent of German wine drinkers, so I read, prefer to buy and collect from a grower. There are also the *Domänen*, state-owned wine-making establishments, one in every important region, which maintain a high standard, their knowledge and experience available to all.

Two great years

Some sunless summers, such as made the 1970s a dismal decade apart from 1971, 1975 and 1976, have to be expected. But this was soon forgotten when 1982 brought a record yield of almost sixteen million hectolitres, followed by 1983 with 13·3 million, of a quality even better than its predecessor.

Britain, where 71 per cent of all wine sales are white, is Germany's best customer in volume and in cash. Our wine-drinkers are increasing and the white, medium-dry to medium-sweet styles are what most newcomers to table wines prefer (the drier taste comes later, with, ironically, a swing back towards a 'sweet tooth' when they are long and, maybe, mostly false). Thanks to the duty reduction in the 1984 Budget, their prices, as low as £1·50 a bottle, became attractive and about one in four bottles Britain imported in 1983 was German.

Of course we have long been among Germany's best customers, abbreviating to 'Hock' the town of Hochheim on the river Main to denote any Rhenish or Rhine wine in the days of King Charles II. In 1971 the Germans also went in for an abbreviation; they reduced their 52,000 vineyard names to a mere 3,000 in a new series of wine laws.

Liebfraumilch

A report from the Wine Institute at Mainz that we are drinking 37 per cent of their exported quality wines gives the impression that we find the new laws quite simple and their labelling clear as a bell. But all Liebfraumilch now counts as quality wine and it is mainly Liebfraumilch that Britain is drinking.

There are many sound brands, the best known — highly advertised on television — recovering this expense in the price. Hugh Johnson, after sympathising with people giving up the struggle with the laws and labels, who then get no further than Liebfraumilch, writes in his *Wine Companion*:

> The law requires only that the wines should be 'of pleasant character', and be made of certain grapes in certain regions — those which in any case produce the greatest volumes of wine. Learning the pleasures of German wine starts with abandoning Liebfraumilch.

Clearly my object in the pages that follow must be to aid this abandonment by the clearest exposition of laws, labels and districts, at the risk of being shot against the wall of the Liebfrauen-Kirche itself, Liebfraumilch St Dominic being Peter Dominic's best selling wine.

The wine laws

The 1971 German laws, subsequently liable to EEC legislative changes, created two classes: Table, *Tafelwein* and Quality, *Qualitätswein*.

Tafelwein Wines that are 100 per cent German grown and made are now called Deutscher Tafelwein, usually followed by one of five rivers — Rhein, Mosel, Main, Neckar or Oberrhein — which are the regions of Tafelwein. One example is Deutscher Tafelwein Mosel from the Zentralkellerei (co-operative) at Bernkastel-Kues. A site name is not permitted for any Tafelwein.

Introduced in 1982, Landwein is the German equivalent of *vins de pays* and with a 0 · 5 per cent minimum higher strength is meant to be superior to any Deutscher Tafelwein from the same area. Landwein can come from fifteen Landwein areas and their names precede or follow 'Landwein' on the label.

Tafelwein alone can denote an EEC requirement for blended wines of two or more EEC countries. Known as 'Euroblends', they are mainly blended and bottled in Germany from wines not of German origin, usually Italian and sometimes of the poorest quality. This is disguised by decorative labels, embodying illegible Gothic-script German names like Moselgarten, with the obligatory words in German 'Blend of table wines from several countries of the EEC' or 'Wine made in . . . from grapes harvested in . . . (country of origin)' barely visible amid the decor. Though not illegal, this unscrupulous practice is of growing concern to the honest majority of German wine-makers as damaging to their national reputation. The simple foreigners could be conned into believing that these wines are the pride and joy of Europe and Germany, when in fact by *Tafelwein & Lyleburger* out of *Lago de vino Italiano* is nearer the truth.

Qualitätswein bestimmter anbaugebiete (QbA) 'Quality wine from a designated region', QbA for short, is the first of two classes. The second — and better class — is *Qualitätswein mit Prädikat* (QmP) which has special attributes, for example a particular site or style from Kabinett to Trockenbeerenauslese. Provided it meets with its own specification (see page 133), all Liebfraumilch ranks as QbA wine.

The most important requirement for wines aspiring to either class is that they must be submitted to official analysis and tasting before bottling. Each grade, Kabinett, Spätlese etc., must reach the minimum must weight in degrees Oechsle prescribed for it, and correspond in appearance, smell and taste with a typical wine of identical origin. Only then will it be given the control number that must appear on the label.

Thus, the laws provide for promotion and relegation. The wine of a great site, normally Qualitätswein mit Prädikat, would be down-graded to Deutscher Tafelwein if it was badly made or bad weather had ruined it. Similarly — and more likely — a modestly sited vineyard could reach the higher grade by skilful viticulture and viniculture in a good year. This is an advance on the system of *Appellation d'Origine Contrôlée*, which guarantees geographical origin but not quality, a fact clearly recognised by the French now introducing tastings for the wines of St. Emilion.

The special attributes making QmP a superior class are either a site, or a style, of distinction. Kabinett and all wines from late-harvested or specially selected grapes are QmP. No sugar (i.e. no chaptalisation) may be added to increase the alcoholic content of QmP wines.

ELEVEN WINE REGIONS

Geographically there are eleven wine regions (*Gebiet*), each sub-divided into various districts called *Bereich*, comprising groups of villages making similar wines. The Bereich name is often that of the principal town or village in the region (for example, Bereich Bernkastel, Bereich Johannisberg) and on a label the word *Bereich* must precede that of the town or village.

Before 1971 every village had a bewildering number of vineyard names. Now only those of five hectares (12 · 5 acres) or more are recognised. Each district (*Bereich*) is divided into two or more vineyard areas (*Grosslagen*), which in turn break down first into villages, parishes or communes (*Gemeinden*) and finally into sites (*Einzellagen*) under different ownership. The system is similar to the region — commune — vineyard — plot or *climat* sequence in Burgundy, but with more names, pointless to memorise and better looked up.* The total comes to 11 Regions, 33 *Bereich*, 150 *Grosslagen*, which divide into 2600 *Einzellagen*. As to villages, I have counted 1368, hundreds of them in Baden and Württemberg, where the people are great wine drinkers.

From the system a clear pyramid of origin, with the region as the base, ascends to the Single Vineyard, for example;

1	Region	Mosel-Saar-Ruwer
2	District	Bereich Bernkastel
3	Vineyard group *(Grosslage)*	Michelsberg
4	Village *(Gemeinde)*	Piesport
5	Site *(Einzellage)*	Goldtröpfchen

---

* Cyril Ray's *The Wines of Germany* gives them all.

All five locations are of course rarely necessary on a label. In this case, village and site are so famous that Piesporter Goldtröpfchen is sufficient. *Grosslage* rarely appears; it is a collective term introduced to cover wines from several little-known *Einzellagen*. Bereich Bernkastel describes a wine of that district just as Saumur describes a wine of the Anjou region.

Wine?
Have you tried that Niersteiner
Trockenbeerenauslese 1959?
They say it's quite nice —
At the price.
(R. L. Chambers, Stourbridge)

Drink sweet, get high
On Tokay.
Then drink Niersteiner Auflangen Orbel
Riesling und Sylvaner Trockenbeerenauslese
As a chaser.
(W. E. Weeks, Truro)

Wine Mine Clerihews 1969

Ahr

With only 1010 acres, this little tributary is unlikely to set the Rhine on fire. Nevertheless, its pretty valley — holiday country for the people of Bonn, Remagen and Koblenz — has undisputed fame as the most northerly red wine district of the world. Pinot Noir vines, known locally as Spätburgunder, were brought across from Burgundy in the seventeenth century. There are white wines too — Riesling and Müller-Thurgau — and good beer for the 'locals'. There is also a famous mineral water, Apollinaris. I remember in London's theatre bars when a small 'split' came as a matter of course with every whisky or brandy and soda — and we never even said 'Ahr' as we poured out that 'baby Polly'.

GERMAN WINE LAWS – A TABULATED GUIDE

German Wine Law — Three Statutory Grades			Table
Grade	**Legal Requirements**	**Classification**	**Limits of Origin**
Tafelwein (German Table Wine)	Only for suitable vine types from approved vineyards 8.5° minimum alcohol content	Light, digestible wine for quenching thirst	Exclusively home-grown wine from German table wine regions
Qualitätswein from defined regions (Q.b.A.)	Official testing, must have typical taste, free from errors; fixed min, natural alcohol according to district; inspection number	Full-bodied wines typical of district with tested quality; for daily consumption	Exclusively from single defined area. Total number of defined production regions: 11
Qualitätswein mit Pradikat		According to official control of vintage, based on testing of analysis and taste: without any enriching of the must with sugar		stylish, fully matured wines of high class	
'Kabinett'					
'Spätlese'		Late vintage of grapes in mature condition		rich fullness of taste	
'Auslese'		Selection and separate pressing of any mature grapes		a noble growth for special occasions	Exclusively from a single area within a defined growing region
'Beerenauslese'		Selection of overripe grapes only			
'Trocken-beerenauslese'		Selection of shrivelled grapes of highest taste concentration			
'Eiswein'	Grapes frozen to ice during gathering and pressing	Rare in all grades		

In the Qualitätswein mit Pradikat rows, the second column reads vertically: "graded statutory minimum requirements of natural ripeness (must weight)" and the fourth column reads vertically: "highest quality grades up to the highest grade".

Mosel-Saar-Ruwer Area: 30,370 acres. White wine: Riesling 57 per cent; Müller-Thurgau 23 per cent; Elbling 10 per cent; others 10 per cent. Production: 1 · 8 million hectolitres (about 20 million cases), QmP 52 per cent, QbA 42 per cent, Tafelwein 6 per cent.

314 tortuous miles from a source in the Vosges, past Nancy and Metz through Luxembourg into Germany, the Mosel decants itself into the Rhine at Koblenz. The fame of its wines begins along the Saar, a large tributary joining it above Trier, then below it on the little Ruwer, pronounced

Qualitätswein and Qualitätswein mit Prädikat			
Defined Regions *(Gebiet)*	**Districts** *(Bereich)*	**Vineyard** *(Grosslagen)*	**Single Vineyards** *(Einzellagen)*
1 Ahr	Walporzheim-Ahrtal		
2 Baden	Bodensee Markgräfeland Kaiserstuhl-Tuniberg Breisgau Ortenau Bad Bergstr-Kraichgau Bad Frankenland		
3 Franken	Steigerwald Maindreieck Mainviereck		
4 Hess Bergstrasse	Starkenburg Umstadt		
5 Mittelrheim	Bacharach Rheinburgengau	Names of Grosslagen, the large sites or vineyard areas. Each Bereich has two or more Grosslagen.	Names of single vineyards within the Grosslagen. There are about 2,500, size between 5 and 10 hectares.
6 Mosel-Saar-Ruwer	Zell-Mosel Bernkastel Saar-Ruwer Obermosel		
7 Nahe	Kreuznach Schloss-Böckelhein		
8 Rheingau	Johannisberg		
9 Rhein-hessen	Bingen Nierstein Wonnegau		
10 Rheinpfalz	Sudl Weinstrasse Mittelhaardt-Deutche Weinstr		
11 Württemberg	Remstal-Stuttgart Mittelhaardt-Unterland Kocher-Jagst-Taubertal		

REGIONS AND DISTRICTS (TABLE LEFT)

'Roo-ver', reaching a climax on the Middle Mosel from Trier downstream to Bernkastel-Kues and Traben-Trarbach as far as Cochem. Here, in a cold climate between precipitous slopes, where the river twists and turns like a corkscrew, the poor slate soil reflects just enough warmth for wine to be made from grapes; and, miraculously, the Riesling vine achieves a unique potion with a marvellous bouquet and refreshing acidity.

The siting of a vineyard — the direction it faces, its incline, the amount of sun reflected from the river (and the new canal) — can make one wine better than that of a close neighbour, and this is why their descriptions have to be detailed. The slate itself is so vital that any washed away is replaced. Slow to ripen, the Riesling vintage can run into late November, increasing the risks from bad weather; replaced by Müller-Thurgau, a better cropper, the wine lacks the Riesling's fruity acidity.

The charm of good Mosel lies in its greenish tinge, lively bouquet, 'slatey' fresh taste and low strength about 9°; summer thirsts can be slaked — from Lord's to every village green — from those traditionally tall green bottles with less anxiety about breathalysers 'as the run-stealers flicker to and fro'.

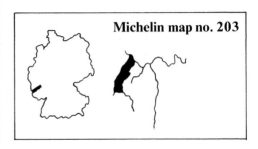

Michelin map no. 203

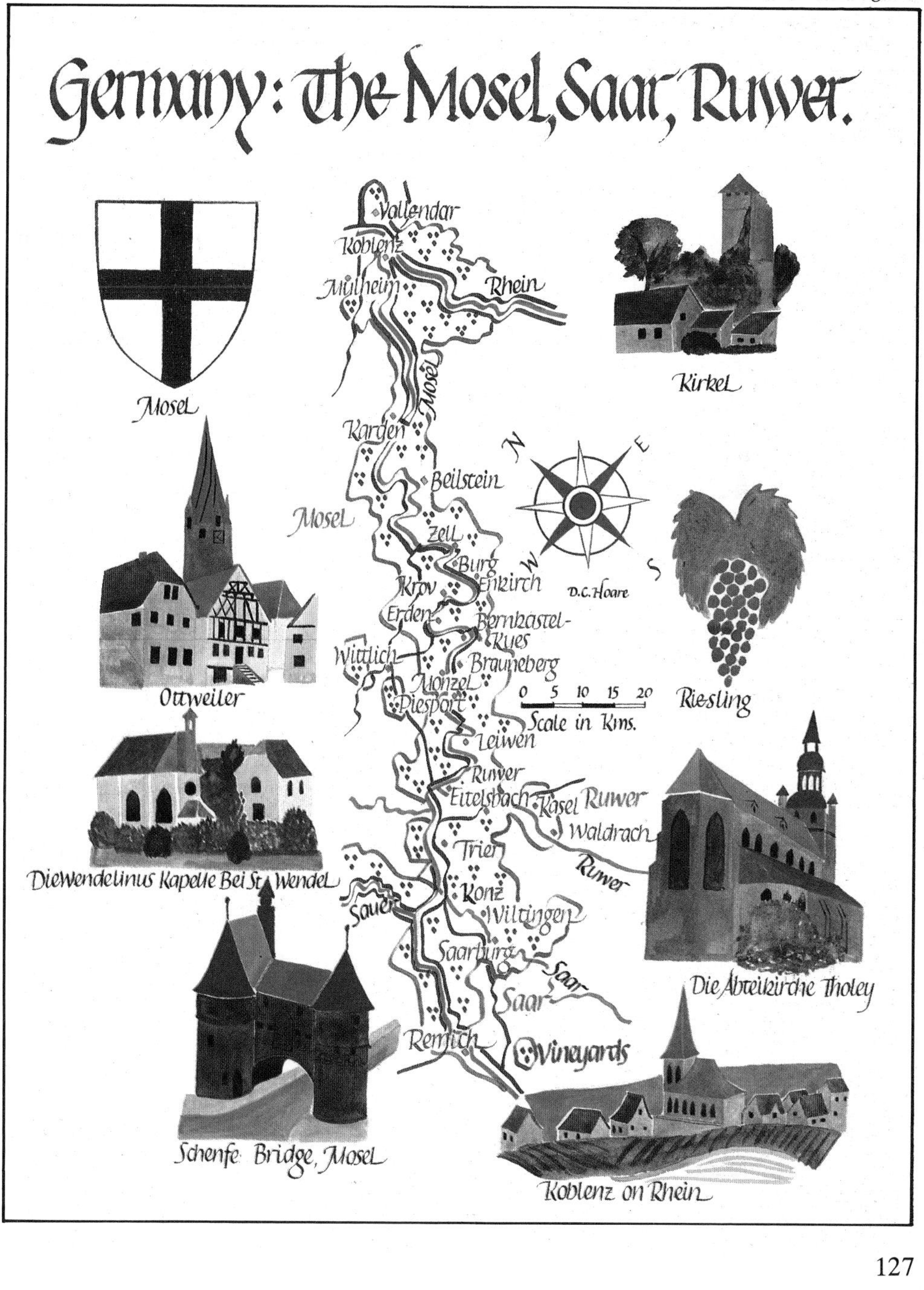

Germany: The Mosel, Saar, Ruwer.

Mosel

Vallendar
Koblenz
Mülheim
Rhein

Kirkel

Karden
Beilstein
Mosel
Zell
Burg
Krov
Enkirch
Erden
Bernkastel-
Kues
Wittlich
Braumeberg
Wonzel
Piesport

Riesling

N
E
W
S
D.C. Hoare

Ottweiler

Leiwen

Ruwer
Eitelsbach
Kasel
Ruwer
Waldrach
Trier
Ruwer

0 5 10 15 20
Scale in Kms.

Die Wendelinus Kapelle Bei St. Wendel

Konz
Wiltingen
Saarburg
Saar
Saar

Die Abteikirche Tholey

Remich
Vineyards

Schenfe Bridge, Mosel

Koblenz on Rhein

127

The finest wines are wholly Riesling, nowhere finer in great years of 1982 and 1983 class, than from the two tributaries, Saar and Ruwer. When their Rieslings ripen properly, Wiltinger, Serriger, Ayler (Saar) and Kaseler, Eitelsbacher and Maximin Grünhäuser (Ruwer) come into their own.

On the Mosel itself, the middle reach between Longuich and Zell now called 'Bereich Bernkastel' makes the best wines, on average fuller and less acid than those of Saar and Ruwer. They come from nine *Grosslagen* with nearly 150 *Einzellagen* between them, the right bank from Bernkasteler Doctor downstream past J. J. Prüm's parcels of Graacher Himmelreich and Wehlener Sonnenuhr being Arcadia for the Mosel worshipper.

The low-priced wines are mainly Müller-Thurgau, which yields more and ripens in fifty-two days against the Riesling's sixty-eight.

Mittelrhein

This region, a belt ten miles wide on either side of the Rhine, runs downstream from Bingen at the mouth of the Nahe almost to Bonn. With 1882 acres, about 80,000 hectolitres (900,000 cases) are either drunk or turned into Sekt (sparkling wine). Though much appreciated by *Weinkenner* (connoisseurs) in the region, Mittelrhein wines are rarely met in other parts of Germany or in Great Britain.

Rheingau

7240 acres. White wine: Riesling 83 per cent, Müller-Thurgau 9 per cent, others 8 per cent. Production: 270,000 hectolitres (about 3 million cases) QmP 71 per cent, QbA 29 per cent, Tafelwein 0 per cent.

Here, where the north-flowing Rhine turns west-south-west for fifteen miles, the Riesling vines on the south-facing slopes of the north bank reach their pinnacle of perfection. The Rheingau is small, just a river front of fifteen miles, with a deep brown soil, going back for about three miles towards the Taunus mountains that protect it from the northern blast. The slope gets little rain and the reflected warmth from the river, about half a mile wide, not only ripens the Riesling fully but brings the mists that aid the *Edelfäule* — that same noble rot or *pourriture noble* — as essential for Germany's sweet Beerenauslese and Trockenbeerenauslese dessert wines as it is for France's Sauternes.

Much the same climate benefits Hochheim, where the Rhine's turn westward begins and its tributary the Main flows in from Franconia, far away to the east. Thus the vineyards of Hochheim on its north bank also form part of the Rheingau, and Victorians learnt about them in 1850 when their Queen, on a visit, thought them so good that a vineyard was renamed Königin Victoria.

Approaching the Rheingau from the Channel ports along the right-bank road, the first village, Assmannshausen, makes a little of what the Germans lack and love — red wine; this constitutes the last red wine stop until Baden, sixty miles on. The great Rieslings now begin at noisy, tripper-ridden Rüdesheim, where the car ferry across to Bingen affords escape to a tranquil Nahe.

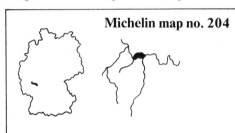

Michelin map no. 204

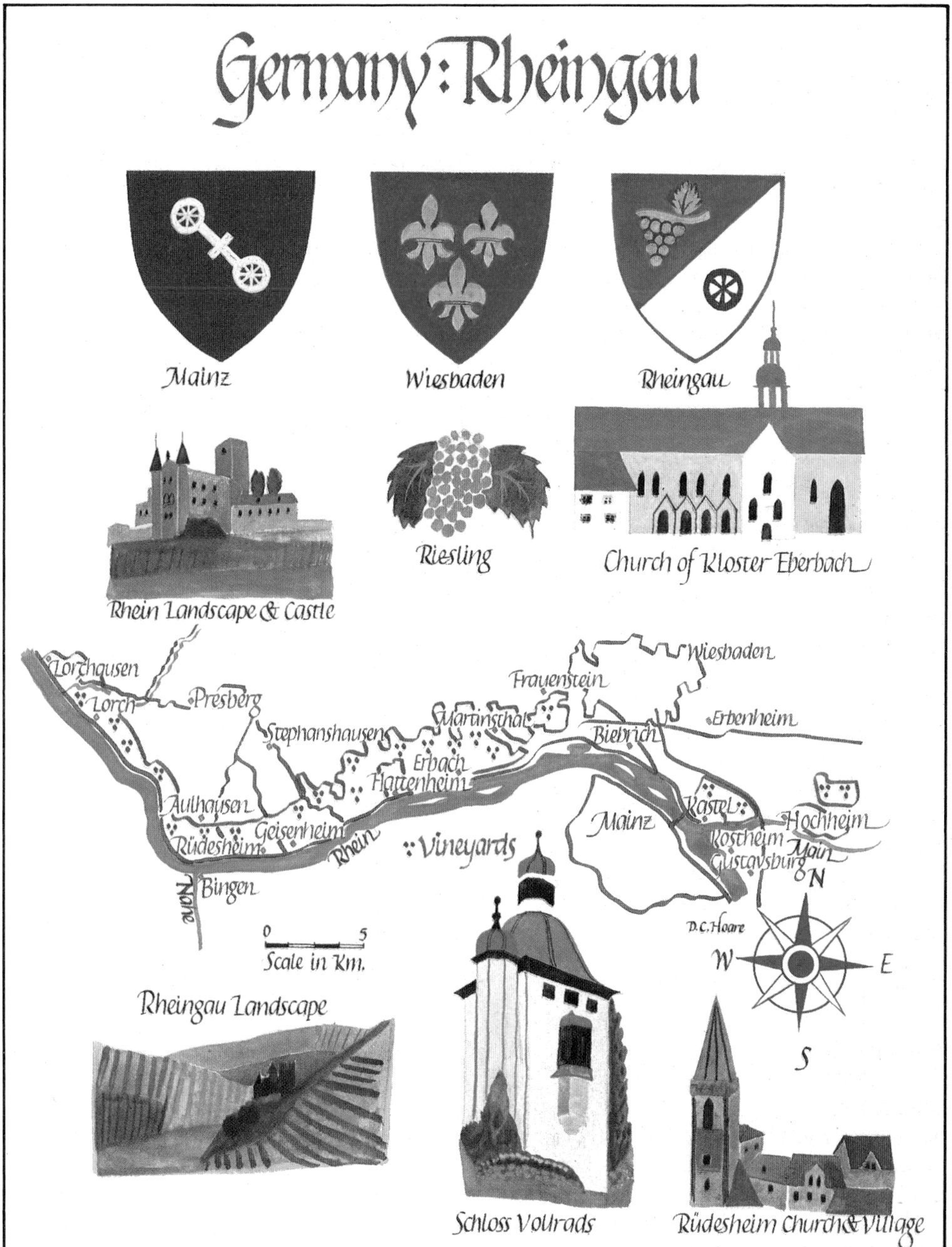

Germany: Rheingau

Mainz

Wiesbaden

Rheingau

Rhein Landscape & Castle

Riesling

Church of Kloster Eberbach

Lorchausen
Lorch
Presberg
Stephanshausen
Aulhausen
Rüdesheim
Geisenheim
Bingen
Nahe
Rhein
Martinsthal
Frauenstein
Erbach
Hattenheim
Biebrich
Erbenheim
Wiesbaden
Mainz
Kastel
Kostheim
Gustavsburg
Hochheim
Main

:: Vineyards

D.C. Hoare

N
W — E
S

0   5
Scale in Km.

Rheingau Landscape

Schloss Vollrads

Rüdesheim Church & Village

129

Along the Rheingau river road, at little more than one mile intervals, come Geisenheim, Winkel, Mittelheim, Oestrich, Erbach and Eltville. A mile or so higher up, the aristocracy look over these villages from their great estates to the river. Fürst von Metternich from his Schloss Johannisberg, Count Erwein Matuschka-Greiffenclau from Schloss Vollrads, the Princes of Prussia from Schloss Reinharts-hausen, families that continue to play great parts in wine-making. There are others too, enough to compile a list that reads like a German growers' *Debrett.*

Another show place, the twelfth-century Cistercian monastery, Kloster Eberbach, is open to the public and belongs to the Hessian state. It is used as a venue for tastings and courses; in the cellars lie all the wines of the thirty-two-acre Steinberg, the State's ancient walled vineyard nearby.

But numerous commoners and co-operatives also own fine sites and make fine wines in the Rheingau. And, believe it or not, one *Bereich,* 'Johannisberg' does for them all, even though 'all' does mean 10 *Grosslagen* and 126 *Einzellagen.*

Nahe Area: 11,080 acres.
White wine: Müller-Thurgau 30 per cent, Silvaner 27 per cent, Riesling 23 per cent. Production: 579,330 hectolitres, (about 6,437,000 cases) QmP 47 per cent, QbA 46 per cent, Tafelwein 7 per cent.

Rising in the Hunsrück hills, this pretty little Rhine tributary enjoys a loop or two reminiscent of Mosel before ending its life at Bingen. The vineyards grace the last fifteen miles from the town of Schloss-Böckelheim, which is the first Bereich, with scores of villages (*Gemeinden*) and sites (Einzellagen). The other Bereich is Kreuz-nach, Bad Kreuznach being the spa town on either side of the Nahe six more miles downstream.

Serena Sutcliffe M.W., in *Great Vineyards and Winemakers,* likens the Riesling wines to fine Mosels with a little more body; those blended from Müller-Thurgau and Silvaner are more like good Rheinhessen with greater elegance. A Kreuznacher Mönchberg Riesling Auslese 1976 from Reichsgraf von Plettenberg of Bad Kreuznach I have found sweet enough to substitute for Sauternes with my home grown raspberries.

The State Domaine with offices and cellars at Niederhausen-Schloss-Böckel-heim owns some fine sites, including Kupfergrube and Felsenberg among the best in the valley.

Rheinhessen Area: 58,040 acres.
White wines: Müller-Thurgau 27 per cent, Silvaner 15 per cent, Riesling 6 per cent, Scheurebe 9 per cent, Bacchus 8 per cent, Faber 7 per cent, Kerner 7 per cent, Morio-Muskat 5 per cent, others 16 per cent. Production: 3,418,240 hectolitres, (about 38 million cases) QbA 52 per cent, QmP 47 per cent, Tafelwein 1 per cent.

On the southern side of the Rhine opposite the Rheingau, Germany's largest region (20 by 30 miles) stretches eastwards

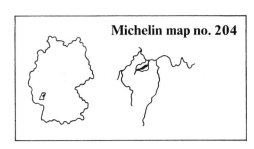

Michelin map no. 204

Germany: Nahe

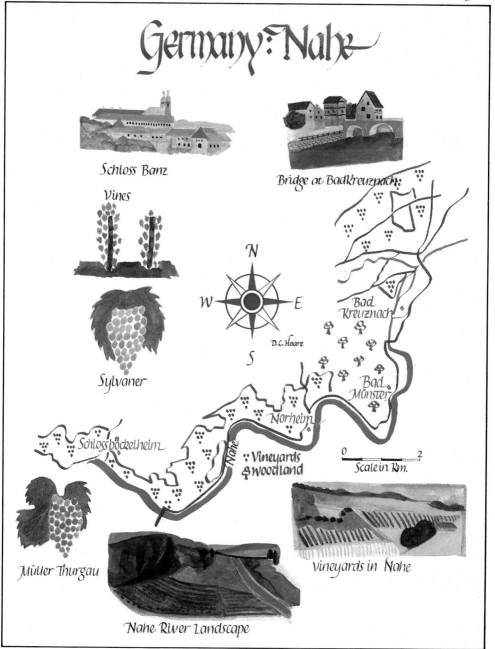

Schloss Banz

Bridge at BadKreuznach

Vines

Sylvaner

N

W E

S

D.C. Hoare

Bad Kreuznach

Bad Münster

Norheim

Schlossböckelheim

Nahe

Vineyards & Woodland

0   2
Scale in Km.

Müller Thurgau

Nahe River Landscape

Vineyards in Nahe

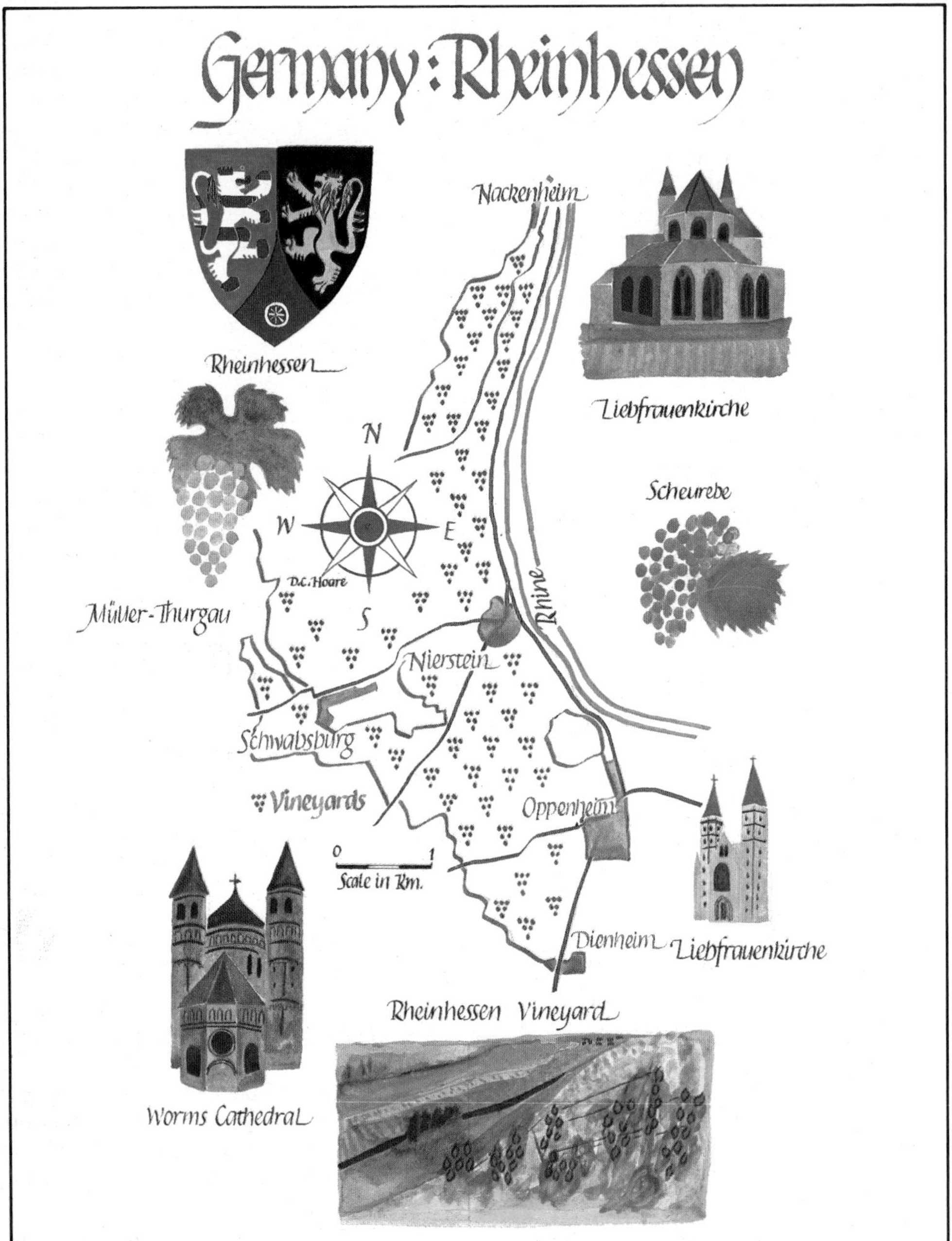

Germany: Rheinhessen

Rheinhessen

Liebfrauenkirche

Scheurebe

Nackenheim

Müller-Thurgau

N

W · E

S

D.C. Hoare

Rhine

Nierstein

Schwabsburg

Vineyards

Oppenheim

0 1
Scale in Km.

Dienheim   Liebfrauenkirche

Worms Cathedral

Rheinhessen Vineyard

from Bingen to Mainz, then south along the Rhine to Worms and finally north-west back again to the Nahe. Flat and uninteresting country, the best wines are made on the fringes by the two rivers.

Driving down the Rhine road from Nackenheim through Nierstein, Oppenheim and Dienheim, the steep red slopes thick with Riesling greenery reveal celebrated site names capable of Edelfaüle wines as great as those of the Rheingau. The Bereich is Nierstein. Within it there are eleven *Grosslagen,* their names Auflangen, Gutes Domtal, Rehbach, being better known than the scores of sites that comprise them. Among Nierstein winemakers Anton Balbach, Heinrich Seip and Louis Guntrum are outstanding firms and C.A. Kupferberg, suppliers of sparkling wines to British Kings and Lords, keep open house in Mainz. Bereich Bingen, the western half of Rheinhesse bordering the Nahe, has some wines of good quality seldom exported.

Liebfraumilch: New rules Bereich Wonnegau, third and last of Rheinhessen divisions, covers the hinterland of Worms, where Liebfraumilch originated in the vineyard of the Liebfrauen Kirche (Church of Our Lady), still a green preserve in summer in a city rebuilt after the Second World War. German legislation of 1983

requires all Liebfraumilch to be Qualitätswein QbA, wholly from grapes grown either in Rheinpfalz, Rheinhesse, Nahe or Rheingau, but not from any combination from these regions. Fifty per cent must be Riesling, Silvaner or Müller-Thurgau. The minimum sugar content of the must is 60° Oechsle. The names of vines must not be declared. And as a QbA wine, it will have to be tasted before and after bottling to obtain the official AP. (Amtliche Prüfungsnummer) number that must be on the label. number that must be on the label.

I wonder how these rules will be enforced. How many brands are there in the world besides the dozens in Britain? Who will volunteer to taste them day after day? It could be a fate more monotonous than that of Lambert Simnel sentenced to be a scullion permanently peeling potatoes in Henry VII's kitchen.

The Liebfraumilch League table in Britain is currently led by Blue Nun, and Saccone's Black Tower in a fancy bottle held by marketing men to create 'Brand Loyalty'. There are so many fancy names, the entertaining Richard Stilgoe should have no difficulty in composing a Liebfraumilch libretto from *Black Tower, Blue Nun, The Bishop of Riesling,* the *Sleeping Beauty, Goldener Oktober, Rhine Bear* and *St Dominic.*

Rheinpfalz Area: 53,920 acres.
White wine: Müller-Thurgau 28 per cent, Riesling 14 per cent, Silvaner 12 per cent, Kerner 11 per cent, Morio-Muskat 9 per cent, Scheurebe 7 per cent, Red Portugieser 8 per cent, others 11 per cent. Production: 3,017,700 hectolitres, (about 33 million cases) QbA 54 per cent, QmP 43 per cent, Tafelwein 3 per cent.
Being well south of the Rheingau and

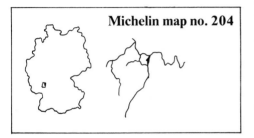

Michelin map no. 204

Rheinhesse this region, (protected to the north-west by the Haardt mountains, an extension of the Vosges) gets more sunshine and makes more wine than any other. The term Pfalz for this flat plain comes from the Latin, 'Palatinus', the first of Rome's seven hills, where Augustus built a palace. Thenceforward buildings in which Roman emperors stayed became, in German, 'palast', *Pfalz* being a later corruption. In English 'Palatine' is a Count with territorial jurisdiction (Count Alma-viva in *The Marriage of Figaro* springs to mind) but 'palatine', an adjective relates to the palate, so our name Palatinate for this region seems doubly suitable.

Deutsche Weinstrasse, a celebrated wine road, starting south-west of Worms, runs for 54 miles through gaily-painted villages to the monumental gateway at Schweigen, ending eventually in Alsace, still among the Rieslings but of drier fame.

Bereich Mittlhaardt Deutsche Weinstrasse Rheinpfalz divides into two; this Bereich is the northern half, from Dackenheim to Neustadt, where the great wines are made at Kallstadt, Ungstein, Dürkheim, Wachen-heim, Forst, Deidesheim and Ruppertsberg, seven outstanding villages.

About the third week in September, the town of Dürkheim (12,000 strong) holds the largest of Germany's many wine festivals known as the Sausage Fair, a riot of eating, drinking, dodgems and coconuts. People pour in from all over the country. Every wine fair has its queen and princesses, chosen for their local wine knowledge as well as their looks.

The leading producers are three old family firms, Dr von Bassermann-Jordan, Reichsrat von Buhl, both of Deidesheim

and Dr Bürklin-Wolf of Wachenheim. Their wines stand comparison with the best of the Rheingau and can be as long lived (a Forster Ungeheuer Riesling Auslese 1937 tasted at Christie's in 1969 could still be described as 'magnificent').* Others with smaller estates include Johannes Karst and Söhne of Bad Dürkheim, whose fascinating selection of estate-bottled Scheurebe, Gewürztraminer, Silvaner and Riesling, some of them blends of two grapes, were a feature of Wine Mine from the 1959 vintage onwards.

Bereich Südliche Weinstrasse The southern half can supply plenty of excellent wine for Liebfraumilch. Until 1971 most of it was going to the Mosel under an organisation set up by the Nazis. Re-organised by co-operatives, quantity and quality have increased enormously, and there has been an enterprising spirit in experimenting with new grapes, notably Bacchus, Kerner and Morio-Muskat in this *Bereich* running south from Neustadt, with Landau the main town.

Hessische Bergstrasse Only 926 acres, this region lies on the Rhine's right bank north of Heidelberg and what little wine it makes goes to the Hessen State Domaine at

---

* *The Great Vintage Wine Book,*
Michael Broadbent.

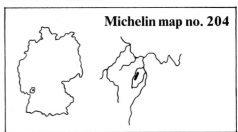

Michelin map no. 204

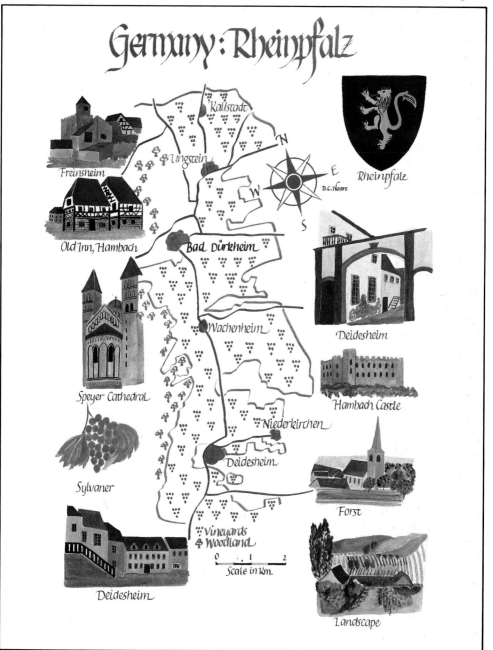

Germany: Rheinpfalz

Kallstadt

Freinsheim

Ungstein

Old Inn, Hambach

N

W E

S

D.C.Hoare

Rheinpfalz

Bad Dürkheim

Wachenheim

Deidesheim

Speyer Cathedral

Hambach Castle

Sylvaner

Niederkirchen

Deidesheim

Forst

Deidesheim

Vineyards
Woodland

0 1 2
Scale in km.

Landscape

135

Eltville. Researching his book, *The Wines of Germany,* Cyril Ray could find no local wine at the local hotel and nobody who knew why this locality was one of the national XI.

Baden Area: 35,310 acres.
White wine (77 per cent): Müller-Thurgau 45 per cent, Ruländer 15 per cent, Gutedel 10 per cent, Riesling 8 per cent, others 22 per cent. Red wine (23 per cent): Spätburgunder 95 per cent, others 5 per cent. Production: 1.8 million hectolitres (about 20 million cases) QmP 53 per cent, QbA 46 per cent, Tafelwein 1 per cent.

Baden competes with Mosel-Saar-Ruwer for third place as Germany's biggest producer. The region is a strip 130 miles long on the right bank of the Rhine from Heidelberg abreast Rheinpfalz to Basle in Switzerland.

Until the phylloxera destroyed the vineyards about 1870, Baden was Germany's biggest producer and, given the chance, every inhabitant still drinks wine daily like a Frenchman. Between the two world wars the hybrid vines* that replaced them were ordered to be pulled up, in order to plant better vines and make better wines. This is still going on under efficient co-operatives and more will surely be heard about Baden abroad.

Württemberg Area: 21,400 acres.
White wine (53 per cent): Muller-Thurgau 50 per cent, Ruländer 20 per cent, Gutedel 14 per cent, Riesling 11 per cent, others 5 per cent. Red wine (47 per cent): Trollinger 65 per cent, Müller Rebe 25 per cent,

---

*An unsatisfactory cross between European noble grapes and American species outlawed in Germany and France for quality wine.

others 10 per cent. Production: 1.4 million hectolitres (about 15.4 million cases) QbA 62 per cent, QmP 37 per cent, Tafelwein 1 per cent.

North and south of Stuttgart these vineyards lie on both sides of the Neckar, a sizeable Rhine tributary. Little, if any, wine is left for export; Baden and Württemberg being politically and administratively one since 1953, the patriots are zealous in consuming it.

Franken Area: 10,630 acres.
White wine: Müller-Thurgau 50 per cent, Silvaner 25 per cent, Bacchus 7 per cent, Kerner 5 per cent, others 13 per cent. Production 673,500 hectolitres, (about 7.5 million cases) QbA 54 per cent, QmP 45 per cent, Tafelwein 1 per cent.

Seventy-five miles north-north-east of Stuttgart lies Würzburg, centre of Franconian wine and for those who delight in Baroque, one of Europe's most pleasing places. At the gigantic Residenz palace, the art of architecture and the Winzer could hardly be closer: the Bavarian state cellars are underneath it.

Standing on the quay by the pleasant hotel Walfisch contemplating the Main, the massive Marienberg fortress towers above with its little Leiste vineyard below it. Cross the bridge and away to the north, outside the city, the Stein vineyard comes into view. Only wines from these two ancient sites are entitled to the name Steinwein (stone wine) and, in its original form, its fame was based on sweet Beerenauslese wine, which lived as long as Malmsey Madeira.

On the other hand, Franken wines in their *Bocksbeutel* flasks were never sweet. They were the driest in Germany, more like a white burgundy and better suited to the dinner table than Hock or Mosel. The grape

MANNER OF HARVESTING AND WHEN TO DRINK

Deutscher Tafelwein 5°/44	As required
Q.b.a. 7.5°/60	Keep 1—2 years
Kabinett 9.5°/73 Lowest grade of Q.m.P. An above average beverage wine originally good enough for the grower's cellar	Keep 2—3 years
Spätlese 11.4°/85 Late picked Q.m.P. Fuller than Kabinett; not necessarily sweeter	Keep 3—4 years
Auslese 13°/95 Late picked *and* 'specially selected' Q.m.P. from ripest bunches	Keep 5—6 years
Beerenauslese 17.7°/125 Q.m.P. Ripest single grapes selected, infected with Edelfaüle. Rare, sweet and expensive	8 years plus
Trockenbeerenauslese 21.5°/150 Q.m.P. As for Beerenauslese but from drier grapes kept on the vine until they were raisins. Rich, rare, very sweet. very expensive	8 years plus
Eiswein Q.m.P. From grapes picked frozen solid in mid-winter. With water content frozen, the juice when separated makes a very fruity wine. Unique, expensive novelty of indeterminate vintage when picked in January.	8 years plus

was the Silvaner. Now, understandably in a continental climate liable to sharp frosts, the higher-yielding Müller-Thurgau — earlier to ripen — replaces Riesling and Silvaner. Other aromatic grapes, Bacchus and Kerner, are being tried. Will the character of Franconian wine change? One can only wait and see.

Prominent among the dozen villages on the Main above and below the city are Escherndorf, Randersacker and Iphofen. Gebietswinzergenossenschaft Franken, the Würzburg Co-operative, has been a good source of supply (£1.17 a bottle in 1972). But the finest wines are those of the Bayerische, the Bavarian State Institute, and the two vineyards owning charitable foundations (similar to the Hospice de Beaune) the Juliusspital and the Bürgerspital. All three have headquarters in the city. Details are in my *Guide to Visiting Vineyards.*

The vintage

In other countries when *der Tag* is declared either ripe grapes are picked as fast as possible from each vineyard to make table wines, or overripe grapes are picked later to make dessert wines. In Germany they do both in the same vineyard. Each grower has his own plans remembering that every day of fine weather will increase the must weight by one degree Oschsle and that rain will reduce it.

Hauptlese is the general harvest and *Vorlese* any harvest authorised to begin earlier, as when exceptionally bad weather is expected. Though no sugar may be added to QmP musts, *Süssreserve* (the unfermented grape juice, maximum 1° alcohol) approved for each style may be added to the newly-made wines, which are likely nowadays to be kept in modern steel or glass lined vats protected by inert gas from further fermentation, and later by sterile bottling. The sweet reserve, added to dry wine immediately before bottling, is kept separately in stainless steel or glass-lined vats. Thus a good vintage will produce the choice tabulated above.

---

*The figures are percentage alcohol and their equivalent degrees Oechsle as required for the Rheingau. Other regions vary slightly.

1983 — Vintage

Detzemer Würzgarten — Vineyard area (Grosslagen)

— Vineyard

— Grape variety

Riesling - Spätlese — Manner of harvesting indicative as to the style

Qualitätswein mit Prädikat — Quality level

Mosel-Saar-Ruwer — Defined region

A. P. Nr. 2576280 17284 — Control number

Abgefüllt in Bernkastel für **WEINKELLEREI VILLA EDEN GMBH** Bingen 70cl e — Merchant's name

GEWA BINGEN

Bottled in Bernkastel

Bottled by the producer

ERZEUGER-ABFÜLLUNG

Neck label

Switzerland

The three wine-making communities in Switzerland (French, German and Italian) all make good wines, besides being good Burgundy customers. If Chasselas (called Fendant in Switzerland) and red Pinots and Gamays are seldom seen in Britain it is because there are so many similar wines, from other parts of Europe, which cost less.

Italy

In the summer of 1956 when I was promoted from Worthing branch apprentice to Mail Order Manager at Horsham, Peter Dominic had ten branches, a price list, no mail order department and no Italian wines. With thirty clarets – mostly 1949 and 1950 – including Pontet-Canet at 11s 6d and Mouton-Rothschild at 21s, supported by plenty of white Bordeaux and Burgundy at under £1 a bottle there was no

Total Production 1983: 77,000,000 hectolitres, about 856 million cases
1980 (record): 86,545,000 hectolitres, about 961 million cases
DOC Production About 10 per cent of total annually
Further information The Italian Trade Centre, 37 Sackville Street, London W1 Tel: 01-734 2412

Region		Total production cases 12 bots. 75cl.	DOC cases 12 bots. 75cl.
1	Piedmont	50,044,444	11,345,577
2	Valle d'Aosta	466,666	4633
3	Lombardy	26,100,000	4,175,544
4	Trentino Alto Adige	16,500,000	8,921,600
5	Veneto	97,055,555	20,608,033
6	Fruiti-Venezia Guili	13,300,000	5,133,777
7	Liguria	3,811,111	86,877
8	Emilia Romagna	119,344,444	8,388,000
9	Tuscany	50,288,888	17,788,355
10	Umbria	10,477,777	1,965,266
11	Marches	30,200,000	3,480,777
12	Lazio	69,777,777	5,966,755
13	Abruzzi	37,155,555	3,107,455
14	Molise	5,844,444	–
15	Campania	30,611,111	130,455
16	Puglia	131,644,444	2,034,255
17	Basilicata	5,511,111	96,011
18	Calabria	15,144,444	498,900
19	Sicily	115,722,222	29,739
20	Sardinia	26,577,777	1,436,022

market for them. And, outside Soho, except for Chianti the public — and quite a few fashionable wine merchants — would have had difficulty in naming an Italian wine.

But Paul Dauthieu, ex-sommelier of Claridges had long known Federigo Secondo Matta, ex-sommelier of the Café Royal, who had started a wine shop in 1919 close to Waterloo Station, as Paul was to do in Horsham twenty years later. By 1957 *F.S. Matta* was shipping five out of every ten bottles of Italian wine in this country, so with his supplies and a Matta Patter parody of the *Ruddigore* Trio we launched our 'Italian campaign', building a list of nearly thirty table wines for the first *Wine Mine* published in 1959.

F.S. Matta became part of the Beecham group; the old man, retiring to Italy, died there in 1974. His son John is proprietor and manager of Castello Vicchiomaggio, one of the great estates of Chianti Classico.

DOC laws take shape

Doubtless inspired by this 'Dominican effort', the Italian government also decided they too could sell more wine. The nation already grew vines in haphazard fashion from top to toe loosely controlled by a *consorzio* of growers in each region working with the ministry of agriculture. Now the same combination set to work, devising by July 1963 a set of new laws.

These divided Italian wines into three kinds but the first, *Denominazione d'Origine Semplice (DOS)* was so simple that the EEC persuaded the Italians to put two other groups in its place. Now there are four:

Vino da Tavola Corresponding to *vin de table* in France and *Tafelwein* in Germany, *vino da tavola* means table wine. A place name can come after it. Sometimes, however, it can be much better than table wine because many growers are experimenting nowadays with foreign grapes for which no better classification was made in the new laws.

Vino tipico Created to correspond with French *vin de pays* and German *Landwein*. Further details are awaited.

Denominazione di Origine Controllata (DOC) Corresponding to the French AOC and German QbA (all of which are *vins de qualité produits dans de régions déterminées* — (VQPRD) this is the hub of the new Italian law, drafted by local *consorzii* and approved by government decree. Wines may be shipped in bulk for bottling by the purchaser, though in practice now they seldom are.

Slowly but surely, with firmness, integrity and tact the DOC committee have conferred DOC on 200 zones making some 450 district wines. This may be only 12 per cent of grape production but when that comes to seven billion litres, one litre of fine wine in every nine is quite impressive. A limit of 20 per cent is envisaged to match French AOC.

Denominazione di Origine Controllata e Garantita (DOCG) These wines are intended to be a small élite bottled only where they are made. They will display a government DOCG seal of quality. The first DOCG district was announced in 1983 as Vino Nobile de Montepulciano, a highly controversial choice Burton Anderson, an American whose book on Italy *Vino* had been acclaimed on both sides of the Atlantic two years earlier, tasted five samples in Montepulciano itself, finding them far below the standard of Barolo, Barbaresco and Brunello di Montalcino, declared DOCG districts in 1984.

Award-winning wines should be on sale from 1985, but several vintages will be needed to assess a system in which wines have to be tested, tasted, aged, tasted again, approved and distributed. Individual makers in DOGC districts will declare in advance their intention to submit samples, and only those reaching a required standard will be awarded the DOCG seal by the government on the recommendation of the panel. Wines that do not reach the standard required will have to be sold as *vino da tavola* at a much lower price.

Given an adequate and incorruptible inspectorate, DOC and DOCG should control origin, grape varieties, yields, alcoholic strengths and other matters relating to quality. Except that this is the land of the all-pervasive Mafia! In Sicily it took Danilo Dolci seventeen years to build the Iato dam, which still does not irrigate the vineyards properly, because his opponents divert most of the water at source into the sea.*

It is intended that DOC wines will also submit to tasting panels but with 200 zones making 450 district wines this could be a tall order. Chaptalisation is not allowed in this warm country, where raising alcoholic strength is rarely necessary.

Recalling the 1950s when Matta bottled some pretty lifeless liquids under Waterloo station, these laws have improved the quality and consistency of Italian wines beyond recognition. Italy makes a fifth of the world's wine and even after the Italians have drunk 90 litres a head per year, 1.5 billion litres are exported, about one third of the wine world's exports.

Britain's imports at 13 per cent follow Germany's 30 and France's 39, while in America, Italian wines are so cute that the USA drinks more Lambrusco than can possibly have frothed its way across the Atlantic from a few Emilia villages.

Improving quality

Though the number of individual wine makers has diminished, the co-operatives *(Cantini sociale)* have increased since 1956 from 264 to 800 with a 40 per cent share of the production. Private firms have attracted capital to modernise equipment and techniques. Concern however is felt for those experimenting with vines like Cabernet Sauvignon, not traditionally Italian, because their efforts can claim no better description than *vino da tavola*. Not being learners an L plate would hardly be appropriate, but to my simple mind the suffix X could be. Subject to tasting, why not DOC (X) for experimental?

Improving quality involves trial and error. Plant a few acres of Cabernet Sauvignon in place of your Nebbiolo, wait for them to bear, blend the new with the old in various proportions, wait again for the blends to age; these experiments can go on for years. Yet already there have been successes: try Count Bonacossi's Carmignano, Tenuta di Capezzana for example.

'A matchless source for good medium price wines, the variety is almost endless', concludes Serena Sutcliffe *Great Vineyards and Winemakers*, a book designed for the coffee table but much more useful in the study.

---

*Margot Speight, Travel 2 *The Times* 27.2.84.

Italy: Piedmont

Castle of Grinzane Cavour

Alba

Barolo Castle

Piedmont Landscape

N
W E
S

D.C. Hoare

Lake Maggiore

Ghemme

Gattinara

Novara

Po Vercelli

Turin

Freisa
d'Asti Dolcetto
Grignolino d'Asti Asti Alessandria
d'Asti Nebbiolo Moscato d'Asti
d'Alba Asti Spumante
Alba Barbaresco

Tanaro Barbera d'Alba

Wine Types Barolo
Towns

Nebbiolo

White Muscat

Fontanafredda

Castle Of Costigliole D'Asti

0   20   40
Scale in Km.

Fontanafredda Landscape

Basilica of the Sidon Turin

THE REGIONS

Italy's twenty wine regions, stretching from the Alps to Sicily, include Sardinia and the tiny island of Pantelleria in the Malta channel. The Veneto and Emilia-Romagna (Province of Bologna) in the north, Sicily and Puglia (province of Bari) in the south — are the four biggest producers. Wine in the Veneto and Tuscany is largely DOC; Trentino-Alto Adige likewise, planted with Alsace and German varietals. Piedmont wines would almost all be red but for sparkling Asti Spumante.

South of Rome once upon a time luncheon spaghetti and free *vino* would put us out for the count till 5.00 p.m., but these heavy weights now vanish into tankers bound for southern France, where the Frenchman's daily litre has needed a little strengthening from within the EEC since Algeria became independent. In its place the south offers lighter and fresher reds, whites and rosés made by the new methods.

Valle d'Aosta Entering Italy through the Mont Blanc tunnel or over the St Bernard Pass, whether heading for Turin or Milan, you cannot avoid Aosta and its nooks and crannies planted with Nebbiolo and Carema. Production matches local demand, but apart from giving a first view of Italy's classic black Nebbiolo grapes this region is not important.

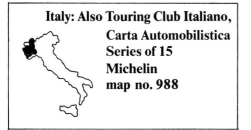

**Italy: Also Touring Club Italiano,
Carta Automobilistica
Series of 15
Michelin
map no. 988**

Piedmont

'Foot of the mountain', Italy's north-west province bordering France and Switzerland keeps the red flag flying with the three Bs - Barolo, Barbaresco and Barbera. The Nebbiolo vineyards for the first two and other potable table wines lie along the slopes of the Monferrato hills, 25-30 miles south-east of Turin close to the river Tanaro, an impressive tributary of the Po rising miles to the south in the hills backing the Italian Riviera. After skirting the Barolo district it passes the wine towns Alba and Asti, before turning east to reach the Po near Alessandria.

Barolo Min. 13°. Three years ageing (two in wood). Riserva four years. Riserva Speciale five years. Production 400,000 cases.

This village gets the name but Morra, Fontanafredda and Serralunga also comprise a district that is only five miles by five. This big wine needs ten years to develop its superb nose and flavour with four years in wood for Riserva, and five for Riserva Speciale. Drink when ten to fifteen years old and I would add decant ten hours before drinking.

Barbaresco Min. 12.5°. Two years ageing (one in wood). Riserva three years. Riserva Speciale six years. Production 167,000 cases.

Barolo, near the Tanaro, is five miles south-west of Alba. Barbaresco another village making it a close relative is on the river about three miles north-east of Alba. As indicated above, the DOC rules for Barbaresco are less exacting. Softer and with more fruit, best drunk when seven to twelve years old, decanting seven hours before hand should suffice.

In 1984 wines of the 1978 vintage were being offered in Britain at £7-8 a bottle, one list advising purchasers not to drink them before 1986-88. Growers in the future are almost bound to make them ready sooner.

Barbera Min. 11.5°. Production 3.2 million cases.

Not a village this time but an Italian grape that is also doing well in California; the wine it makes is plentiful and cheap. For the Piedmontese it is as Beaujolais to the Lyonnais, a highly satisfactory beverage in a hot summer. There are three DOC; Barbera d'Alba and Barbera d'Asti are both exclusively from this grape, strength 11.5°/12°, Barbera del Monferrato needs to be only 85 per cent Barbera.

Dolcetto from the grape of this name, once sweet, now dry, gives similar satisfaction and can be *frizzante* meaning slightly sparkling.

Nebbiolo Mist in Italian and the vine's name thrives in the mists that rise from the Po and its tributaries. Barolo and Barbaresco have some good imitations; Carema is grown near Turin, Gattinara and Ghemme are villages in the Novara hills to the north of the city.

Home of the white truffle the gourmets concentrate at Alba for the annual truffle fair in October. The Savona is a pleasant hotel and there are good restaurants in some Barolo villages.

Aromatic sparkler A line joining Acqui, a fourth 'A' town, to Alba, Asti and Alessandria encloses Moscato d'Asti, a green landscape in which Muscat grapes for the sweet, aromatic, sparkling Asti Spumante must be grown. Delicious with a peach — also grown to perfection here —

Asti Spumante is fermented naturally in closed tanks; far quicker and cheaper than the *méthode champenoise*, this *autoclave* system keeps the price low and the fragrance high. Moscato d'Asti, 8°-9° is *frizzante*, a weaker sparkler.

The only *still* white wine of Piedmont is from the Cortese grape, Cortese di Gavi near Alessandria being the most acceptable.

Lombardy

The plains of the Po do not sound the ideal location for bouquet and flavour and, sure enough, Lombardy is uninteresting wine country. The exception lies at Chiuro, near Sóndrio east of Lake Como, close to the Swiss border, where the Chiavennasca grape, alias Nebbiolo, makes red wines called Valtellina, Sassella and Inferno, all hey nonny nonny and less hotchacha than the last name suggests.

Liguria Along the Mediterranean, from the Riviera round the Bay of Genoa to Spezia, Liguria is another unimportant region. Rossese-di-Dolceacqua, a claret sort of wine of Imperia, has one of its two DOCs; the other, far better known, is Cinqueterre, the dry white wine of Monterosso and four adjacent villages at the foot of the cliffs north of Spezia. As the map shows, access by road to some of them

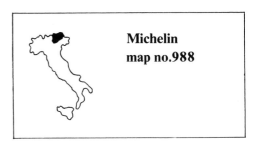

Michelin map no.988

Italy: TrentinoAltoAdige

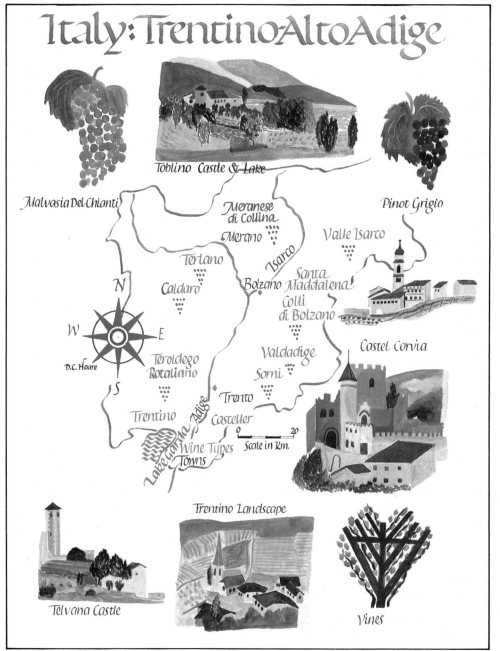

Toblino Castle & Lake

Malvasia Del Chianti

Pinot Grigio

Meranese di Collina

Merano

Valle Isarco

Terlano

Isarco

Caldaro

Bolzano

Santa Maddalena

Colli di Bolzano

N

W   E

S

D.C. Hoare

Teroldego Rotaliano

Valdadige

Sorni

Castel Corvia

Trento

Trentino

Casteller

0   20
Scale in Km.

Lake Garda, Adige

Wine Types
Towns

Telvana Castle

Trentino Landscape

Vines

is impossible but the railway line serves them all.

Trentino-Alto Adige

Plenty of this region's wines are on sale in Britain even though Austria, just across the Brenner Pass, is the best customer. Fifty per cent of total production achieves DOC and, of that total, thirty five per cent is exported. All the vineyards are in the valley of the Adige, flowing south to Verona and the Adriatic. Running down the valley the motorway connecting Austria with the tip of Italy and to the rest of the network, expedites distribution.

The higher northern part, which includes the capital, Bolzano or Bozen, is the German-speaking Alto Adige, known as the Süd-Tirol when Austrian before 1918. The southern part, the Trentino around Trento, is Italian-speaking. Together they form an autonomous province with an Italian-speaking majority. Wines may be described in either language or in both, for example, Colli di Bolzano (Bozner Leiten), Meranese di Collina (Meraner Hugel) Lago di Caldaro (Kalterersee), Santa Maddalena (St Magdalener).

These four examples (with German names in brackets) happen to be the best red wines of Alto Adige. The majority go to Austria but the last two (best known) are offered in Britain. Trentino has three native grapes, Schiava, Lagrein and Teroldego giving red Valpolicella style wines, that famous Veronese district being under fifty miles further south.

Abroad, the popularity of Trentino-Alto Adige wines lies in the astonishing number of French and German grapes grown there. In Britain it should be possible to find Rheinriesling, Riesling Italico, Sylvaner, Müller-Thurgau, Pinot Bianco, Sauvignon and Gewürztraminer at prices less than those for their north European counterparts. On labels Terlaner, from Terlano best for white wines, usually precedes the grape name. And similarly for red wines try Cabernet, Merlot and Pinot Nero.

Though there are numerous private firms, *Cávit Cantina Viticoltori* at Trento, said by one expert to be the world's most efficient co-operative, makes seventy per cent of Trento wines, not all under its own label.

Veneto

With the gentlemen of Verona and the merchants of Venice, the wine trade of this region, started by the Romans, has never lacked for customers. After 1814 when the Veneto became part of the Austro-Hungarian empire, the imbibers were joined by the Viennese, and in the last twenty years by the Americans, taking to Soave like tourists to gondolas.

Verona's three DOC wines, named after villages, have come to be appreciated world wide, consequently the Veneto region makes more DOC wine than any other. The vineyards are scattered in hilly, wooded country north of Verona, where the vines are allowed to sprawl up trellises in the cooler air above ground to gain more acidity.

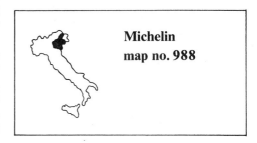

**Michelin
map no. 988**

Italy: Veneto

Italian Arms

N
W   E
S

D·C·Hoare

Vines

Belluno

S·Antonio Padua

R. Piave

Piave

Cabernet Merlot

Treviso

Valpolicella
Bardolino
Verona
Soave

Breganze

Vicenza

Lake Garda

River Adige

Padua

Venice

Pinot Bianco
Sauvignon

Adriatic Sea

Marano
Wine Types
Towns

River Po

Rovigo

Rondinella

0   15   20
Scale in Km.

Corvina

Campanile Padua

A.S. Zeno Maggiore Verona

Villa Capra Vicenza

Bardolino. Min. 10.5° Superiore 11.5°. Production 2.25 million cases. Principal grapes: Corvina, Molinara, Negrara and Rondinella.

This village is on the south-eastern shore of Lake Garda, some fifteen miles from Verona. From a frontage of about ten miles along the shore, the district extends eastwards for about five miles to the right bank of the river Adige. The half nearest the lake constitutes Bardolino Classico, historically Classico meaning the original part, usually still making the best wine.

The wine itself, a lighter version of Valpolicella, can be pale red or a rosé like Chiaretto from the other side of the lake. Possibly as much as half the production is made by Lamberti, based at Lazise who own 250 acres in the Classico portion. Lamberti are part of Winefood, a Swiss group. Like Beaujolais, Bardolino is for drinking in twelve to eighteen months; they have even been known to make a Bardolino Novello.

Valpolicella. Min. 11°, Superiore 12°. Production: 3.66 million cases. Principal grapes: Corvina, Molinara, Negrara and Rondinella.

The Classico portion, about seven miles by seven miles, lies north-west of Verona and runs eastwards from the left bank of the Adige. The rest of Valpolicella spreads eastwards for another eight miles as far as the Soave boundary, the Valpantena valley reputed to make slightly more robust wines being a part of it. The nearest Italian vines get to claret, except arguably at Torgiano, Valpolicella should be light, ruby coloured and delightful to drink when young; a pleasing tenor as it were to the bass that is Barolo.

In the Italian chapter of *Wines of the*

World, Phillip Dallas explains that fourteen major Verona *négociants,* led by Bolla and Lamberti, as well as many smaller firms make both Valpolicella and Valpolicella Superiore. Sound wine but not exciting, these *négociants* buy the former mostly from the co-operatives, but the *Superiore* is from grapes grown in their own vineyards with additions as necessary bought from small holders. This wine will be aged for two years in wood, although DOC only requires one. In short *Superiore* is the *négociant's* pride, which he hopes will be the customer's joy. Made too by numerous individual small holders, *Superiore* is worth keeping two to three years from the vintage.

Recioto della Valpolicella. Whereas in Bordeaux and Germany the grapes become shrivelled on the vine to obtain sweet wines, the Italians pick them first and then spread them out to dry for a month or so before crushing. Two luscious dessert Valpolicella — the sweet Recioto and the dry Amarone can then be made.

Recioto Amarone. Recioto is a 14°–18° sweet red wine made from selected bunches grown high up for maximum sunshine, bunches that stick out like 'ears' (*recioto* being derived from *orecchio,* an ear). If these grapes are dried on racks, pressed after Christmas and then fermented for forty-five days, with a further eighteen months in wood before being bottled, the result is Amarone (Amaro means bitter), a dry autumnal brown wine with a unique bouquet and flavour, best drunk when four to seven years old as an aperitif or a liqueur.

Soave. Min. 10·5°. Superiore 11·5°. Production: 4·65 million cases. Principal grapes: Garganega and Trebbiano di Soave.

This little village with its castle, in the

south-west corner of the small Classico zone is conspicuous from the Milan-Venice Autostrada. Expanded, the zone now goes east as far as Roncà and north to San Giovanni Ilarione. Pale straw with a greenish tinge, this light, dry white wine is made — like the other two Veronese wines — for one to two-year drinking. A little becomes Soave Spumante, and Recioto di Soave is sweet and luscious.

Fruili-Venezia Giulia Until the disastrous earthquake struck this region in 1976 even Italians were apt to forget that their country ends at Trieste, a hundred miles east of Venice by road. Northwards among the hills a multitude of grape varieties have been planted in the hope of making this last-to-be-declared region the promised wine land.

Few wines have as yet reached export markets but Burton Anderson's chapter in *Vino* speaks of Italy's 'finest and freshest' and Count Attems's estate in Fruili is one of four great Italian vineyards chosen by Serena Sutcliffe in her book already mentioned, so it looks to be a case of 'up Masters of Wine and Attem!' Some Fruili wines have reached Adnams and Oddbins already.

Emilia-Romagna A glance at the map shows Autostrada A1 running diagonally across the Emilia plain past Piacenza, Parma, Modena and Bologna in succession. When A1 turns south through the Appenines, A14 takes over, heading south-east below the hills on the right, past Ravenna and Forli to the Adriatic coast. The towns named are those of Emilia-Romagna, associated with Albana di Romagna and other local DOC red and white wines, well suited to *cucina Bolognesi.*

Another four DOCs go to Lambrusco, a grape that gives its name to a dry red fizzing, foaming, finally prickling wine made in several places near Modena. Names that follow Lambrusco on the label are Grasparossa di Castelvetro, Reggiano, Salamino di Santa Croce and Sorbara and it is as well to see them there because, greatly discredited, Lambrusco has become a craze in America. The Bolognese, seeing containers galore being loaded, re-named it 'Lambrusco-Cola'. The genuine article Elizabeth David has described as perfectly delicious with Bolognese hams, poultry, white truffles and Parma cheeses. The best that can be said for the totally different export variety, declares Victor Hazan in a new Penguin *Italian Wine,* is that for many people it could be a first step from soft drinks to wine. Of course being a grape it can be grown anywhere and its wine sold as *vino da tavola.* Pedrotti in Trento-Alto Adige is doing this and most of the Emilia towns named on A1 have long done so. It can now be made white to order.

Tuscany

Everybody seems to have heard of Chianti, probably because the original vineyards, Chianti Classico, were owned by the noble families and have formed one big zone between Florence and Siena for centuries. Chianti — like claret — is made principally from one grape, Sangiovese, with several others in much smaller quantities. Since the late eighteenth century there have been two kinds, each from the same mixture, one for immediate drinking going into the straw-covered *fiaschi,* which kept the women busy, and the other matured for some years in cask, which made a finer wine if aged longer still in the bottle.

The younger variety was much improved

in the nineteenth century by *Governo all'uso toscana,* a system whereby 3 to 10 per cent of rich must from dried grapes is added to the young wine being racked during the winter after the vintage. This provokes a secondary fermentation enhancing the flavour of fresh grapes.

Chianti Classico. Min. alc. content Vecchio (age two years) 12 · 5°. Riserva (3 years) 13°. Regional production 1 · 33 million cases. Principal grapes: Sangiovese 75—90 per cent. Canaiolo 5—10 per cent. Trebbiano and Malvasia 5—10 per cent.

Thirty miles long by a dozen wide this zone was delimited in 1932 and is said to coincide with that of the fourteenth-century League of Chianti. Its symbol on every flask or bottle, is the *Gallo Nero* or Black Cock and there are over 700 producers using it, some of them (for example, Melini, Bertani, Bertolli, Ruffino) being firms of world renown. Equally distinguished, Ricasoli (part of the Seagram group since the mid 1970s) and Antinori, still independent, resigned from the *Classico consorzio*; too blue-blooded for this red wine association perhaps.

A typical Chianti will be Sangiovese 75 per cent, Canaiolo 10 per cent, with white grapes Malvasia and Trebbiano 15 per cent. Ordinary Classico will be bottled after 12—18 months, Vecchi after two years ageing in wood (or other materials now). Riserva after 3 years. When Chianti is declared DOCG, permissible white grapes will be reduced to 5 per cent making for a mellower wine.

Some of the best properties still use the *governo* system for their best wines, the slow secondary fermentation taking up to two months; as in Bordeaux it can be combined with, or followed by, malolactic fermentation, likely to need the cellar heating on between November and April. Growers striving for DOCG status may well show the world that there is more to Chianti than at present meets the palate.

Chianti Putto. Surrounding Classico there are six more zones which, with Classico and other small isolated pockets, bring the total to 425,000 hectares, the largest DOC in Italy. These six form their own *Consorzio*, Chianti Putto, *putto* being the pink cherub that is their emblem. Allowed a maximum yield of 87 · 5 hectolitres a hectare, more than Classico's 80 · 5, the latter's overall quality should be slightly better and its prices higher. Each has its own office in Florence for promotional and informative purposes. The Putto zones, comprising 1960 properties are: Montalbano, Colli Fiorentini, Rufina, Colli Aretini, Colli Senesi and Colline Pisane.

Two Independents. Fifteen miles east of Florence in the hills near Vallombrosa lies DOC Rufina where the Frescobaldi family have made great wine since 1300. West of Florence a separate DOC was necessary for Carmignano because the Bonacossi family have made Tenuta di Capezzana with 10 per cent Cabernet Sauvignon for centuries. The Count, appearing at Peter Dominic's Winchester Wine Festival with

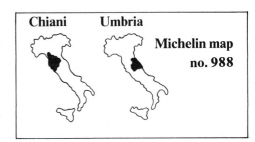

Chiani   Umbria

Michelin map
no. 988

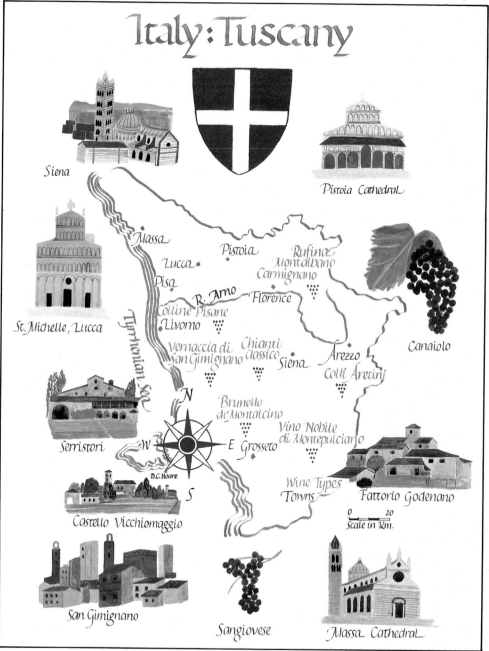

Italy : Tuscany

Siena

Pistoia Cathedral

St. Michelle, Lucca

Massa

Lucca

Pisa

Pistoia

Rufina

Montalbano

Carmignano

R. Arno

Florence

Colline Pisane

Livorno

Tyrrhenian Sea

Vernaccia di San Gimignano

Chianti Classico

Siena

Arezzo

Colli Aretini

Canaiolo

Serristori

N

Brunello di Montalcino

W

E

Grosseto

Vino Nobile di Montepulciano

D.C. Hoare

S

Wine Types
Towns

Fattorio Godenano

Castello Vicchiomaggio

0   20
Scale in Km.

San Gimignano

Sangiovese

Massa Cathedral

151

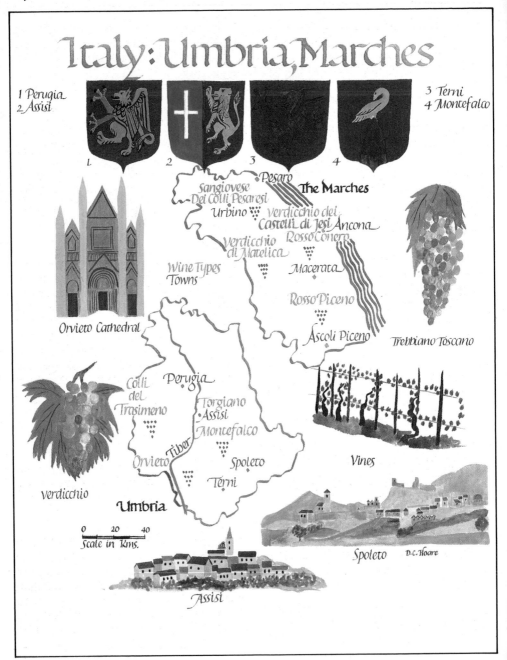

Italy: Umbria, Marches

1 Perugia
2 Assisi

3 Terni
4 Montefalco

1. 2. 3. 4.

The Marches

Pesaro

Sangiovese
Dei Colli Pesaresi

Urbino

Verdicchio dei
Castelli di Jesi

Ancona

Verdicchio
di Matelica

Rosso Conero

Wine Types
Towns

Macerata

Rosso Piceno

Ascoli Piceno

Orvieto Cathedral

Trebbiano Toscano

Colli
del
Trasimeno

Perugia

Torgiano
Assisi

Montefalco

Orvieto Tiber

Spoleto

Terni

Vines

verdicchio

Umbria

0   20   40
Scale in kms.

Spoleto

D.C. Hoare

Assisi

twenty cases, had sold them in no time.

Two DOCG. Matured for at least four years in wood. Brunello di Montalcino is an outstanding Chianti from carefully selected Sangiovese Grosso grapes called Brunello, now made by a dozen growers of this village, fifteen miles south of Siena. Developed by five generations of the Biondi-Santi family, Dr Franco and his son Jacopo, both oenologists, supervise their own 45-acre estate Il Greppo, purposely making wine that needs at least ten years before it should be drunk and may be twenty. Other estates like Altesino halve the time and the price.

The second DOCG award went to Vino Nobile di Montepulciano, a wine I have drunk in a Montepulciano hotel just opened for the summer, where the staff knew less about it than I did. An expert verdict is at best a superior Chianti; at worst unworthy of DOCG.*

White wines No white wine can be called Chianti. The most attractive Tuscan white wines, both dry, are Vernaccia di San Gimignano and Montecarlo, a Trebbiano from Lucca. Vin Santo from dried grapes is sweet and more often white than red.

Sassicaia is a Cabernet Sauvignon made south of Livorno, aged in wood and bottled and sold by Antinori in Florence. Tignanello, under trial by Antinori, replaces the white grapes in Chianti with red Cabernet Sauvignon.

The combination of cypress, olive and vine make the Chianti Classico zone unique. From Florence take N222, the Via

---

* Letter from Italy, Burton Anderson, *Vino Nobile: DOCG or roulette* — *Decanter* magazine, December 1983.

Chiantigiana to Greve, Castellina and Radda, a slow drive through the heart of Chianti to Siena. Lunch in the Piazza. The return can be made on the fast Siena - Florence 'superstrada', after a detour to San Gimignano if time permits.

Umbria
Besides Perugia and Assisi, Umbria — the province immediately south of Tuscany — has many smaller hill towns and I look back to a week in 1977 based at Assisi's quiet Umbria hotel when our explorations included all three Umbrian DOC's — Orvieto, Torgiano and Colli del Trasimeno.

Orvieto, up above the Autostrada, remains a peaceful overnight stop after the heat of the plain between Florence and Rome, but it's naturally aromatic, golden, slightly sweet Abboccato bit the dust after the Second World War. The big producers spent a lot of money on equipment to make it Secco and Burton Anderson wittily concludes they are unlikely to put the clock back to the golden days that pleased Etruscans, Renaissance painters, Popes and Christie's Master of Wine, Michael Broadbent. On the contrary if experimental plantings of Pinot and Chardonnay are successful, Antinori, closely involved, foresee at least some silver medals for the new wine-makers selling wines better suited to the business of eating than their predecessors.

Torgiano With picture and profile Dr. Giorgio Lungarotti, very rightly, gets half a page to himself in Hugh Johnson's mammoth *Wine Companion.* Would that I had the space here to repeat the tributes *Wine Mine* first paid to Estate-bottled Rubesco Torgiano and Estate-bottled white Torre di Giano when Peter Dominic

153

first brought them to Britain in the autumn of 1971.

Though made from the same grapes in much the same way as Chianti, the soil of Torgiano, only a few miles out of Perugia, and the skill of a trained oenologist, made Rubesco Torgiano more like a claret, given its customary three to five years in wood and a further two in bottle. A year later Wine Mine Club members a hundred strong found Torgiano the highlight of a weekend in Italy, enthusiastically reported in *Wine Mine* by John Mahoney, who had retired as Secretary of the Wine & Spirit Association after twenty-four years.

In 1977 my wife and I went out to see the new *Museo del Vino* created by Lungarotti's wife, Maria-Grazia described by Burton Anderson as 'the most stimulating display of the glories of the wine's past I have ever witnessed'. This confirmed the opinion of Moran Caplat, since retired as General Administrator at Glyndebourne, who was with us and had been more impressed here than in the museum at Château Mouton-Rothschild, which gets so much more publicity. Then, across the road, came *Le Tre Vaselle*, the beautifully restored hotel.

Rapid success brings problems of supply and demand but research must go on. Since the 1974 vintage prospects of Cabernet Sauvignon from Torgiano have looked promising.

The Marches

Verdicchio dei Castelli di Jesi. Min12°. Production 1 million cases.

Verdicchio is an indigenous white grape. Mixed with a little Trebbiano and Malvasia and aided by Fazi-Battaglia, the leading firm's bright idea of a green amphora-shaped bottle, its wine swept Italy in the 1950s and is now a good second to Soave in world markets. Twenty miles wide by thirty long the delimited district is on either side of the river Esino between Fabriano and Ancona, close enough to the Adriatic for the fish to be fresh.

With vines, shrines, sunshine, rivers and Appennine greenery, *cognescenti* find this peaceful region attractive, particularly as it can be part of a day out from Perugia or Assisi to the Ducal Palace at Urbino further north, or indeed from Rimini sixty miles up the coast along the Autostrada.

For twenty years excellent Verdicchio has been coming to Britain from the *Cantina Sociale* at Cupramontana close to Jesi. I still remember the luncheon they gave us at the restaurant in a monastery where only two monks were left. With the success of Verdicchio perhaps they've joined the wine-makers by now.

Southern Italy

Nine regions — Latium, Abruzzi, Molise, Campania, Apulia, Basilicata, Calabria, Sardinia and Sicily — remain. They make plenty of sound wine but the few of higher quality offered at times by British wine merchants have largely been withdrawn through lack of support.

Among many Mediterranean dessert wines, Marsala — named after the port on the west coast of Sicily which makes it — is the best. The basic style *fine*17° is rather ordinary. *Superiore* 18° aged for two years, is more acceptable. *Vergine* 18°, aged for five years, is the finest of all. Production: nearly four million cases a year. Florio, owned by Cinzano, is the largest company but John Woodhouse born 1730 in Liverpool first made the wine.

Spain

Spain's acreage under vine is greater than that of any other European country. But poor soil, old vines and old peasants possibly, put her in third place after France and Italy with about forty million hectolitres a year. 65 per cent home consumption and 15 per cent exported leaves a 20 per cent surplus distilled for industrial purposes. The policy is therefore to improve exports by raising the overall quality and to bring standards into line with her EEC membership.

Latitude 36° 0'N to 43° 47' N puts Spain in the middle of that ideal band for viticulture 30° to 50° and the grapes also benefit by being cooler, 1000-2000 feet up

Land under vines 4 million acres of which 2.5 million are Denominación de Origen (DO)
Production Annual average: 33 million hectolitres (367 million cases). Annual average yield: 20 hectolitres/hectare. Exports: 73 million cases.
Regions 24, given below with yields permitted − 1984 figures.

	hl/ha		hl/ha		hl/ha
Alella	20	Málaga	12	Ribeiro	54
Alicante	13	Mancha	30	Rioja	44
Almansa	17	Manchuela	12	Tarragona	24
Ampurdan−Costa Brava	10.5	Méntrida	9	Utiel-Requena	26
Cariñena	10	Montilla Moriles	57	Valdeorras	64
Huelva	33	Navarra	22	Valdepeñas	38
Jerez (Sherry)	86	Penedès	47	Valencia	26
Jumilla	40	Priorato	4	Yecla	11

Information Vinos de España, 22/23 Manchester Square London W1M 5AP Tel: 01-935 6140 or (for Sherry Institute 01-487 5826).

Best customers

	For Rioja (cases)	For Sherry (cases)
UK	244,000	8,000,000
Switzerland	229,000	—
Denmark	227,000	—
USA	223,000	500,000
Netherlands	—	5,000,000
West Germany	—	1,500,000

on the plateau that forms most of the country. Wet and sunless days make the north coast unsuitable, though Portugal's Vinho Verde region does extend a little way north of the frontier into two small Spanish districts, Ribadavia and Valdeorras. Otherwise Spain has twenty four demarcated districts, the majority east of a line joining Bilbao to Huelva, (west of Seville) the vine preferring the warmth of the inmost sea to the cold winds of Alanticus.

Denominación de Origen
Spain's *Denominación de Origen* is similar to France's *Appellation d'Origine*, a *Consejo Reguladores* in each region deciding grape varieties, yields, alcoholic strengths and so on. There is an inspectorate but not as yet any submission of wines to tasting panels. Irrigation is not permitted, though in the light of California and Australian success that too could come. The words *Denominación de Origen* are either printed on the label or stamped on the cork.

THE REGIONS
The two outstanding table wine regions are in the north, Rioja bestride the River Ebro, Penedès near Barcelona. The south, Andalucia, with its summer heat and little rain, belongs to *vinos generosos*, a term embracing sherry, Montilla and Malaga, fortified wines of 14 to 23° alcohol. Jerez de la Frontera is near Cadiz on the Atlantic, Montilla the hottest patch in Spain south of Córdoba, and Málaga, a Mediterranean sweet dessert wine from the hills behind the town. Known as 'Mountain' a century ago, it still makes a small contribution to the excellent profits achieved by Laymont & Shaw of Truro, a principal importer of Spanish wines to Britain.

In the centre an enormous rectangle stretches inland for 200 miles from the Mediterranean ports of Alicante and Valencia made up of some ten small regions as far as La Mancha and Valdepeñas. This is the main source of cheap wine for quaffing, blending and distilling into alcohol.

La Rioja
Recognised by the wine trade as being second only to Bordeaux and Burgundy, ever since French growers re-organised wine-making here a century ago when the phylloxera was rife in the south of France, it is only in the last ten years, as claret prices have risen, that the British public have been shown what fine red wines Rioja has to offer for less money.

Seventy miles long and about fifteen wide, well protected by the Cantabrian mountains, the vineyards are on either side of the big river Ebro, ninety miles south of Bilbao, the port of exportation less than two hours away on the new dual carriageway. The best wines come from Rioja Alta and Rioja Alavesa on the western side; Rioja Baja, the eastern half with less rain being less good. The name *Ree-oc-a* is a contraction of the small Ebro tributary, Rio Oja and from west to east the wine towns are Haro, Cenicero, Fuenmayor and Logroño, where the growers had already formed their own society by 1588 the year when the Armada set sail for England.

The organisation is not unlike that of Champagne. There are nearly fifty firms making and marketing *tinto, blanco* and *rosado* wines, some of the grapes being bought and others coming from their own vineyards. Over thirty have *bodegas* and offices in Haro. Traditionally red Riojas have been matured for up to three years in 225-litre oak casks, the minimum

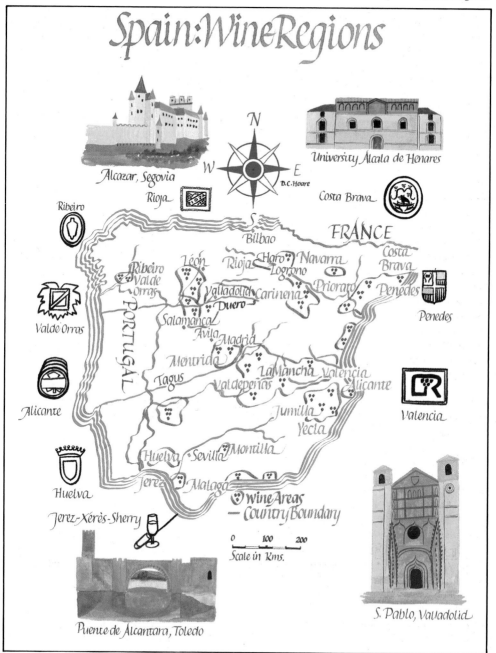

Spain:WineRegions

Alcazar, Segovia

University Alcala de Henares

D.C.Hoare

Rioja

Costa Brava

Ribeiro

FRANCE

Bilbao

Ribeiro
Valde
Orras

León

Rioja
Haro
Logroño

Navarra

Costa
Brava

PORTUGAL

Valladolid
Duero

Carinena

Priorato

Penedes

Penedes

Valde Orras

Salamanca

Avila

Madrid

Alicante

Montrida

Tagus

La Mancha

Valencia

Valdepenas

Alicante

Valencia

Jumilla

Yecla

Huelva

Huelva

Sevilla

Montilla

Jerez

Malaga

Jerez-Xerès-Sherry

Wine Areas
— Country Boundary

0   100   200
Scale in Kms.

Puente de Alcantara, Toledo

S. Pablo, Valladolid

Spain: Rioja

Hill Top Town

L'abastida · Laguardia

Haro

Rio Oja

Logroño

Rio Ebro

Najera · Navarrete · San Adrian

Rio Najerilla · Rio Iregua

Arnedo · Aldeanueva

1 Rioja Alta
2 Rioja Baja
3 Rioja Atavesa

0 5 10
Scale in km

Reus

Tempronillo

Burgos Cathedral

Spain: Catalonia

N

W · E

S

D.C. Hoare

Barcelona Cathedral

Landscape near Tarragona

Llobregat

Barcelona · Alella

San Cugat
del Vàlles · Mongat

Barcelona

ZERIDA

Cornudella

Villafranca
del Penedés

Priorato · Valls · Penedés

Francoli · Gaya · Vendrell · Sitges

Mora · Reus · Villanueva
De Ebro · Tarragona · y Geltrú

Gandesa · Tarragona

Ebro

0 10 20
Scale in Km.

Wine Areas

Garnacha

requirement being two years with only one in these casks.

It was never clear whether a year on a label of an old Rioja meant a wine wholly of that year (as elsewhere in Europe) or a blend to some extent based on it. To conform with a 1977 EEC labelling Act, a 1979 Spanish law decrees that the words *cosecha* (harvest), *añada* (vintage), *vendimia* (year) must indicate a wine from grapes picked in the year stated.

If, however, wine is released for sale during the first, second or third years after the harvest, the three terms may be replaced by *primer año* (1st year) *segundo año* (2nd year) *tercero año* (3rd year). And because evaporation loss in cask has to be replaced, a vintage wine is now one in which at least 88 per cent is of the year stated.

There is only one white wine in ten of Rioja output and, at least seven out of the ten now are probably the light fruity variety, products of a long cool fermentation at 14°C to 18°C in stainless steel fermentation vats. A few wines are still fermented old style and matured in oak casks, great care being taken against oxidisation, to give that full oaky flavour not unlike old white burgundy.

Among the wine-makers Marqués de Murrieta, founded 1860, keeps rigidly to ageing in cask as exemplified by his rich golden Ygay, while of the same seniority the Marqués de Riscal has planted forty nine acres of Cabernet Sauvignon in order to add 5 per cent to his best wines. Frederico Paternina (1898) exporting 0.75 million cases must be doing very well with their brand Banda Azul. La Rioja Alta is the group that makes that 'old smoothie' Vina Ardanza and Peter Dominic has one white and two reds from Lagunilla, a sister company belonging to International Distillers & Vintners.

Catalonia

Tarragona is Catalonia's largest region, stretching down the coast for forty miles. Its best table wine is Priorato, a big dark 14.5° astringent beverage, made inland up in the hills. On the coast seven miles north of Barcelona is Alella, another spot with a small acreage and wines all its own, the better it seems for a grape called Parisa (Xarel-lo in Catalan). Red, white or rosé, the label *Allela Legitima* exudes confidence and the co-operative's version is labelled 'Marfil' sounding like a tonic for Mum.

Penedès Wines to be taken more seriously with eager anticipation are those of Penedès, roughly a thirty mile square south west of Barcelona, around Villafranca del Penedès and San Sadurní de Noya. The former is the still wine centre with a magnificent wine museum (closed Mondays) in the mediaeval palace opposite the Cathedral; the latter the world's largest sparkling wine centre where Codorníu make three million *Méthode champenoise* cases a year. They like visitors (guided tours from 10.30 to 16.30) to see the *Cavas*, which means both the deep cellars and the Spanish sparkling wines made in them.

But the exciting wines of Penedès are those of the Torres family established here

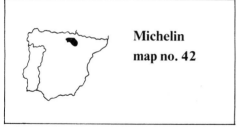

Michelin

map no. 42

in 1872. Some of the region's 990 acres, 2200 feet up in the hills around Pontons, are proving ideal for Chardonnay, Chenin Blanc, Merlot and Pinot Noir grapes. Trained at Dijon University in viticulture and oenology, Miguel Torres joined his father and his sister, experimenting only in the last twenty years with a score of varietals and the long cool fermentations in stainless steel now the talk of our trade.

Here are four examples out of a dozen Torres wines in Britain, complete with a brief, but highly informative, subsidiary label on each bottle:

Gran Vina Sol: Spanish Parellada grapes with 30 per cent Chardonnay; *Vina Esmeralda:* 70/30 Parellada and Sauvignon Blanc, both now established white wines exported to many countries. *Tres Torres:* a youthful red, dry but fruity wine from Spanish Garnacha and Cariñena grapes. But the firm's Gran Coronas *'Black Label',* largely Cabernet Suavignon with considerable bottle age, having been preferred to Château Latour 1970 by experts at a blind tasting in Paris, is of course the star turn. (Château Latour, as everybody knew, is the renowned slow developer, but the merit of the Torres wine was clearly demonstrated.)

Other Catalan wine-makers include Masia Bach bought by Codorniú but still in the Florentine folly they built, René Barbier taken over by the huge Spanish Rumasa company now nationalised and Freixenet, runners-up to Codorniú in sparkling production.

Ribera del Duero

Finally on the Duero east of Valladolid, around Peñafiel and Pesquera, lies Spain's latest DO region, home of Vega Sicilia, her most expensive wine costing around £25 a

bottle. There will only be 10,000 cases from the 300 acre vineyards around Don Eloy Lecarda's impressive château. Cabernet Sauvignon, Malbec and Merlot have been growing here for at least a century, the wine maturing in oak casks for ten years. Down at Peñafiel, the local co-operative's Riserva Especial 1966 may be just coming on the market at £8 a bottle.

SOME SPANISH WINE TERMS

Añada	Vintage
Blanco	White
Bodega	Almost anywhere where wine is kept
Clarete	Light red
Coseja Regulador	Controlling body of a region
Cosecha	Harvest
Crianza	Aged for 3 years
Denominación de Origen	Designation of Origin
Dulce	Sweet
Espumosa	Méthode Champenoise
Reserva Gran Reserva	Mature quality wine (likely to be at least 4 and 6 years old respectively)
Rosado	Rosé
Seco	Dry
Tinto	Red
Vendimia	The gathering of the grapes (vintage)
Vino de Calidad	Quality wine
Vino Rancio	Mellow wine

Other Regions

In La Mancha, bulk supplier of cheap wine to bars and brandy distillers, experiments are under way in the hope of producing quality wines of moderate strength from French and Spanish varietals. At *Rueda* south-west of Valladolid, for centuries their wine has been like a dry Montilla. Now Marqués de Riscal is making a light, fruity table wine in a new Bodega equipped for long cool fermentation. Toro, a town on the Duero (Douro) between Tordesilles and Salamanca on the way into Portugal at Miranda do Douro, makes red wines as strong as the white wines of Rueda, which Jan Read in *The Wines of Spain* declares are to the Dons of Salamanca University, as vintage port to those at Oxbridge. Having already organised Inter-University tastings in Britain, Peter Dominic will surely invite the Spaniards if they bring their Vega Sicilia with them.

Sherry

Spain's finest wine, a blend of white wines slightly fortified with brandy to a strength of 15° to 18°, needs a book to itself and fortunately there is a very good one, *Sherry* by Julian Jeffs QC. Second only to beer among popular alcoholic drinks, Britain takes 43 per cent of sherry exports, only beaten occasionally by the Irish and Dutch; real sherry, of course, which by British law can only come from the demarcated region around Jerez de la Frontera, near Cadiz.

In September each year they harvest the Palomino grapes from the chalky hillsides, taking them to modern presses in the bodegas. There the new wine will ferment in clean oak casks or stainless steel tanks and the curious process of making sherry begins. Within two months a nasty looking film of yeast cells, *mycodermi vini* or *flor*, appears in some of the casks, growing into a white layer of varying thickness covering the entire surface of the wine. No attempt has been made — as with claret — to keep the casks topped up. The wine has been left on ullage; the *flor* covering now protects it from the danger of becoming vinegar through exposure to the air.

Flor is natural but unpredictable; some vineyards' wines grow it for a vintage or two and then cease doing so. The one certainty is that Fino sherries develop from the flor-growing wines and Oloroso sherries from the others. These are the two basic styles of sherry and in their natural state both are dry. Finos remain dry. If sweeter sherries are required, sweet wine made from Pedro Ximenez grapes dried in the sun will be blended with the dry Oloroso sherries.

Whereas table wines become oxidised in casks not fully filled, sherries thrive in the Andalusian ozone. The bodegas are above ground and open to the air; the casks are purposely kept partially filled. After a year, sometimes longer, wines are moved to a *criadera* or nursery and then, batch by batch, to a *solera*.

Solera system

For explanatory purposes the *solera* system, dating from about 1800, can be visualised as a collection of butts arranged to form three or more sets of tiers, or 'scales', in which wines of the same type, but of different ages, are fractionally and progressively blended. Imagine a scale of forty butts on the floor, with three more scales, each of forty butts, on top, one above the other. Suppose the bottom one contains the oldest wine, the top one the youngest. Two or three times a year the shipper will draw off his requirements from the bottom scale, taking not more than one-third to a half out of each butt during one year. On each occasion the wine is replaced by a similar quantity from the scale above, the top scale being topped up with younger wine taken from the *criadera.*

This game of 'general post' suits sherry; aeration through movement does it good and the new wines soon blend with the old in these *soleras,* most of which were laid down scores of years ago. The well-known brands however, from Crofts, Domecq, Garvey, Gonzalez Byass, Harveys, Sandeman, Williams & Humbert and others — are seldom drawn from one solera but from several.

The merit of the system is consistency. The shipper can export numerous brands that never vary and can also match samples sent to him by trade customers wanting their own house brands. From it the different styles of mature sherry emerge.

Principal styles

*Fino.*Pale, light, dry and delicate; the ideal aperitif served slightly chilled.

*Manzanilla.*A Fino from grapes grown and wine matured north west of Jerez in or near the sea-side town of Sanlucar de Barrameda, where it acquires a lovely 'bite' and a salty tang. (Taken to mature in Jerez, only fifteen miles away, Manzanilla loses its character and develops as a normal Fino).

*Amontillado.*This word should describe a Fino matured longer in cask, becoming darker and stronger (naturally). It should have a rich, nutty flavour and cost much more than a Fino. Those that do not, are sweetened blends usually described, all too aptly, as 'medium'.

*Oloroso.*Not easily obtained as a naturally dry, matured, nutty dark golden wine, Oloroso is blended to be sweet or very

sweet and styled Amoroso, Cream, Golden or Brown accordingly. By no means the cheapest of sherries, these are what we see in the television advertisements; and, in any house with only one bottle of wine, it is almost sure to be that one.

A recent survey breaks down British consumption into: dark cream 30 per cent, medium sweet 30 per cent, pale cream 20 per cent, fino and amontillado 14 per cent. The remaining 6 per cent goes to the dry olorosos, and the palos cortados, a style between amontillado and oloroso, full, dry, expensive and rare.

Montilla

Twenty-five miles south of Córdoba and 120 north-east of Jerez is an even hotter patch of white *albariza* soil forming the region Montilla-Moriles. Here the Pedro Ximenez vine, used for sweetening in Jerez, is pruned short to provide the basic wine, which traditionally is fermented in *tinagas,* huge earthenware or cement pots open at the top. Otherwise the wines are so like sherry that it was Montilla that inspired the description 'Amontillado' adopted by the Jerezanos about 1805.

Until demarcation in 1933 much of Montilla went to Jerez for blending, but in 1967 the Jerez shippers obtained a settlement in the British High Court restricting not only 'sherry' but the

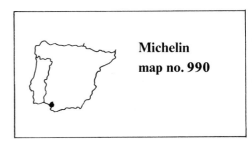

Michelin map no. 990

Spain : Sherry

N
NW
E
S

D.C.Hoare

Guadalquivir

Vine Street Jerez

Lebrija
Trebujena

Castle of San Marcos

Chipiona
Torrebreba
Macharnudo
Guadrónales
Añina
Carrascal
Tehigo
Balbaina

Casa Lonja Seville

Golden Tower Seville

Jerez de la Frontera
Los Tercios
Puerto de Santa Maria
Cadiz
Guadalete

San Fernando
Wine Areas

Chiclana de la Frontera

Portal of Seville Cathedral

Palomino Grapes

0 10 20 30
Scale in Km.

Church of St Lucas Jerez

The Giralda Seville

163

descriptions 'amontillado', 'oloroso', and 'fino' wholly to their own products.

The dry, fino-like Montillas reach the strength of Jerez without fortification and the medium dry and cream styles are no less popular.

Other countries
Because the British High Court decision of 1967 restricted the word 'sherry' to the wines of Jerez, other countries may only use it with a prefix, for example, Australian sherry, Cyprus sherry.

Drinking sherry and Montilla
Contributing the chapter on sherry to *Wines of the world* (Serena Sutcliffe) Julian Jeffs comments that no wine is more regularly ruined by being served badly. Make sure of the bouquet by using a tulip-shaped glass, ideally a Spanish *copita*, now easily found in the shops. Twirl it round, get your nose over the top! And if you have no cellar, keep your fino in the door ledge of the refrigerator.

Unlike other sherries, the light dry finos lose some of their flavour after a few days once opened. With spare half bottles in which to decant, this can be avoided.

Málaga
Heading south from Montilla, the Pedro Ximinez grape is again in evidence in the hills around Archidona and Antequera. Its natural wine is like an amontillado-style Montilla, but over 60 per cent, laced with boiled down grape juice called *arrope*, becomes the sweet dessert wine called Málaga or formerly just Mountain.

Muscat grapes are also grown on the hills east of Antequera and at least ten varieties of dessert wines qualify for the name if they have been aged in the town of Málaga.

Portugal

A rosé called Mateus

As a nation we are not very interested in architecture (when did you last see, let alone read, an article by your daily newspaper's architectural correspondent?). So the extent to which we — and the rest of the world — have been captivated by a Portuguese Baroque mansion is surprising.

In 1942 Fernando Guedes, head of a new firm called SOGRAPE, blended a rosé wine, which he wanted to sell in a flagon shaped like a Portuguese soldier's water bottle. He asked his cousin, the Count of Vila Real, if he could reproduce the Count's Vila Mateus as the label and the Count agreed.

First shipments reached Britain in 1951, the year I first tasted it at Floresta, the fish restaurant at Cacilhas across the Tagus from Lisbon. Today, with a million bottles sold each week, Mateus Rosé is the world's leading wine brand and SOGRAPE Portugal's largest wine company. The palatial Vila, open to the public, two miles south of Vila Real, is easy to combine with a visit to spectacular port vineyards in the Douro valley lower down. The grapes — now needed from many parts of North Portugal — are processed in a modern factory at Avintes, a southern suburb of Oporto.

Land under vines   350, hectares (868,000 acres)
Production   9 million hectolitres (100 million cases)
Growers   180,000. 87 per cent produce less than 100 hectolitres (1100 cases). 96 per cent produce less than 250 hectolitres (2800 cases)
Rural Workers   Some 235,000 are part-time employees in the wine trade.
Co-operatives   113
Consumption   Home: 75 per cent; Export: 25 per cent
Exports   Table wine: one million hectolitres (11 million cases). Port: 600,000 hectolitres (6.7 million cases)
Demarcated wine regions   10: Vinhos Verdes, Douro Port wine, Dão, Bairrada, Bucelas, Carcevelos, Colares, Moscatel-Setúbal, Algarve, Madeira
Grape varieties   Portuguese; names are not important
General information   Portuguese Government Trade Office, 1/5 New Bond Street, London W1Y 9PE. Tel: 01-493 0212

'There is no such thing as a great rosé and anybody who uses the phrase is either drunk or has shares in the company', wrote Raymond Postgate*. True, but this Portuguese *rosado* with it's Vinho Verde prickle does make a refreshing introduction

---

Portuguese Wine 1969

165

to Portugal's better beverages, among them the fruity white Mateus, also in the familiar flagon, for which SOGRAPE have built a separate production centre at Anadia in the Bairrada, a new region with an old history demarcated in 1979.

Portugal's first demarcations were in the early 1900s, long before other countries. Now there are ten regions, nine mainland and one Madeira. Three — Colares, Carcavelos and Bucelas — are so near Lisbon's encroaching suburbia that exports are negligible. Three more — Douro, Madeira and Setúbal — principally make fortified wines. A reorganisation now that Portugal has joined the EEC seems probable. Annual table wine production of nine million hectolitres puts her in seventh place among the wine-producing countries and one in five of a large agricultural population are occupied with wine.

PORTUGUESE WINE TERMS

Vinho Branco	White wine
Vinho Clarete	Light red wine
Vinho Consumo	Ordinary wine
Vinho De Mesa	Table wine
Vinho Engarrafada	Bottled wine
Vinho Espumante	Sparkling wine
Vinho Garrafeira	A wine of exceptional quality which has been subjected to a compulsory period of ageing in cask and bottle.
Vinho Reserva	A selected wine of a good year
Vinho Rosado	Rosé wine
Vinho Tinto	Red wine

The Regions
Vinhos Verdes
The 'green wines' are in fact 70 per cent red and 30 per cent white. It is the country washed by Atlantic rains that is green; the vines, trained up trees, poles and *pergolas* to prevent the grapes rotting, give the wines acidity besides leaving space and shade to grow vegetables below.

The region, highly populated with peasant farmers, is the whole of North Portugal from the Minho river that forms the frontier, to a point south of the Douro. It's six sub-regions — towns or rivers — are Monção, Basto, Lima, Braga, Penafiel and Amarante. Only the Portuguese relish the tart taste of the red wine, but the light dry 9°/11.5° white wines with a 'prickle', first advertised in 1983, have become so popular in Britain with the fish dish or

before it that consumption has doubled annually since.

Twenty-one modern co-operatives and a few private *adegas* make these wines — with a malolactic fermentation to reduce the high malic acidity, cooling and filtering in time to market them, ready to drink, by February through the summer.

Dão
This is Portugal's best table-wine region making a little dry white wine and much

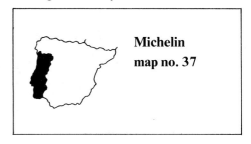

Michelin map no. 37

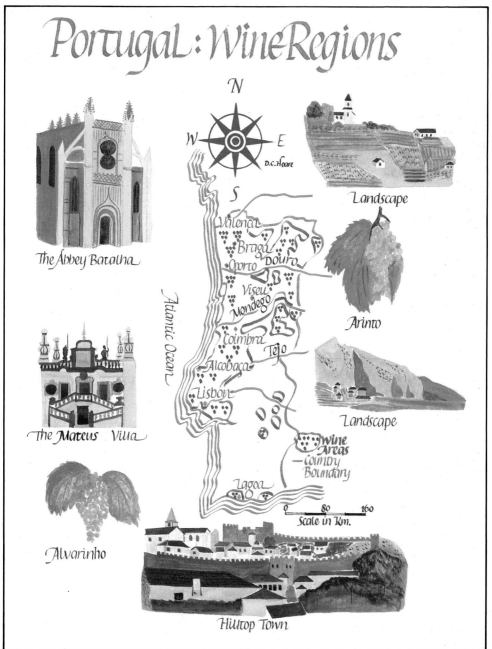

Portugal: Wine Regions

N
W E
S

D.C. Hoare

Landscape

The Abbey Batalha

Valença
Braga
Oporto Douro
Viseu
Mondego
Coimbra
Tejo
Alcobaça
Lisbon

Atlantic Ocean

Arinto

Landscape

The Mateus Villa

Wine Areas
Country Boundary

Lagoa

0 80 160
Scale in Km.

Alvarinho

Hilltop Town

167

PRINCIPAL GRAPE VARIETIES – PORTUGAL

Vinho Verde (white)	Alvarinho Azal
Vinho Verde (red)	Amaral
Dão	Touriga Tinta Pinheira Preto Mortagua
Colares	Ramisco
Torres Vedras	Many varieties
Bucelas	Arinto
Setúbal	Moscatel de Setúbal

more of a full dry red, far better than the pronunciation 'Dawng', 'Dong' or even 'Dung' might suggest. There is nothing 'farm-yardy' (an expression used at one time by tasters) about the bouquet, indeed a London tasting panel found twenty-five different Dão very good value for money and far more consistent than comparable groups they had tried, reported Jan Read in *The Wines of Portugal.*

Only a twentieth part of a huge demarcated area is planted, so there is room for expansion in the flattish plain of the Mondego and it's tributary Dão, where the best grapes grow protected by the Serra da Estrela to the south and the Caramulo mountains to the north.

Most of the 40,000 growers take their grapes to one of the ten co-operatives, whose customers include the private firms marketing the wines, because the law forbids them to vinify grapes they have not grown. Red wines must have eighteen months in wood, normally two years in practice, with at least two months in bottle. As the co-operatives must clear stocks before the next vintage, maturing rests with the purchaser; a firm like Vinicola do Vale

do Dão in Viseu uses the large plastic-lined concrete 'balloons' now apt to disfigure many wine lands, before transferring to large wooden barrels. Given at least three years in wood and a little more bottle age, Dão Tinto is very good; the *reservas,* with a year longer, even better. But no wine is given the *selo de origem* without passing tests for colour, bouquet, flavour and stability set by the regional Federation.

Viseu (Viz-a-oo)

A pleasant market town, is a comfortable overnight stop, where the museum, the hotel and the best Dão are all named after Grão Vasco, the painter who was the nation's Giotto. Grão Vasco Branco with real river trout has a touch of the Grand Master too.

Bairrada

Between the Dão region and the Atlantic, with Aveiro to the north and Coimbra to the south, the Bairrada may become a serious rival to Dão. 7000 growers with 45,000 acres make over five million cases of red wine a year and a little white for a Portuguese *méthode champenoise,* sparkling wine from French grapes made here in the past, Bairrada being an old wine region left undemarcated until 1979.

A grape called *Baga* gives the red wines so much tannin that long ageing is required, posing a problem for the long-established research station at Anadia, centre of the region, in how to reduce this time without spoiling a wine that first landed in Britain during the autumn of 1984.

Visitors to Portugal will also find sound local wines from undemarcated regions almost everywhere. On the Algarve those of Lagoa, Tavira and Portimao are in this category and the recent elevation of the Algarve to demarcated may increase their status and price but not their quality.

Port

> Proceed, great days! till learning fly the shore,
> 'Till Birch shall blush with noble blood no more,
> 'Till Thames see Eaton's sons for ever play,
> 'Till Westminster's whole year be holiday,
> 'Till Isis' elders reel, their pupils sport,
> And Alma Mater lie dissolv'd in port.
> Alexander Pope (1688—1744)
> Prologue to Addison's *Cato* (1713)

In 1678, the year Croft was founded, two young Englishmen discovered a new red wine in a monastery near Pinhão, a small town fifty miles up the Douro, still the heart of the port vineyards today. The abbot explained that he had added local brandy during the fermentation, which conserved the grape sugar in the wine. This new, sweet, fortified wine became fashionable with the literary lions in London, thanks largely to the Methuen treaty of 1703, a British act of war against the French, reducing the duty on Portuguese wines to one third less than that on French wines.

By 1756 the wine district had been demarcated. Between 1758 and 1784 the squat bottles became slimmer until they could be laid horizontal and binned, making possible vintage port — matured in bottle as opposed to wooden cask. By 1790, the British Association (of Merchants) founded in 1727, had built a handsome granite 'Factory House' in Oporto as their club, with two identical dining rooms, the second to drink, on formal occasions, their vintage port after the meal in an atmosphere unsullied by culinary smells.

Like sherry, port is really a wood wine, matured in oak casks for five, ten, twenty, even forty years, it's colour mellowing to ruby and then to tawny, these being the two basic styles. Vintage port is the exception, taken out of the wood and bottled between 1 July in the second year after the grapes were gathered and 30 June in the third year.

Vintage port Made on average every four years when the shipper has declared the year as a vintage, vintage port — a blend of the finest wines of a single year — only amounts to about two per cent of all port production. Yet, curiously, the reputation of port as a whole is founded on this two per cent. It so happened that from 1788 to 1811 there were a dozen great vintage years and some of these wines would have greeted Wellington's victorious officers returning to London from the Peninsular War just before Waterloo in 1815. After anything they had drunk in the lines of Torres Vedras, these vintages must have seemed glorious, so much so that two Scotsmen, Cockburn and Graham, went back to Oporto to start their own companies.

In Britain, Norfolk squires and Lincolnshire poachers, with nothing but the north-east wind between them and Siberia, are said to be it's greatest imbibers. Elsewhere — including Portugal — the regular drinkers keep to tawny, a much lighter, any weather, drink. Nevertheless, for special occasions from now until 2000 AD it would be nice to have a cellar with a case each of 1960, 1963, 1966 and 1970 — '63 being the great stayer, to be left until last.

In the next decade, 1977 is the big one and 1975 the lighter year. Some shippers declared a 1980, but for my grandson, born in November 1982, I must lay down a case of that same year, being bottled in Oporto during 1984/5. There are good reports of Sandeman, Graham, Croft, Quinta do Noval and Delaforce at £73 to £83 a case, with VAT and duty at about £18.50 to be added when shipped. Other shippers have now declared a 1983 vintage.

Crusted port Similarly matured in bottle, crusted port is a blend of different years, lighter, cheaper and usually ready sooner. Often a bargain, Cockburn's Crusted, bottled 1974 at £6.65 and Taylor's Crusted 1978 at £9.00 are examples offered as ready in 1985.

The wood ports Ruby, tawny and white are the three basic styles. Young, fresh and relatively inexpensive, rubies were the base of 'port and lemon', that huge pub trade hit by the introduction of 'Babycham' between the wars. Tawnies, growing lighter in colour with age, may be 10, 20, 30, even 40 years old and, like fino sherry, they are best chilled in hot weather. White ports are from white grapes and any tawny colour gained from the wood has to be removed. Nearly all brands are dry or medium dry, making acceptable aperitifs which can be chilled too.

Late-bottled vintage (LBV) This is a 'convenience' style, ready to drink without decanting, often chosen for Rotary Club luncheons and similar functions where the 'loyal toast' will be drunk. Spending twice as long in wood as real vintage port, bottling must take place between 1 July of the fourth year and 30 June of the sixth. LBV costs less than real vintage port. Late-bottled, Reserve, Vintage character are all terms indicating lesser wines of this style not conforming to the bottling dates prescribed

for LBV. Nothing, however, in my view surpasses Tawny port, the older the better, up to twenty years.

The Douro region
The demarcated zone lies on either side of the Douro from a point below Régua for some fifty miles to Barca d'Alva near the Spanish frontier. This wild, mountainous land of rugged grandeur, it's white *quinta* buildings conspicuous among the terraced vineyards, is described in some detail with a *route de vin* in my book, *Travellers' Portugal.*

About 60 per cent of port is made by British firms, principally Croft, Cockburn, Sandeman, Taylor and Warre, which now have their own wineries, where auto-vinificators make port more efficiently than rows of peasants treading barefoot in the stone trough *lagares* of the *quintas.* Yet the *lagares*, being nearer the vineyards, involve less delay than when transporting large lorry loads to distant wineries. Many experts still believe treading gives better quality, so feet are far from finished. Either way, Douro brandy is added when the fermented must attains 4−6° alcohol, the rate being 100/150 litres of brandy to 400 litres of must. This stops the fermentation, leaving the sweetness desired and the wine will be taken to the Lodges in Vila Nova de Gaia by road the following spring.

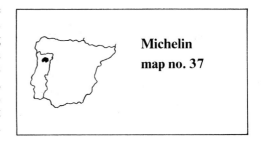

Michelin map no. 37

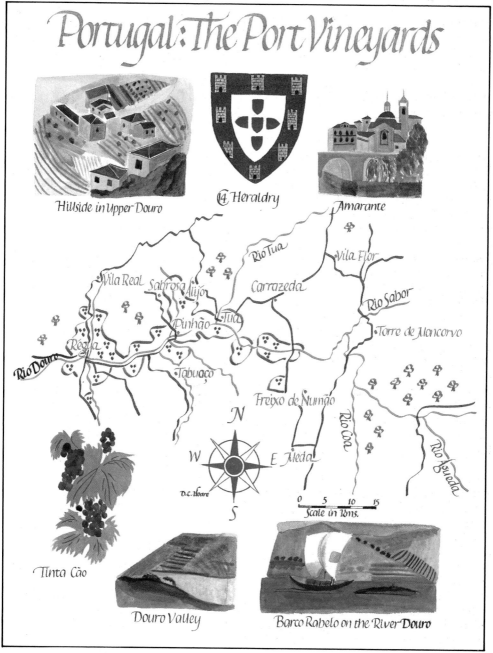

Portugal: The Port Vineyards

Hillside in Upper Douro

(4) Heraldry

Amarante

Vila Real — Sabrosa Alijó — Rio Tua — Carrazeda — Vila Flor

Pinhão — Tua — Rio Sabor

Régua — Rio Douro — Torre de Moncorvo

Tabuaço

Freixo de Numão

Rio Côa

Meda — Rio Águeda

N — W E — S

D.C. Hoare

0 5 10 15
Scale in Kms.

Tinta Cão

Douro Valley

Barco Rabelo on the River **Douro**

Working in Oporto at the Lodges, the shippers use their *quintas* for holiday weekends and to entertain the occasional visitor to the vineyards. The new 70-room hotel Columbano at Régua with a restaurant opposite has increased accommodation. In October 1984 a Government sponsored international auction of vintage ports (20th and 19th century) with fourteen shippers participating was held at Quinta do Noval, majestically sited high above the Douro at Pinhão. Attracting buyers from the leading wine countries, this could grow into an annual event like the *Hospice de Beaune* sale each November. The hosts, Cristiano van Zeller and his sister Teresa, both in their twenties, now direct Quinta do Noval, the family firm since 1813.

> 'Oh! God of Wine deliver me
> Now half across life's stormy sea
> From Snares and gins of every sort
> And bring me safely back to Port
> *Neil Hogg in Visitors' Book at Quinta de la*
> *Rosa, Pinhão*

Madeira

I have read many good wine books in the course of writing this one, but my 'Booker prize' would go to the newest, Noël Cossart's *Madeira the Island Vineyard*, published by Christie's on 6th November 1984, my seventy second birthday, a trifling age for a Madeira.

Raymond Postgate described Cossart Gordon as the firm 'whose records are such a joy to the historian', adding that at one time a good half of the total Madeira wine trade was in its hands.* Mr. Noël Cossart born there in 1907, has written this book from those records, which start with the founder's first letter, dated 1748.

---

*Portuguese Wine 1969

Malmsey Madeira is the longest lived of all wines, save Tokay Essence which hardly exists. To illustrate just how long, J. Pierpont Morgan, the American banker, had a collection that included 1774 and 1795 vintages. When opened in 1934, these wines had lost nothing in fragrance and vinosity. In Britain, Sir Stephen Gaselee, the Cambridge scholar, Foreign Office librarian and, at one time, tutor to Lord Louis Mountbatten, was the great collector who died in 1943. As recently as *Wine Mine* 1973, Peter Dominic was offering four centenarians, including Cossart Gordon's Waterloo Bual Solera 1815 at £3.78 and Blandy Malmsey Solera 1863 at £3.17. Doubtless they are still obtainable, but not at those prices!

By 1680 Portugal's charming 6000-foot mountain-island, 360 miles off West Africa with volcanic soil and a sub-tropical climate, had twenty-six shippers, ten of whom were British. Fortified with brandy from about 1753, Madeira wines, rolling in their casks through tropical seas, delighted Clive's officers in India; while in America, Washington, taking his daily pint at dinner, started a fashion that kept the ports busy from New Orleans to Baltimore.

By 1800 the sea-going aeration was being simulated by *estufagem*, the production process that puts the new wine in a 120°F hothouse for a few months. Then in 1852, mildew practically destroyed the vineyards and by the time the cure, sulphur dioxide, was discovered, the phylloxera, from 1872 onwards, destroyed what was left. Foolishly, American vines were planted instead of grafting the old vines — white: Sercial, Verdelho, Bual, Malvasia and black: Bastardo — on to American root-stocks as was done in Europe. Since 1970 unsatisfactory species have been replaced with others approved by the EEC, anticipating Portugal's entry into the Community. In the next century the great quality of Madeira could gradually be matched once more by quantity. Meanwhile, Blandy's popular Duke brands — Sussex, Cambridge, Cumberland and Clarence — are all about £5 a bottle and Madeira remains the wine *par excellence* in the kitchen.

Laying down, standing up One last point. I recently saw a car sticker that said "Surfers do it standing up". Madeiras likewise it seems! Bottles should be 'laid down' standing up on a strong shelf and never moved. A dark airy cupboard, temperatures from 9°C/48°F to 18°C/65°F, allows them to breathe through the cork. Damp, swelling the cork a little, is welcome. Bottles should be recorked every 20—25 years. The more conventional horizontal position with one bottle on top of another is not of course a disaster but Mr Cossart at 77 is definitely a surfer.

The five styles
   Sercial (Sair-see-ahl), the dry amber

Madeira, worth trying chilled with soup or (says Mr Cossart) with salt and pepper to mash an avocado pear.

Verdelho (Ver-dayl-yo), medium to rich golden wine with a dry finish. Postgate declared it was appropriate for aldermen drinking turtle soup.

Rainwater. Treat as the two above. Originally named from a consignment of casks that got drenched waiting on a Funchal quay for a ship from America, where eventually, in spite of water possibly in the casks, it was drunk with rapture.

Bual. A sweet dessert wine like Malmsey but often cheaper. Suited to reviving that 11.00-a.m.-glass-with-a-biscuit custom next time you chair a morning meeting.

Malmsey. Greatest of the five. Decant three to four hours before passing it with, or in place of, the port. The finest wines spend at least twenty years in cask. Single vintage wines are rare and less reliable when old than those described as Solera (date), the date being when the Solera was started.

One place name, Cama de Lobos, given further fame when Winston Churchill painted there, is sometimes met on labels.

Eastern beakers

And not from western winelands only,
The cases come for your delight,
A few, may be, mature too slowly
But eastwards, look the timing's right!

With apologies to Arthur Hugh Clough

In terms of British table wine consumption Yugoslavia follows Spain (seven bottles) with four bottles out of every hundred we drink. The other central European countries providing the 'beakers' are Hungary, Bulgaria and Austria scoring about one apiece. But of course there is no interminable wait until they are ready, nor an enormous price to pay, as there is with 1961 claret and will be with 1982 and 1983.

Prominent in all these Rhine and Danube lands is the Riesling grape. In Germany it is the real Riesling, sometimes with 'Rhein' in front of it, but more often standing alone as if to indicate it's august quality, like a British peer signing himself just 'Lapper-Litre'. Elsewhere, a more prolific variety, the Welschriesling or Wälshriesling, makes many dryish fruity wines of less distinction under different names in every country. The best guide I have seen to this intricate subject is the chapter 'Grapes' in the Pamela Vandyke Price *Penguin Wine Book*. Here are her Welschriesling synonyms:

Riesling Italico (Italy), Olasz Risling (Hungary), Italianski, Rizling (Bulgaria), Laski Risling, Grassevina, Grasica, Italianski Risling, Taljanska grasevina, Bliea skadka grasica (all Yugoslavia), Risling vlassky (Czechoslovakia).

Until very recently, in America and Australia anything labelled Riesling was likely to be something else. The pronunciation incidentally is *Reesling,* so that jokes such as 'Bottled in Betws-y-Coed' are quite in order.

Yugoslavia
The largest country of the four is the largest producer with up to half a dozen white, German-style wines at attractive prices in good off-licences, some in wine boxes as well as bottles.

Slovenia, the most important province is 45°N, a parallel of latitude that could form an aerial *route des vins* over Bordeaux, the Rhône valley, Rumania and Bulgaria. In the north corner, Ljutomer, Maribor and Ptuz are the three towns of a very old district, forty miles long by twenty wide, between the two Danube tributaries, Mura and Drava. The Alps' protection in winter and a cool Bora wind from them in summer combine with Adriatic warmth to achieve

YUGOSLAVIA

AUSTRIA

ITALY

Slovenia

Rijeka

Zagreb

Croatia

Trogir

Bosna-
Herce Govina

Sarajevo

Rumania

Belgrade

Laski Riesling

Labin

Dubrovnik

Montenegro

Serbia

N

W   E

D.C. Hoare

S

Kosovo

Macedonia

St Nagoricavi

Gewürz-
traminer

Wine Areas

Country
Boundary

0   50   100
Scale in km.

Vodice

175

Bijelo	white
Biser	sparkling
Crno	red
Čuveno	selected
Kvalitetno	quality
Modri	black
Ružica	rosé
Slatko	sweet
Stolno vino	table wine
Suho	dry
Vhrunsko	finest quality

Ljutomer Riesling, Sylvaner, Sauvignon, Pinot, Muscat and Gewürztraminer. There is also a small quantity of real Rhine (Renski Riesling). The famous Tiger Milk, a Spätlese, is from Ranina Radgona, on the right bank of the Mura. Many of these white wines are also made in Vojvodina, the province north of Belgrade, Novi Sad being the wine centre.

Wines of Dalmatia I first met in 1936 as a Sub-Lieutenant serving in the destroyer *Grafton*, escorting King Edward VIII in the yacht *Nahlin*. Charles Firth, our smart handsome captain, had been nicknamed 'Champagne Charlie' in Alexandria, so it was fitting that we wardroom officers should take to wines of lower station as we moved between the islands from Rab to Korčula and on to Dubrovnik and Kotor.

Easier to drink than to say, the Plavac grapes make the red Plavac, the 17° Dingac and the sweet Postup. Pošip from Korčula and Bogdanusa from Hvar are fresh and fragrant white wines, while Grk from Korčula is more like sherry. Further north the Merlots and Cabernets of Istria are good, but for Yugoslavia's best dry white wine, Žilavka, we must go inland to Mostar in the hills north-west of Dubrovnik.

Further information
Yugoslav Wine
Information Centre,
6 Vigo Street,
London W1X 1AH.
Tel. 01-437-5927.

Hungary
From Ljutomer it is less than fifty miles to the Hungarian frontier, where Route 7 runs north-east for another 120 miles to Budapest along the southern shore of Lake Balaton. Continuing north-east for a hundred more miles would first pass Eger and then reach Tokay in the gentle hills just short of the Czech border.

Tokay Aszu Walloon growers are said to have brought the Furmint vines here about 1250. Tokay is the town, surrounded by some twenty villages. Left to ripen in the autumn sun, the dull yellow Furmint and Hárslevelü grapes develop that welcome precursor of great sweet wine — the 'noble rot'. These Aszu grapes, late-gathered like the German *auslese*, are kept a week before being kneaded into a paste, which is added to sweeten the base wine made earlier from normally ripe grapes. It is added in a measure called a *puttony*, which holds 20-25 kilograms of the paste. Three, four or five (exceptionally six) *puttonyos* are added to 136-140 litres of the base wine.

The blend needs maceration and stirring for about two days before being fermented in 140-litre barrels called *gonci* from Gonca, the village where they are made. Racked and fined the *gonci* are left unbunged in dark old narrow twisting tunnels that abound, like Dordogne caves, in this region. The free air above the wine develops a flor yeast on it's surface, as happens with sherry, giving a dry finish to a

HUNGARY

C14 Hungarian Heraldry

Harslevelü

Furmint

Budapest

Mount Badacsony

N
D.C.Hoare
W E
S

Danube

Eger

Tokaj

Győr

Somló

Budapest

Debrecen

Tapolca

Siófok

Lake Balaton

Tisza

Szekszárd

Szeged

Pécs

Country Boundary
Wine Areas

0   100
Scale in Kms.

Fishermen's Bastion Budapest

Eger

Pinot Noir

Cabernet

Wine Cellars

Ruins of Füzér Castle

Dome of Parliament
Budapest

177

sweet wine. The sweeter the wine the longer the maturing necessary, adding two years to the number of *puttonyos* (for example, 7 years for a 5 *puttonyos* wine) being the rule of thumb. Bottling is in the traditional half-litres, strength 13°/15°.

There are four grades of Tokay:

1. Essence, free-run juice allowed to drip from late-picked Furmint and Harslevelü grapes before pressing, is so rich and rare that it is seldom on sale.

2. Aszú Essencia, a slightly less rich variety from hand-selected grapes of the best vineyards, matured for ten years.

3. Aszu, the sweet Tokay of three, four, five and even six *puttonyos* referred to above.

4. Szamorodni ('as it was grown'), more of a table wine, production being greater when autumn weather is unsuitable for much late-picking and hand selection. The final wine is sweet or dry according to the amount of summer sunshine and the number of Aszú grapes added to the must.

Eger About half-way between Tokay and Budapest, this old Baroque town is known for Egri Bikavér or 'Bull's Blood of Eger'. It's deep red colour, owed neither to bulls nor to blood, comes from the local Kadarka grape. The dry white Egri Leányka, is also exported.

Balaton Lacking access to the sea, Hungarians like to make the most of Europe's largest lake for summer recreation. Though thick with villas, the shores are thick with vines too, especially on the northern side around the hill of Badacsony. Balaton is thus the chief white wine district of Hungary, with Olasz Riesling Furmint, Pinot Gris and Kéknyelü among the best.

Mór This is a district north-east of Lake Balaton making Móri Ezerjó, the dry golden wine.

Sopron In the extreme north-west corner, Sopron is part of the Burgenland (see Austria), where both Haydn and Liszt composed. Though many good red and

GRAPES AND PLACES — HUNGARY

Grape	Grown at	Wines
Ezérjo 'A thousand boons'	Mor	Dry white
Furmint	Tokay	Tokay Aszu
	Lake Balaton	Light white
Hárslevelü 'Wine leaf'	Debro	Sweet white
Kadarka	Great Plain	Red and some rosé
	Eger	Egri Bikaver, some rosé
Kékfrankos	Sopron	Gamay sort of wine
Kéynelü 'Blue stalk'	Mt. Badácsony	Full bodied white
Léanyka 'little girl'	Balaton and Eger	Egri Léanyka
Nagyburgundi	Villány — Siklós (southern border near Drava river)	Soft red
Olasz Riesling	Widely	White
Szürkebarát 'Grey Friar'		White
Pinot Gris		

Agker	Controls state farmers
Aszu	See Tokay
Edes	Sweet
Fehér	White
Hungarovin	Controls state cellarage and bottling
Monimpex	Controls imports/exports
Puttonyos	See Tokay
Száraz	Dry
Vörös	Red

white table wines are made, it's fame rests on the fresh young red wine, Soproni Kékfrankos.

Péc-Villány In the extreme south, near the frontier with Yugoslavia, this district produces some good Olasz Riesling and other white wines. Parts of it have made good red wine in the past and, from the Kadarka, there are rosé wines in abundance.

Kiskunhalas Seventy miles south of Budapest this is the wine town of the Great Plain, a huge sandy space east of the Danube growing Kadarka and Wälshriesling.

Hungary's 400,000 acres are nearly all state-owned with seven regional *combinats* operating them. All exports are handled by one organisation, Monimpex, and most of the wines come through Budafok, the State Cellars near Budapest. The State seal on the bottle and the words *minöségi bor* (equivalent of AOC) on the label are the marks of authenticity.

Further information Commercial Section, Hungarian Embassy, 46 Eaton Place, London S.W.1. Tel. 01-235-8767.

Bulgaria

In my early days in the Navy my instructors were always saying, 'Hogg you're all astern' and, because my bottom happens to stick out like a sore thumb, this caused uproarious mirth among my fellows. It is therefore with pride that at least in the matter of Bulgarian Chardonnay and Cabernet Sauvignon I have been 'all ahead'; I first persuaded Peter Dominic to offer these two wines in the mid-sixties.

By 1968 Edmund Penning-Rowsell was commending them to his *Financial Times* readers as 'Sound authentic *vins de table*'. In 1982 to Master of Wine, Bill Gunn, tackling Eastern Europe in *Wines of the World*, they had become the wines of the future, while Hugh Johnson's *Wine Companion* now summarises Bulgaria as 'some of the world's best value for money in familiar flavours'.

The modern wine industry only began in 1949 with all the problems of persuading peasant-farmers to change their ways in order to supply the best grapes to state-controlled wineries that had yet to be built. By the mid 1970s noble grapes had been planted on a large scale, a new *Appellation Contrôlée* system being introduced in 1978.

Today, with 400,000 acres of vineyard — about the size of Bordeaux — Bulgaria has become a major wine exporter, sending sparkling wines and traditional white Dimiat and Misket white wines, besides the old Mavrud and Pamid reds, to Russia in bulk, while the new quality Chardonnay, Cabernet Sauvignon and Merlot come to the West, where in 1984 they were being sold retail for about £2 a bottle.

In 1983 sales to Britain went up from 130,000 cases to 300,000, not a great figure, but a 130 per cent improvement in a

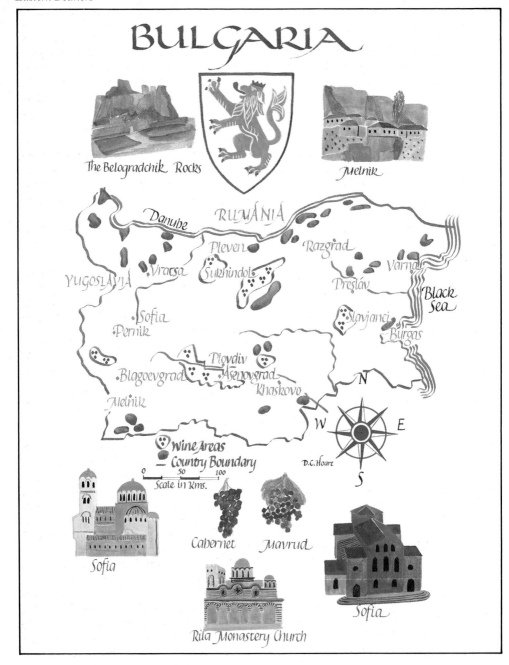

BULGARIA

The Belogradchik Rocks

Melnik

Danube

RUMÁNIA

Pleven

Razgrad

Vratsa

Suhindol

Varna

YUGOSLAVIA

Preslav

Black
Sea

Sofia

Slavjanci

Pernik

Burgas

Plovdiv

Blagoevgrad

Asenovgrad

Khaskovo

Melnik

N

W

E

D.C. Hoare

S

🍇 Wine Areas
— Country Boundary

0   50   100
Scale in Kms.

Sofia

Cabernet

Mavrud

Sofia

Rila Monastery Church

single year must be rare in the annals of export. At present her wines are going to seventy countries, including Japan, where one in three bottles of wine imported is Bulgarian.

The word Bulgar or Bougar means a cultivator or ploughing peasant and there are nine million of them in this land 300 miles long and 200 broad. To the east is the Black Sea. To the north the Danube, flowing east, forms the frontier with Rumania. To the south the Meritsa also flows east and between these two rivers lies the high range of Balkan mountains, splitting a small country in two.

At present the 'Dominican' Cabernet Sauvignon is likely to be made at Sukhindol on the northern side, where the Yantra and it's tributaries flow through deep valleys to the Danube. To the south Plovdid, second in size to the capital Sofia, and it's neighbour Asenovgrad make the best Mavrud, sampled by Wine Mine Club members as 'Wine of the Month' in April 1982.

The white wine regions are in the plain inland from Varna on the Black Sea, and Vinimpex, the state marketing organisation, hope that Riesling, Aligoté and Ugni Blanc will soon follow their successful Chardonnay. Meanwhile after 500 years of Turkish temperance, and with a good supply of mechanical cultivators, the Bougar's lot must surely be a happy one.

Further information Bulgarian Vintners Co. Ltd., 156 Caledonian Road, London N1 9RD Tel. 01-278-8047.

Austria

After Czechoslovakia, Austria's remaining frontiers are with West Germany, Hungary, Yugoslavia, Italy and Switzerland. That, as far as wines are concerned, is some competition! She has only 147,000 acres of vineyard (Hungary alone has 400,000) which are all in the eastern half of the country, mainly within fifty miles of Vienna, where the Viennese drink enormous quantities, fresh from the cask.

This is *Heurige* wine, new and prickly like Vinho Verde in Portugal, *Heurigen* being the taverns and gardens where the grower displays a green bush when it is ready to drink. Thus a green bush became the sign of a tavern and the origin of Shakespeare's 'If it be true that good wine needs no bush, 'tis true that a good play needs no epilogue' in *As You Like It.*

Eighty per cent of Austrian wines are white, half from the country's own grape, Grüner Veltliner and half from Wälschriesling, Pinot Blanc, Pinot Gris and others with which we are now familiar. The laws of 1973, very similar to Germany's of 1971, decreed four regions: Lower Austria 33,387 hectares, Burgenland 30,351, Styria 2,226 and Vienna 607 hectares.

Lower Austria. Wachau, the best-known district, is that charming stretch of the Danube below Krems, with vineyards on either side, that runs north-east for some forty miles to the Czech border. Village names, Weissenkirchen, Dürnstein and Loiben go with well-balanced flowery wines from Rheinriesling, Grüner Veltliner and Muskat Ottonel. Those of Krems and Langenlois come a good second.

But by far the most successful wine of this region in Britain is the brand of Lenz Moser called Schluck ('luck') which many retailers have been selling without a break for the best part of twenty-five years. Better still and more expensive is Prinz Metternich's Schloss Grafenegg, a Veltliner from his own

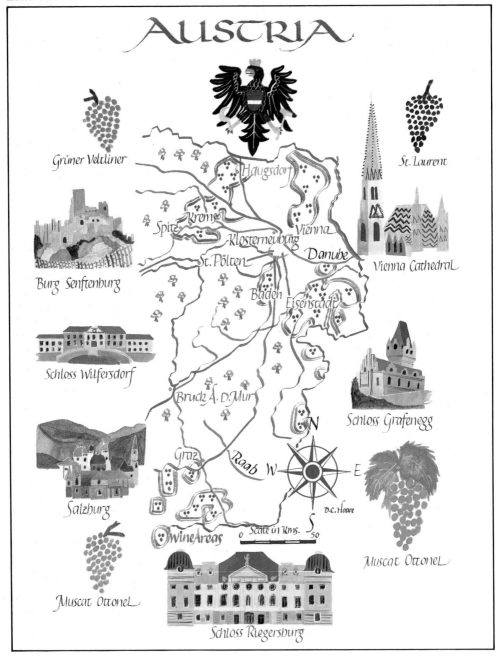

AUSTRIA

Grüner Veltliner

St. Laurent

Burg Senftenburg

Vienna Cathedral

Schloss Wilfersdorf

Haugsdorf

Spitz Krems

Klosterneuburg

St. Pölten

Vienna

Danube

Baden Eisenstadt

Bruck A. D. Mur

Schloss Grafenegg

Salzburg

Graz Raab

N

W E

S

Scale in Kms.

0 50

D.C. Hoare

Wine Areas

Muscat Ottonel

Muscat Ottonel

Schloss Riegersburg

estate, in the family since 1169. Bottled in his cellars in Krems, people have now trusted it for over fifteen years in spite of the adage about princes.

Weinviertel. This inverted triangle, north-east to the Czech border with Vienna as the apex, is forty miles long by twenty wide. Grüner Veltliner wines come from *Am Wagram*, the stretch along the northern bank of the Danube and some light reds from Retz, Pulkau, Poysdorf and Falkenstein near the border.

Burgenland Some twenty-five miles south-east of Vienna these vineyards surround the large reedy lake of Neusied, it's southern end jutting into Hungary. The climate is mild where Rust, the old town on the western side, has long made a dessert wine like Tokay from the Furmint and other grapes. Ruster Ausbruch was once famous and Lenz Moser might well revive it's fame with Ruster Beerenauslese 1982, selling here at £4.79 a bottle in 1985. Ruster Blaufrankisch Spätlese at £3.74 is a sweet red, the sweetest red known to Tanners of Shrewsbury who list it.

Styria These vineyards are to the south, on the Yugoslav border only fifty miles from Lutomer. Traminer is outstanding among the usual Austrian white wines and there are some light reds from Blau Portugieser and Blau Fränkisch grapes. Graz is the capital of this rich farming countryside.

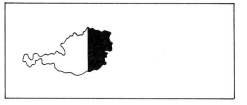

Further information The Austrian Trade Commission, 1 Hyde Park Gate, London SW7 5ER. Tel. 01-584-4411.

Greece

Hot dry summers tend to make sweet dessert wines such as the red Mavrodaphne, exported largely by Achaia Clauss of Patras in the Gulf of Corinth. White Muscats of similar style are to be found in Crete, Rhodes, Santorin, Samos and most of the other islands. Demestica (red and white), Castel Danielis (red), Domaine de Kantza (red), Santa Helena (white) and Pendelis (white) are the best brands of light table wine. Retsina can be any dry white wine to which pine essence has been added, giving it a curious waxy flavour.

An EEC member since 1981 there is now an appellation system and experimental Cabernet Sauvignon vineyards have been planted.

Further information The Commercial Counsellor, Greek Embassy, 1A Holland Park, London W11 3TP. Tel. 01-727-8040.

Cyprus

Between 1945 and 1960 when Cyprus became independent, the British Government helped to modernise an industry which now produces very good sherry style wines. Commandaria, the dessert wine dates from the Crusades; Aphrodite and Arsinoe are good dry white wines; Othello a good red; Bellapais, a good slight sparkler. Experimental work goes on and a surprise from the mass of vineyards on the south side of the Troodos mountains is quite a possibility.

GREECE & CYPRUS

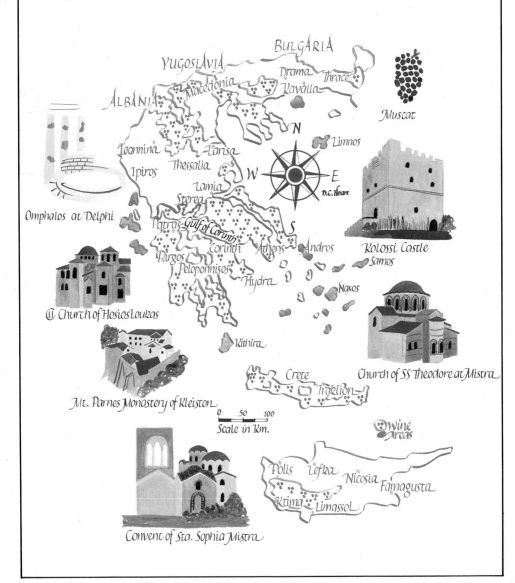

BULGARIA

YUGOSLAVIA

Drama

Thrace

Macedonia

Kavalla

ALBANIA

Muscat

N

Limnos

Ioannina

Larisa

Thessalia

W   E

Ipiros

D.C. Hoare

Lamia

Kolossi Castle

Sterea

S

Omphalos at Delphi

Patras Gulf of Corinth

Corinth

Athens

Andros

Pirgos

Peloponnisos

Samos

Hydra

Naxos

(I) Church of HosiosLoukas

Kithira

Crete

Church of SS Theodore at Mistra

Traklion

Mt. Parnes Monastery of Kleiston

0   50   100

Scale in Km.

Wine Areas

Polis   Lefka

Nicosia   Famagusta

Ktima   Limassol

Convent of Sta. Sophia Mistra

Further information The Commercial Counsellor, Cyprus Trade Centre, 213 Regent Street, London W1R 8DA. Tel. 01-437-3831.

Lebanon

One of the few pleasant surprises from this wretched corner of the Mediterranean has been — and miraculously may still be — the red wine of Château Musar at Ghazir, sixteen miles from Beirut, first presented here at the 1979 World Wine Fair in Bristol.

In the 1930s when Lebanon was French, Gaston Hochar planted Cabernet Sauvignon, Cinsault and Syrah in the Bekaa Valley near the ruined temple to Bacchus at Baalbek. When his son Serge, trained in Bordeaux, brought eight vintages to London in 1981, Peter Dominic's tasting at 2-8 Orange Street showed beyond doubt that these wines, aged in barriques, were Bordeaux's very respectable relatives.

Since then the vineyards have been part of the battleground between Israelis and Syrians, Maronite Christians and Druze Moslems, shells and rockets falling on and around them. How Serge, his brother Ronald, the Bailiff and the Bedouin families picked the vintages of 1982 and 1983 without casualties is so miraculous that *Decanter Magazine* acclaimed Serge their 'Man of the Year 1984'. His health can be drunk in his 1978 vintage, just ready, price £5.09. There will be no 1984, the one year they have failed to make wine.

United States of America

California

Wine in California is still in the experimental stage; and when you taste a vintage, grave economical questions are involved. The beginning of vine-planting is like the beginning of mining for the precious metals: the wine-grower also "prospects." One corner of land after another is tried with one kind of grape after another. This is a failure; that is better; a third best. So, bit by bit, they grope about for their Clos Vougeot and Lafite. Those lodes and pockets of earth, more precious that the precious ores, that yield inimitable fragrance and soft fire; those virtuous Bonanzas, where the soil has sublimated under sun and stars to something finer, and the wine is bottled poetry: these still lie undiscovered; chaparral conceals, thicket embowers them; the miner chips the rock and wanders farther, and the grizzly muses undisturbed. But there they bide their hour, awaiting their Columbus; and nature nurses and prepares them. The smack of Californian earth shall linger on the palate of your grandson.

The Silverado Squatters
R.L. Stevenson, 1883

Nobody can say for certain why, east of the Rockies, all attempts to establish European vines, first made by Thomas Jefferson, US Minister to France 1785-1789, failed. Torrid summers, freezing winters, Atlantic humidity, the phylloxera ... these, maybe, played some part in turning the settlers to spirits — applejack, rum and eventually whiskey.

West of the Rockies it was different; *vitis vinifera* came northwards up the Pacific coast with Jesuit missionaries, and when eventually the phylloxera crossed the mountains the remedy — grafting the vines on to American root-stocks — was known.

Squatters in Silverado

The first Briton of consequence to drink California wines was fortunately a writer, who had been living in France. Robert Louis Stevenson (1850-1894), tubercular and penniless, reached San Francisco by sea in December 1879 in pursuit of Fanny Osbourne, ten years his senior, whom he had met at Fontainebleau. They married the following year, settling as squatters in Silverado, a derelict former silver-mining town overlooking the Napa valley.

At home in Chichester, I was pleased to find *The Silverado Squatters* — regrettably unread by me — in a 1901 Chatto and Windus set, *Works of R.L. Stevenson,* probably a wedding present to my parents.

The Napa wine chapter begins with a lamentation: 'Bordeaux is no more'... 'Chateauneuf is dead' 'the quays at Cette the chemicals arrayed'. Stevenson, having seen devastation by phylloxera, clearly regards France as a Lycidas, 'dead ere his prime', and looks forward to California and Australia 'where the new lands, already weary of producing gold, begin to green with vineyards.'

A prophecy fulfilled

The quotation makes it clear that 'bottled poetry' lay undiscovered for the future; at the time the wine was merely good, 'the best that I have tasted better than a Beaujolais and not unlike'. Chronologically, Stevenson was right: grandsons of the Victorians are drinking California* wines of unsurpassed quality, due primarily to the work of the Department of Viticulture and Oenology set up in 1861 by the University of California at Davis.

Briefly, since the 1930s, it's work has enabled the right vines to be planted in the right places, with the added advantage in the United States that there is much uncultivated, volcanic, fertile, well-drained land suitable for grapes, and enough money for irrigation, insecticides and the latest apparatus for vinification.

Climate zone systems

The vine grows actively in a temperature of 50°F. By taking daily temperatures between 1 April and 31 October, an average above that of 50°F can be obtained over the temperature-taking period. Example: If period was 10 days and average temperature 68°F, 68-50 = 18 × 10 = 180 'degree days'.

California has therefore been divided into five regions ranging from 2500 degree days or less to more than 4000 degree days. Since they might as well have names too, on page 191 I have made them: Very Cool, Cool, Warm, Very Warm and Hot, which is a rough guide and no more to many micro-climates. The coolest regions, as expected, are near the coast, some made cooler by the infamous night fog of San Francisco, so that going north from the Bay it can become warmer.

Students of United States wines — likely to grow in the wake of their success — will find John N. Hutchinson's chapter in André Simon's *Wines of the World* tells the California story up to 1964. The wines were all right; the trouble was, as a leading grower put it, 'the average American is a whiskey-drinking, water-drinking, coffee-drinking, tea-drinking and consequently dyspepsia-inviting subject.' To which the Chairman of the Wine Institute regretted that wine consumption had barely scratched the surface of it's potential, adding 'it is beginning to change'.

That Chairman's name was Robert Mondavi; the fascinating, and sometimes moving, story of how he himself has changed it is extremely well told by Cyril Ray in *Robert Mondavi of the Napa Valley,* a short book packed with interest in every phrase.

Shoulder to shoulder with France

By 1982 wineries had increased from 220 to 540 and vineyard acreage from 170,000 to 343,000.

In Europe few people, even in the wine trade, knew anything of this until on 24 May

---

*To speak of Californian wines nowadays, I have recently learnt, is a solecism. It should be California; just one of those things like saying 'on a ship' to officers RN, who, living *in* them, prefer precision.

1976 at a blind tasting in Paris, nine of France's finest palates judged some California Chardonnay and Cabernet Sauvignon wines from the Napa valley as superior to the finest Meursaults, Moutons and other first growths tasted alongside them. When the horrified headlines had been forgotten, it was discovered that this usually happens, because California wines are stronger in alcohol and more assertive. Subsequent tastings of wines in apposition, not opposition, have all shown that California wines stand shoulder to shoulder with French wines of comparable or identical varietal composition and they are expected to last as long.

The quality of fine wines the Americans call premium (as opposed to jug); in short, palate as opposed to gullet. There are many makers able to produce two or three thousand cases of premium wines a year, these smaller fry being known as 'boutique wineries'. A score or more are represented in Britain by the wholesaler, Geoffrey Roberts. When in 1982 he also became agent for Robert Mondavi, quantity was added to quality: Mondavi premium production at Oakville was 400,000 cases a year and his principal wines, with the percentages of this total, were roughly:

Cabernet Sauvignon, with Cabernet Franc and Merlot for blending	29.7
Sauvignon, with Semillon for blending	26.7
Chardonnay	16.9
Johannisberg† Riesling	9.7
Pinot Noir	8.8
Chenin Blanc	8.2

No wonder Geoffrey Roberts said 'I can think of no other winery in the world which provides wines of such exceptional quality in such enormous quantity.'

No wonder too that 300,000 visitors a year now enjoy the forty-five-minute conducted tour, the pleasant surroundings and the bottles they can buy! Oakville is only closed on New Year's Day, Good Friday, Easter Day, Thanksgiving and Christmas Day. Médoc châteaux are closed every weekend, except for Château Prieuré-Lichine owned and run by Alexis Lichine, another American. Not all Bordeaux growers are as unenterprising as some Californians think: Christian Moueix, of Château Pétrus no less, took his oenology degree at University of California, Davies and Robert Mondavi learnt about malolactic fermentation from him on his annual visits to Europe that included Pétrus.

But Oakville's 400,000 cases and 300,000 visitors pall beside the million cases of high quality vintage jug wines pouring out annually from Woodbridge, the other winery run by this remarkable family whose history in America began in 1906 when Cesare, Robert's father, emigrated from Italy, making just enough money labouring in Minnesota mines to bring back a bride from his home town in 1908. Cyril Ray's book describes the privations of those early years. I have room only for the brief biographies of father and son overleaf.

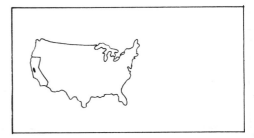

---

†Johannisberg = Rhein in USA.

North America – The Napa Valley

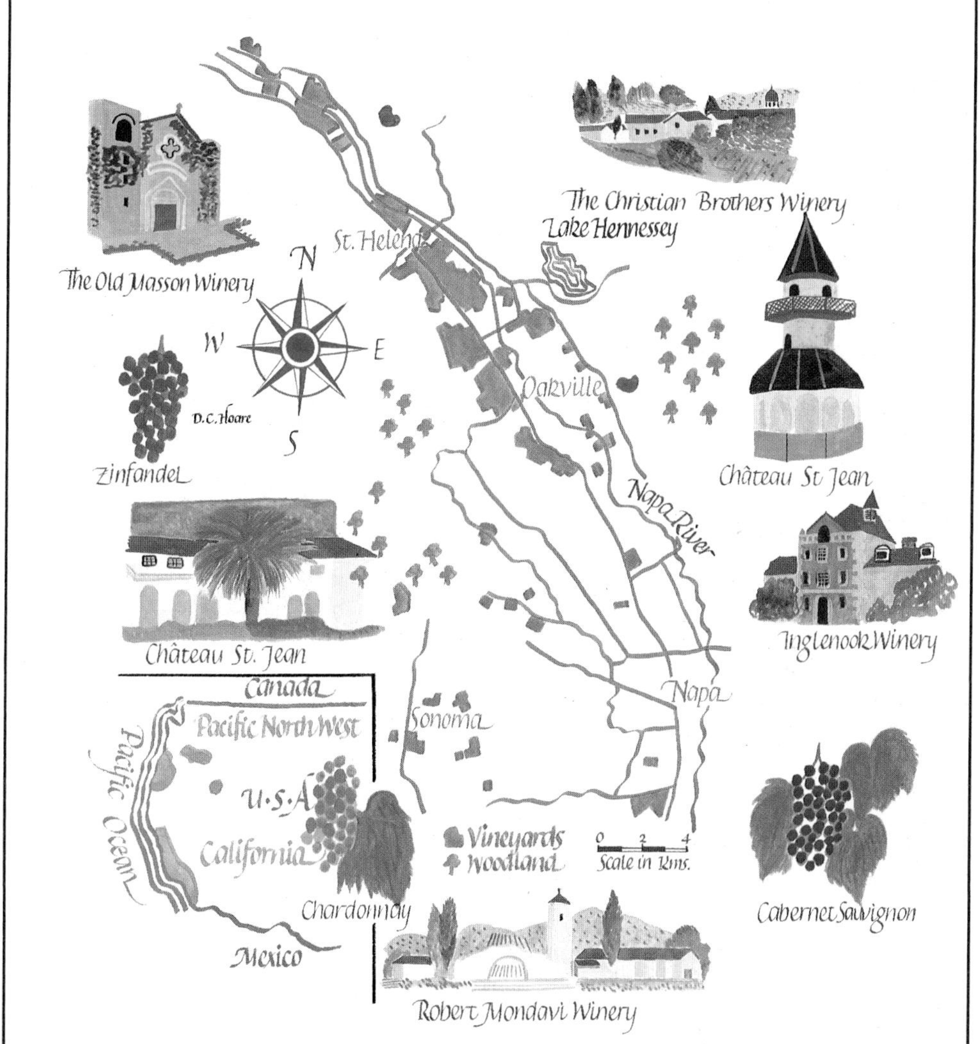

The Old Masson Winery

St. Helena

The Christian Brothers Winery
Lake Hennessey

N
W E
S

D.C. Hoare

Zinfandel

Oakville

Napa River

Château St Jean

Inglenook Winery

Château St. Jean

Canada

Pacific North West

Sonoma

Napa

U.S.A

California

Vineyards
Woodland

Scale in Kms.

Pacific Ocean

Chardonnay

Mexico

Cabernet Sauvignon

Robert Mondavi Winery

189

Noting the success of Chardonnay and Pinot Noir — the grapes of Champagne as well as of Burgundy — the sparkling wine firms of Western Europe have not been slow to move into California, where as yet nothing in the United States law prevents any sparkler being called champagne.

After seven years, Chandon Napa Brut is firmly established as the chic aperitif in Domaine Chandon's *haute cuisine* restaurant. Piper-Sonoma is Piper-Heidsieck, with Freixenet of Catalonia a close neighbour, while the huge Catalan Codorniu has settled half-way to Los Angeles from San Francisco. All have a formidable competitor at Calistoga. The Schramsberg wines were 'bottled poetry' to Stevenson and to the Carlton Club in London. He drank them in the cellar with Jacob Schram, where Jack and Jamie Davies still make the best *méthode champenoise* in the valley.

The Bureau of Alcohol, Tobacco and Firearms, a body with triple lethal responsibilities, has now demarcated the north coast to comprise Napa, Sonoma, Mendocino, Solano, Lake and Martin, counties in which there are 68,000 acres of vineyards and 200 wineries. There is as yet no definition of where premium wines end and jug wines begin. All concerned, however, seem to agree that California jug wines are much better than what we call ordinaire (or sometimes 'plonk') largely because the climate ripens grapes fully every year.

This explains why in Britain we drank over three million of Paul Masson's litre carafes in 1982, 130 years after Etienne Thée from Bordeaux planted vines near Monterey. Thée, not the best name for a wine-maker, it was probably lucky that Paul Masson, an in-law, inherited the firm later.

In 1942 Seagram obtained an interest, leaving three minority shareholders in charge until in 1971 the Canadian firm decided to expand it themselves. With three wineries in California, Paul Masson makes a variety of table, dessert and sparkling wines.

Bob Red, Bob White, Bob Rosé

From 1960 to 1980 the change Robert Mondavi had predicted gathered momentum as a new generation, disdaining their parents' preference for hard liquor, took to wine. Simultaneously the work of the University of California, Davis led to sound, clear, fruity wines at reasonable prices. Mondavi himself, having pioneered premium wines, first at the Charles Krug winery and then at his spanking new Oakville, finished in 1967, bought and modernised a former growers' co-operative at Woodbridge, near Lodi in the Central Valley, where his family had lived before the war. From Woodbridge, operational since 1974, came the jug wines, Robert Mondavi red, white and rosé, followed in the 1980s by Robert Mondavi vintage red and white of higher quality aged in oak, which so surprised his family (all in the business) his friends and a devoted staff that they are known as 'Bob red', 'Bob white' and 'Bob rosé'.

Mondavi Biographies

Cesare. *b.* Sassafarento, near Ancona, Italy 1883. *Education:* 2 years local school. Emigrated 1906, earned sufficient to return home 1809. *Married* 1908 Rosa Grassi *b.* 1890 — *d.* 1976, kitchen maid, no education. Minnesota 1908-1922 Saloon keeper while wife ran their home as Italian immigrants' boarding house for 15 men and reared *4 c.* Mary, Helen, Robert, Peter. 1919-1933 Prohibition. 1922 Used savings to move family to Lodi, Central Valley, California and set up as table

CLIMATE ZONES – CALIFORNIA

Zone	Heat	Locations	Equivalent in Europe	Grapes Theoretically Suitable
1 Very cool	2500 degree-days or less	Mendoza Marine Napa Sonoma Santa Clara Monterey Santa Barbara	Champagne Côte d'Or German Rhine	Chardonnay Riesling Sauvignon Blanc Cabernet Pinot Noir
2 Cool	2500-3000 degree-days	Sonoma Santa Clara Monterey Santa Barbara	Bordeaux	As above though less good
3 Warm	3000-3500 degree-days	Lake Napa (Parts) San Benito Monterey	Rhône Valley	Sauvignon Blanc Semillon Carignan Zinfandel Ruby Cabernet
4 Very warm	3500-4000 degree-days	Sacramento San Joaquin	Southern Spain	Barbera Emerald Riesling Ruby Cabernet Port wine grapes
5 Hot	Over 4000 degree-days	A belt 700 miles long by 60/150 wide parallel to coast and 200 miles inland associated with Sacramento and Joaquin rivers	North Africa	Tinta Madeira Souzao Verdelho

grape wholesaler, exporting table grapes to Middle West and Eastern States.
1937 Bought two thirds share in Sunnyhill Winery, St. Helena, Napa Valley, producing bulk wine. 1943 Bought Charles Krug Winery, St. Helena, founded 1861. *Died* 1959.

Robert. *b.* Minnesota 1913, elder son of Cesare and Rosa Mondavi. *Education:* Lodi High School, family grape-shipping business, Stanford University and privately during vacation from the Davis, University of California, oenologist. *m 1.* 1940 Marjorie Declusin *3 c.* Michael *b.* 1943, Marcia *b.* 1947, Tim *b.* 1951. Marr: dissolved, *m 2.* Margrit Biever.
1937 Apprenticed himself to father learning all aspects of wine making. General Manager Charles

Krug winery. Replanted 100 acres with classic varietals. 1947 First bottlings under Charles Krug label. Pioneered cold fermentation to retain fruit; nitrogen and CO_2 gas to prevent oxidisation; vacuum corking to reduce air intake.
1965 Commissioned Cliff May to design Oakville, first major Winery to be built since Prohibition. Completed 1967.
1971 Acclaimed for his Fumé Blanc 1967, straight dry Sauvignon regarded as superior to comparable Sancerre, Pouilly-Fumé and dry Graves.
1976 Sold his share of Charles Krug Winery to his brother Peter, who continues to run it successfully with his sister Mary and two sons.
1978 Agreed 'Joint Venture' with Baron Philippe de Rothschild.

191

1980 Bought and modernised Woodbridge Winery at Lodi. Followed new California table wines with range of Robert Mondavi Vintage Red, White and Rosé, bringing his firm's annual production to around 1.5 million cases.

1984 Joint Venture on sale as *Opus One*, a Napa Valley Red Table Wine, produced and bottled at Oakville jointly by Mondavi and Mouton-Rothschild teams.

Recreation: Playing with Chardonnay in small oak casks, swimming, *Address:* Robert Mondavi Winery, Oakville, California.

The Pacific north-west

North of California comes the state of Oregon and further north Washington. In the former the Williamette Valley wine-growers have planted 2000 acres out of a possible 3.3 million. In the latter the Walla Walla growers have sixty acres of grapes out of a possible 178,560 acres.

To keep abreast of the North American wine scene, which aspiring Masters of Wine will have to do and others may like to do, Serena Sutcliffe's *Wines of the World* 1981 gives the fullest information, Hugh Johnson's *Wine Companion* 1983 augments it and Cyril Ray's *Robert Mondavi of the Napa Valley* 1984 not only brings the events up to date, but ends with a seven page Bibliographical Note, helpful on how to keep fully informed.

Yet the strength of the dollar has enabled Italy and France to increase their cheap wine sales in America at the expense of American producers, who have replied with wine coolers; mixtures of wine and fruit juices, half the strength of normal table wines.

Hugh Johnson's *Wine Companion* gives names and addresses, with production and other data, of 352 California wineries. The table above gives the leading exporters, many of them represented in Britain by

US WINE EXPORTERS (WITH FOUNDING YEARS)

Beaulieu Vineyard 1900	Freemark Abbey 1895/1967
Callaway 1974	E. & J.Gallo 1933
Chappellat 1968	Stanislaus
Château Montelena 1881/1969	Inglenook 1881
	Heitz 1961
Château St Jean 1974 Sonoma	Charles Krug 1861
	Paul Masson 1852
Christian Brothers Catholic Teaching Order 1920	Santa Clara
	Ridge Vineyards 1959
	Robert Mondavi 1966
Domaine Chandon Moët Hennessey 1977	Robert Pecota 1978
	Joseph Phelps 1972
Dry Creek 1972 Sonoma	Schramsberg 1862
	Spring Mountain 1968
Firestone Vineyard 1973 Santa Barbara	Stags' Leap 1972
	Sterling Vineyard 1964

Geoffrey Roberts Associates, 7 Ariel Way, Wood Lane, London W12 7SN. In the Table two dates indicate founded and later re-founded.

Further information (a) Wine Institute, 165 Post Street, San Francisco CA 94108. The booklet *A guide to Wineries Open to the Public* is available free (but enclose International Reply Coupon).

(b) The US Agricultural Trade Office, 101 Wigmore Street, London W1H 9AB. Tel. 01-499-0024.

Australia

The merits of Australian table or light wines have been known to me ever since the summer of 1945 when, after operating off Japan with the British Pacific Fleet, I spent a week at the Melbourne Club, which kept a fine cellar. But Australians were beer drinkers, as one quickly discovered at 5 p.m. side-stepping the mad male rush from every office to fill up the human tank with pints galore before all the pubs closed at six. (The one civilised state was Tasmania where there were no licensing hours, allowing my aunt and I, after shopping in Hobart, to knock back a 4 p.m. 'horse's neck' before going home to tea.)

The table wine boom

What a transformation there has been! As somebody said of California, counting the wineries was like taking a census in a rabbit warren. These Australian figures show the change in litres to the nearest million.
1959: light wines, 13; fortified wines, 37; 1979: light wines, 143; fortified wines, 48.

Progress has put paid to most of the big sticky wines with names like *Yarra Yarra, Wowser* and *Monsoon,* leaving only Rugger (Whittaker Bros. of — well, yes — Rugby) to uphold the old robust tradition. In their place we have Cabernet Sauvignon and Chardonnay, Semillon and Rhine Riesling, some as good and promising as any wine from California.

The revival came just in time to save from extinction the Hunter Valley in New South Wales, now hailed as a Napa Valley. Slow cold fermentation for white wines, planting of European varietals, immigrants from Europe who became restaurateurs, hoteliers, wine-makers and merchants, good publicity from the media and promotional expenditure by the Australian Wine Board, have all combined to make fifteen million Australians enthusiastically aware of the grape. It was in fact one of them (Once a jolly bagman?) who in the late sixties invented the bag-in-the-box, the container from which they drink 60 per cent of a consumption now said to be twenty litres a head a year.

Although some million litres are exported, trade with Britain was upset when Britain joined the EEC and the fine wines have been imported in small quantities from boutique wineries, difficult to establish without capital. Without a University of California, Davis and a Mondavi, progress has perforce been 'by guess and by God'. In *The Great Wine Book,* describing with wit and wisdom thirty-five of the world's greatest wine-makers, Jancis Robinson tells the astonishing story of how

Max Schubert was 'fired' by Penfolds for inventing Australia's best wine, Grange Hermitage, now made from two separate vineyards near Adelaide.

The firm sent their technically brilliant employee to Bordeaux soon after the Second World War to study under Cruse. But the Shiraz-Cabernet Sauvignon blend from the experimental vineyard, planted on his return carefully choosing the site, was derided when it was first sampled. Max bided his time. When he presented it again after six years in bottle, Australia went wild with what Len Evans, another colourful character, called 'Grangeomania'.

Len Evans, now Australia's leading wine and food author and broadcaster, is also part owner of Petaluma (fine Chardonnay and Cabernet Sauvignon) in the hills above Adelaide and Chairman/Founder of the Rothbury Estate, a shareholders' syndicate in the Hunter Valley.

At Petaluma, Brian Croser is putting into practice all he learnt about oenology in fifteen months at the University of California, Davis a dozen years ago. Since 1977 he has made a late harvest Rhine Riesling and a Traminer of the highest class, moving on to Chardonnay and Cabernet Sauvignon, all from vineyards elsewhere that he has selected. His own vineyard is small, with a winery built to make 20,000 cases from grapes grown a few hundred miles away. Impressed by a sparkling wine from Petaluma, Bollinger has now made an investment in this estate.

The regions
Hunter Valley Cradle of Australian viticulture, where James Busby began it all circa 1820, the Hunter river flows into the Pacific at Newcastle some seventy miles north of Sydney, the humid climate giving the growers more than their fair share of storms and destructive hail.

At Pokolbin, the heart of the region, Gilbeys owned the old Tulloch winery from 1974 to 1983, producing Shiraz, Cabernet Sauvignon, Semillon and Hunter Riesling.* In the Upper Hunter Valley the vineyards of the attractive Rosemount Estate were replanted in 1970 by the Oatley family after being pasture for nearly a century. British retailers, selling their six 1982 wines (Cabernet Sauvignon, Malbec, Shiraz, Fumé Blanc, Chardonnay and Traminer) at under £5.00 a bottle in 1984, were well pleased and the Wine Mine Club met them first at the Royal Festival Hall (a new venue for the Club's Tastings). The Chardonnay could be a serious competitor for white burgundy.

Victoria The spotlight for the time being seems to have moved away from old wineries like Château Tahbilk, founded in 1860 and districts such as the Murray river with it's rich dessert wines, and Great Western where Seppelt produces sparkling wines of high quality. Victoria's wines in British lists are most likely to come from Brown Bros. of Milawa, a family firm founded in 1889 and now run by four

---

*This is in fact a Semillon not a Riesling at all, though none the worse for that.

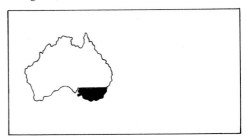

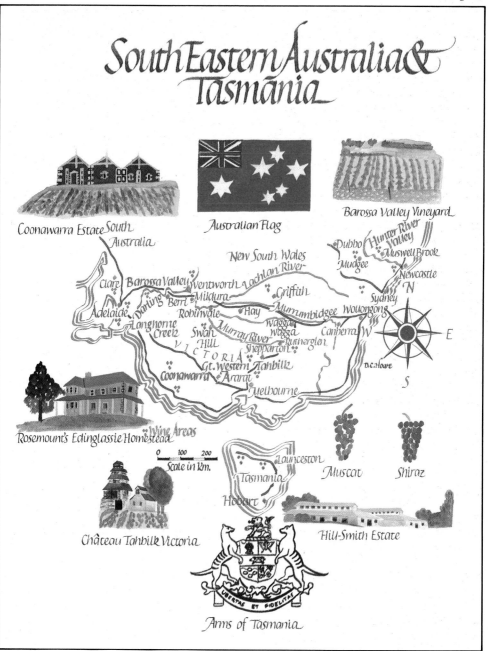

South Eastern Australia & Tasmania

Coonawarra Estate South Australia

Australian Flag

Barossa Valley Vineyard

Rosemount's Edinglassie Homestead

Wine Areas

0   100   200
Scale in Km.

Château Tahbilk Victoria

Muscat

Shiraz

Hill-Smith Estate

Arms of Tasmania

brothers, the third generation. Their dry and late picked Muscats stand out in a wide range.

South Australia Untouched by the phylloxera in the 1890s (though Victoria caught it badly) South Australia became the nation's principal wine-maker. With vineyards from Adelaide southwards for twenty miles inland from the Gulf of St Vincent, where frost does not trouble them, this state still makes 60 per cent of the nation's wines.

Of the big firms Penfold remains in the city while others, facing rising rates, have moved away. But the wines of *Southern Vales*, the maritime district that includes McClaren Vale, Seaview, Ryecroft and Reynella are still many and various, while to the north of Adelaide, Clare-Watervale provides good Rhine Riesling and Cabernet Sauvignon.

Barossa Valley, thirty miles north-east of Adelaide, a pretty district popular with tourists has strong Lutheran links from it's 1840 settlers resulting in fine Rhine Rieslings, some of which come from the Kaiser Stuhl Co-operative taken over by Penfolds, who, since 1962, have been part of Tooths, the brewers. Leo Buring, whose Leonay Rhinegold was a respected 'Australian medium dry hock 8/-' in Peter Dominic's 1954 price list, died in 1961, a year before his firm joined Lindeman, Australia's third biggest wine company. Others still going strong are Johann Cramp's Orlando, owned by Reckitt and Coleman and, still in the Hill-Smith family, Smith's Yalumba, a credit to their 1849 founder Samuel Smith, a Wareham Dorset brewer.

Coonawarra An estate of only ten square miles, Coonawarra was in grave danger of being sold for grazing when times were bad in 1951. Samuel Wynn & Co. bought it just in time. In 1913 — only thirty-eight years before — a young penniless Jewish couple names Weintraub (wine grape) changed their name to Wynn. After a struggle Samuel Wynn succeeded, leaving David (the only one of their three sons not a doctor) to manage a fine company, since taken over by the brewers Tooheys Ltd.

About 6000 acres are under vine so far in this south-eastern corner of South Australia where the soil is red and black over limestone, the climate cool and subterranean water adequate. From their 1718 acres Wynn have been highly successful with Connawarra Cabernet, Coonawarra Shiraz and blends of the two. If this is to be the age of the Cabernet Sauvignon train, Coonawarra could well be it's best (if primitive) station.

Tasmania From Coonawarra, liable to frost, eyes have turned south-east for a hundred miles to the north coast of Tasmania where the micro-climate could be frost free. It is significant that Geoffrey Roberts, the London wholesaler, having become the agent for a score of California wines, rather as Mark McCormack acts for the world's leading golfers, has added the

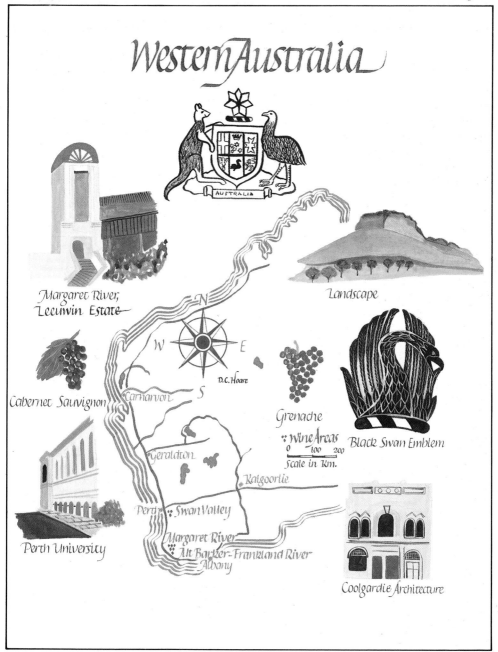

Western Australia

Margaret River,
Leeuwin Estate

Landscape

Cabernet Sauvignon

Carnarvon

D.C.Hoare

Grenache

Black Swan Emblem

Geraldton

Kalgoorlie

:: Wine Areas
0   100   200
Scale in Km.

Perth University

Perth :: Swan Valley

Margaret River
Mt Barker-Frankland River
Albany

Coolgardie Architecture

first Tasmanian to his portfolio. Moorilla Estate, a Cabernet Sauvignon from Berriedale on the north coast, made it's debut in London in 1983. 'Clearly something of a curiosity in the UK but I think it merits it's price, £11 a bottle', he was reported as saying to the trade.* The climate here is similar to that of Bordeaux; who knows, we may yet see the Cabernet Sauvignon Open Wine Championship being won by a Tasmanian?

Western Australia As the city of Perth expands towards the existing vineyards of the Siran Valley, pioneers have been planting others in cooler places down the coast. A selection shown in London by Austral Pacific Vineyards in July 1983, included a Cabernet Sauvignon from the Margaret river, about 200 miles south-east of Perth, where a first planting was made in 1967. A Rhine Riesling and a Gewürztraminer came from Mount Barker/Frankland, about 250 miles south of Perth. A third district, only 115 miles down the coast, was planted in 1977.

Amid all the changes of the last twenty years it is pleasant to find nearly all the companies operating in 1967 still 'in the pink'. Two doctors, both Englishmen, founded Australia's biggest wine companies: Penfold, gave up a thriving practice in Brighton to emigrate in 1844; Lindeman, in 1870 was more extraordinary. Who has ever heard of an RN medical officer foregoing his pink gin and siesta by dashing off to plant vines in Australia? Now, a century later, *The Times* wine correspondent, Jane MacQuitty, has travelled 5000 miles, tasting over a thousand wines, and the Masters of Wine, Britain's chief buyers, have paid their first visit to Australia in 1985.

Further information The Australian High Commission, Strand, London WC2. Tel. 01-438-8205. A Decanter magazine Wine Guide to Australia & New Zealand (free to subscribers) was published in April 1985.

---

*Harpers Wine and Spirit Gazette, 26.9.83.

New Zealand

Te Bono Whata Vino!

Naturally everything is upside down 'down under'! James Busby, the wine lover who planted vines first in Australia and then in New Zealand, became President of the latter's Temperance Society. Concerned with settlers besotted with rum, he wrote: 'If the bodily strength were daily renewed after labour by the use of liquor, which could freely be indulged in without intoxication, the longing for stronger drink would not be felt.'

In New Zealand, 150 years have passed and this has now happened in the last twenty, with a fifteen-fold increase in the area under the wine vine and consumption up from two litres a head a year to a dozen. In 1980 after a month's study, Professor Helmut Becker from the Rhineland declared that the country is closer viticulturally to Germany than any other. Placed at the right latitude on the map of Western Europe, New Zealand would cover South Germany, Alsace, Burgundy and the Loire south to Bordeaux. Her best wine areas average 23°C/73°F in summer with some light rain. No wonder *The Times* wine correspondent, Jane MacQuitty, opines that many New Zealand white wines are 'now of world class and comparable with the finest that France has to offer'.*

I recall a first trial dozen in December 1981, the white grapes being Pinot Gris, Chenin Blanc, Gewürztraminer and Riesling; the red, Cabernet-Sauvignon and Pinotage, a cross between Pinot Noir and Cinsault. Three white wines well below £3 a bottle from Cooks and a Riesling Sylvaner 1980 from Montana are now in the list. Cooks, a young yet public company, are the leading exporters, pleased to see visitors at Te Kauwhata, forty miles south of Auckland. Montana, 40 per cent Seagram owned, have large vineyards at Marlborough in the South Island.

In October/November 1984 Charles Eve, Master of Wine and Peter Dominic's wine Director, was invited to New Zealand as their Overseas Guest Judge in the National Wine Competitions. Travelling and tasting over 700 wines in six days (a seventh was declared a palate rest day), he found the standard of tasting extremely high among the New Zealand judges, the wines correctly made and of good quality. As both vines and wines grow older this should become higher; some red wines were excellent, the oldest was only eight years.

Further information The New Zealand High Commission, New Zealand House, 4 Haymarket, London SW1. Tel. 01-930-8422.

---

* *The Times* 21 July 1984

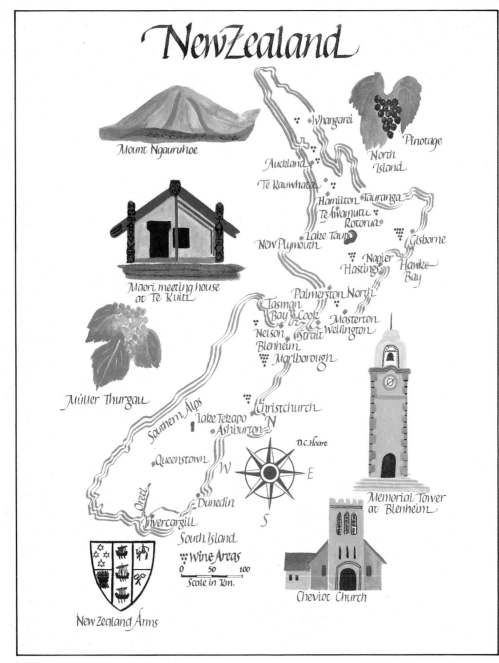

NewZealand

Mount Ngauruhoe

Pinotage

North Island

Whangarei

Auckland

Te Kauwhata

Hamilton · Tauranga

Te Awamutu

Rotorua

New Plymouth · Lake Taupo

Gisborne

Napier

Hastings

Hawke Bay

Maori meeting house at Te Kuiti

Palmerston North

Tasman Bay · Cook

Masterton

Nelson · Strait

Wellington

Blenheim

Marlborough

Müller Thurgau

Southern Alps

Christchurch

Lake Tekapo

Ashburton

N

D.C.Hoare

Queenstown

W   E

Otago

Dunedin

Invercargill

S

South Island

Memorial Tower at Blenheim

Wine Areas

0   50   100

Scale in Km.

Cheviot Church

New Zealand Arms

England and Wales

England's first post-war vineyard was planted by the late Major-General Sir Guy Salisbury-Jones at Hambledon, Hampshire in 1951. Now, having been round the world's wines on a voyage of discovery, which began with England on page 10, let us return to learn what followed. First however we must understand that English (and Welsh) wines are from grapes grown on English (and Welsh) soil as opposed to British wines, which are made from grape sugar, imported in a variety of forms, such as highly concentrated juice or pulps of raisins. By adding water and fermenting the liquid, alcoholic beverages are produced, colour and flavour being added by the makers.

Thirty years of progress

After 1951 ten years passed before Margaret Gore-Browne with 5.5 acres at Beaulieu, Hampshire attempted to add a rosé to a successful white wine from a vineyard planted in 1958. She helped to start the English Vineyards' Association with a dozen members in 1967 and left a silver trophy to be awarded annually to the best wine-maker. No further rosés, nor indeed red wines, of any consequence appear to have been made until 1982 and 1983 when several were submitted to

Decanter magazine's tasters, who found one red called Hesse's Triomphe d'Alsace 1982 quite attractive and awarded a silver medal to a rosé from Kent.

It seems there are now over 300 commercial vineyards including one in Wales, the Croffta at Pontyclun, which in 1983 — the best year ever for English vineyards — made 11,000 bottles from it's three acres. Encouraged by the exceptional summer of 1976, smaller vineyards than this were planted in Cornwall, Devon, Gloucestershire and Nottinghamshire, where wetter weather must surely mitigate against success. The most favoured counties are Sussex 30, Kent 25, Hampshire and the Isle of Wight 20, Essex 15, Suffolk 15, Somerset 12. The Association membership tops 500 and their acreage 1000. An excellent map is available from the English Vineyards Association Ltd., The Ridge, Lamberhurst Down, Kent TN3 8ER. Tel. 0892 890. Price £1.00 + 65p postage.

Feathered enemies

Experience indicates that strong winds lowering the temperature are as great a handicap as lack of sunshine. On the other hand, damage by frost, hailstorms and insects is less than on the continent, but birds (all alleged to be shot by the French)

201

particularly thrushes, blackbirds and starlings, are a menace, requiring expensive, time-consuming bird-proof netting. Frequent sprays against mildew and oidium are also costly and vines that do not ripen until October are more vulnerable to autumn rain.

But in years like 1976 and 1983 the long, slow, ripening warmth gives English wine 'one of the most attractive bouquets in the world: a combination of an English summer garden with the acidity of German wine and the dryness of Alsace makes an irresistibly refreshing, thirst-quenching taste'.* 1982 and 1983 have enabled growers, for the first time, to build reserves.

The grapes
England's white wines come closest to those of the Mosel and Alsace; grapes the EEC recommend are principally, Müller-Thurgau, Reichensteiner, Kerner and Bacchus. The right grapes for a given site can only be determined by trial. Seyval Blanc, a hybrid not recommended by the EEC, suits some English soils and new varieties such as Huxelrebe, Ortega, Wrotham Pinot and Madeleine Sylvaner are now in use.

Taxation
Taxation is a complicated question and a source of English growers' dissatisfaction. To the British Treasury they have to pay Excise duty, Value Added Tax, Corporation and Income Tax — far more than producers in Germany and Italy. Their only relief is a wine allowance for their own consumption of 120 gallons a year, plus 10 per cent of their production above this quantity to a maximum of 240 gallons. This allows the grower, his family and staff to drink their own wine virtually duty free.

With 1982 and 1983 retail prices ranging from £2.44 (Felstar) to £5.50 (Hambledon) further help is necessary to compete with imported wines. As Mae West said, 'A kiss on the lips is one thing, but a diamond bracelet lasts forever'. So far English wines, served at Buckingham Palace and in the Palace of Westminster, have only had the kiss. Consequently producers prefer direct sales to the public 'at the gate', which are more profitable than through a retailer.

The English Vineyards Association (EVA) seal
This mark of excellence on a bottle takes the form of an EVA monogram encircled by the words, 'Certification Trade Mark'. Growers must enter before the vintage; the wine then has to pass laboratory tests as to stability, weight of fruit and yield of must before a final tasting by a panel, usually Masters of Wine giving their services free.

---

*Roger Voss, *Decanter* magazine September 1984. A little doubtful about so fulsome a tribute, I tasted blind with some friends a 1982 Franconia Müller-Thurgau, bought locally, against Chichester's 1982 Chilsdown Müller-Thurgau, grown and made locally and similarly priced. Mr Voss does not exaggerate; the latter's bouquet and flavour were much more marked.

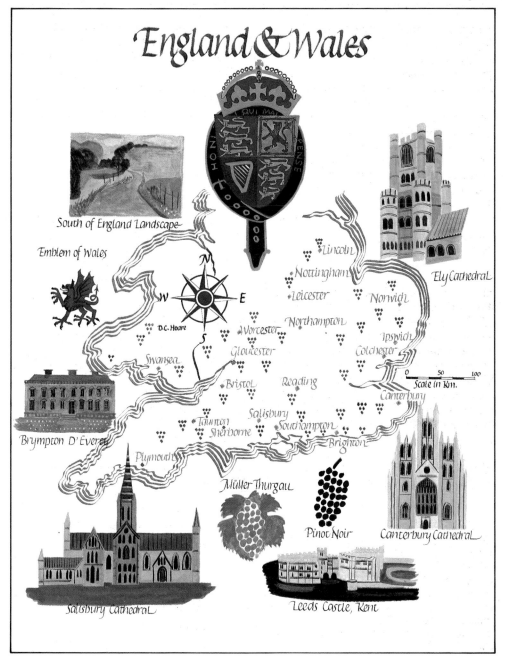

England & Wales

South of England Landscape

Emblem of Wales

Ely Cathedral

N
W · E
S
D.C. Hoare

Lincoln
Nottingham
Leicester
Northampton
Norwich
Worcester
Gloucester
Ipswich
Colchester
Swansea
Bristol
Reading
Canterbury
Taunton
Salisbury
Sherborne
Southampton
Brighton
Plymouth

Scale in Km.
0   50   100

Brympton D'Evercy

Müller Thurgau

Pinot Noir

Canterbury Cathedral

Salisbury Cathedral

Leeds Castle, Kent

Decanter magazine tastings

175 wines, mainly 1982 and 1983 vintages, were submitted and tasted blind in the summer of 1984, a previous tasting having been held in 1982. Two years should mean a noticeable rise in quality from vines planted in the mid-1970s and the panels were impressed with the quality of both years, although most 1983s needed to complete a full year in bottle to reach their best.

Awards

The Gore Browne trophy won in 1983 by Lamberhurst's 1982 went in 1984 to Barton Manor Dry 1983. 'Guyot trained' at Whippingham, Isle of Wight and owned by Mr and Mrs Goddard. A Gold Medal went to Biddenham Ortega 1983 and silver medals to Mr Kenneth McAlpine's Lamberhurst and Mr and Mrs Stephen Skelton of Tenterden for their Spots' Farm Rosé.

Visits

Most English vineyards are open to visitors from May until the end of October. Advance arrangements by telephone are advisable lest nobody should be there. All the necessary information is in the *Decanter Domesday Book of English Vineyards*, part of the September 1984 number, price £1.50 from 2-10 St. John's Road, London. SW11 1PN.

Where to buy

Stockists and prices of all English wines tasted by the magazine's panels are also given in *Decanter*, September 1984. Supplies of course vary according to the size of the vineyard and the vintage. The 1983 yield from Lamberhurst's thirty-five acres certainly sufficed to supply Peter Dominic, Davison, Victoria Wine, Oddbins and others. Wines of smaller vineyards are likely to be restricted to local retailers. The Paget Brothers at Chilsdown, three miles north of Chichester, for example, made 35,000 bottles in 1983, selling them in West Sussex mainly to some 7000 visitors. From 1985 onwards the English Wine Centre at Alfriston, East Sussex, where the Festival of English Wines is held annually during the first weekend of September, will be launching a 'County' series. *Sussex County, Kent County*, etc., blends of the best grapes grown in the county named, will be touring many parts of Britain.

Further information The English Vineyards Association, The Ridge, Lamberhurst Down, Kent TN3 8ER. Tel. 0892-890-734.

Part 2

The Wine-merchants

1st Verse:

COME, come, let us drink to the Vintners'
  good Health,
'Tis the Cask, not the Coffer, that holds the
  true Wealth.
If to founders of Blessings we Pyramids raise,
The Bowl next the Sceptre deserves the best
  Praise.
Then next to the Queen let the Vintners' Fame
  shine;
She gives us good Laws and they fill us good
  Wine.

Chorus:

Come, come, let us drink the Vintners' good
  Health,
'Tis the Cask, not the Coffer, that holds the
  true Wealth.

E. Settle: *Song to the Vintners* 1702.

There used to be a joke that the wine trade
lecturer introduced himself as 'a member of
the oldest trade but not the oldest
profession'. It can't have been a very old joke
because, until 1919, there were no wine
trade lecturers. 1919 was the year in which
André Simon, having persuaded some of
his fellow shippers to form a Wine Trade
Education Committee, found that he was
the only one prepared to give a lecture.
However, 'the oldest trade' goes back at

least to the ninth century when regular
shipments of wine from Rouen reached
London, where Billingsgate merchants had
to pay a tax of six shillings a ship.

After the marriage in 1152 of Eleanor of
Aquitaine to Henry, Duke of Anjou and
Normandy, who became England's King
Henry II the following year, Gascon wine
from Bordeaux poured into London by sea,
and later into other English ports from
Sandwich along the South Coast and round
to Bristol and Chester.

But in 1335 Edward III prohibited the
export of corn and by way of reprisal the
Gascons switched their trade to Flemish,
Dutch and Hanseatic ports, leaving the
English to go and fetch their own wine from
Bordeaux. This they did by building a
mercantile fleet that was to develop into the
Merchant Navy. Twice a year the ships
would sail in convoy — the better for
self-protection from pirates and the cruel
sea — bringing home the 'new wine' before
Christmas and 'the racked wine' in the
spring.

The Inland Revenue, known as
'attorneys of the King's Butler' took two
casks, or the equivalent in money, and some
wine went free to the royal cellars, the army
and the Church before the bulk was landed
and stored by the 'Wine-Drawers', the

'Gauger' checking and recording content.

Sales were made by brokers and retailers under a system that offered 'Anjou' and 'Auxerre', Moselle and 'Oleron' at prices from one to three pennies a gallon during the fourteenth century. With Sweet Vernage from Italy two shillings a gallon, Rhine wine 1s 2d a gallon and Crete 4s a gallon, the choice grew wider. By 1453 when our General Talbot ended England's sovereignty over Western France by losing the battle at Castillon, near St-Emilion, quality too had improved. Gascon wines — later found perfect to distil into Cognac brandy — were relegated to *vin ordinaire* shipped from La Rochelle, *clairette* or claret from Bordeaux taking their place.

In spite of changes in fashions and in duty, as when the Methuen Treaty gave terms to Portugal that were to popularize port, this trade continued unbroken in peace and war until Hitler occupied France in 1940.

Battleship and Bottleship

Such is the popularity of French wine today that in similar circumstances supplies would soon be exhausted. But wine-drinkers then were relatively few and many men and women were away in the Services. With wine merchants rationing their customers, stocks were made to last for some years. But in 1944, when the enterprising Surgeon Lieutenant Norman Burrows RNVR, ward room wine caterer of HMS *Black Prince*, returned triumphantly in a dinghy across Scapa Flow from the French battleship, *Richelieu*, with a cask of red infuriator bartered for what passed for Plymouth gin in those stirring times, I fancy this must have been the only possible source of *vin de table* left in Britain.

Prominent among the London wine shippers before the war and after it, was the firm of Brown Gore & Welch Ltd., started in 1896 by Victor H. Seyd, A.W. Gore and C. Brown. (Gore, incidentally, was the only Englishman to win the Men's Singles at Wimbledon — 1899, 1901, 1908 and 1912 until Fred Perry won in 1934-5 and 6). Their agencies in the 1950s included Bouchard Père et Fils, Bols' Liqueurs, Paul Jaboulet of Rhône wine fame, Offley Forrester ports and Misa sherries. With offices above and cellars below the Corn Exchange in Seething Lane, EC3 they ran a training scheme for apprentices, many of whom are now prominent in the wine trade. 'The Old Brown Gorians', augmented by members of the firm itself when Brown Gore and Welch joined International Distillers & Vintners, Peter Dominic's parent company in 1968, still have their reunions. The President is the one surviving partner, V.L. ('Leslie') Seyd, who succeeded his father Victor.

Having begun my own career on leaving the Navy in 1955 as one of those ten-bob-a-week apprentices, I invited him to continue the tale of 'The wine merchants'. James Long, who succeeded his friend David Peppercorn as Purchasing Executive of International Distillers & Vintners then completes it.

1935-1965 by V.L. Seyd

Before the war a wine shipper was rather a remote person, often conducting his business from a small cellar or basement office in the City around the Minories, Mincing Lane or Eastcheap. Business was almost entirely done on paper, most orders for wine being shipped in cask by the General Steam Co., whose ships — *Grebe*, *Chaffinche* and (more appropriately) *Swallow* — appeared to be all birds.

An order having been given to a shipper

or 'agent', the wines went direct to the shippers' customers, mainly the nation's wholesale and retail wine merchants and some hotel groups; sherry in butts from Jerez, port in pipes from Oporto and a variety of table wines from Bordeaux, Burgundy, the Rhine and Moselle in hogsheads or *aums.*

The Pre-war shipper
The shipper seldom saw, or even tasted, the wines he supplied unless of course there was a complaint to be investigated and put right. There was a continuity in those days. Qualities remained constant and prices stable so that once gained a customer's orders came in regularly and the liaison could last for years. For a shipper, increasing his business could therefore be very difficult. Calling on a firm for the first time in the hopes of meeting a principal, one would be lucky to see the manager or a clerk who was likely to say 'Sorry, we are not wanting anything at present.'

But with perseverance, some tact and a little luck, having eventually gained the inner sanctum, the good salesman made the most of his personality to persuade the prospective new client that he had some fine wines of exceptional quality to offer. Nobody had yet heard of inflation and shippers began to bottle some casks themselves, holding stocks in bottle of wines already supplied in cask against further orders required quickly.

An office lunch
It must be confessed that under these circumstances many of the shippers became rather idle old gentlemen. Apart from passing on the orders they received and signing a few letters and cheques at the end of the afternoon, mornings passed pleasantly receiving a few friends and customers for a glass of tawny port, sherry or champagne. After midday they would clear the office desk for a white linen table cloth and accoutrements to precede a cold chicken, or ham and tongue, accompanied by some excellent wine followed by Stilton cheese and a glass or two of vintage port. For a change they might repair to lunch at the Wine Trade Club, a select establishment in Lloyds Avenue, where port and brandy were consumed well into the afternoon.

When the port or champagne houses showed a vintage, the shipper would allot, from his total allocation, to each of his customers the quantity he considered reasonable. The remainder would be sold in the trade in a few days bringing a nice profit to the shipper and his Principal.

Sample rooms
For Brown, Gore & Welch — and others among the larger shippers — there was plenty of work to be done after the Second World War. Sample rooms were established in which they would keep in Dock sample bottles, those wines which their principals had to offer, enabling them to supply samples from London rather than from abroad. In Brown, Gore & Welch, for example, submitting samples of Bouchard Père et Fils latest vintage Beaune or Volnay could lead to orders for 200 hogsheads.

With ports and sherries many merchants had their 'own label' brands and, seeking a better price they would request 'matching' samples and quotations from different shippers. The prospect of an order for ten butts of sherry made the sample room a hive of activity composing blends and it became an important place in a shipper's life, with an important member of the firm in charge.

The larger merchants, such as the breweries with their own hotels and off-licences, would receive most of their wine in cask, which they would lay-up, fine, bottle and distribute themselves. Orders from small firms such as independent retailers were bottled in our own cellars under the Corn Exchange, British Rail vehicles from the main terminii collecting daily, with delivery anywhere in Britain within a few days.

Bottling, corking and labelling equipment, now much sought after by museums, was hand operated, and in the hands of the apprentices the labelling machine was liable to become as gummed up as a rush hour traffic jam, until Old Bill, one of several Cockney characters in the cellars came to the rescue.

Partners peripatetic

By the 1930s with cars reliable and fun to drive, partners had become more energetic, driving themselves all over the country to get business. The late Jack Rutherford (Rutherford, Osborne Perkin) evidently a believer in 'unto every one that hath it shall be given', always drove a Rolls Royce. Others — perhaps recalling later in the Gospels that treasure in heaven awaits those who give to the poor — would arrive in a clapped out old Ford.

The car undoubtedly counts. For many years I was quite unable to meet Mr Paten, head of his family firm in Peterborough, until one day I drove up in a supercharged 2-litre Bugatti making those exciting noises beloved of sports car fans. In a flash he was out examining the car and asking for a run up the road. The result was a long friendship with the Paten family and many years of rewarding business.

These friendships often led to one being asked to stay the night. In Bristol it was always a privilege to be entertained to dinner by Jack and Carol Harvey or by Ronald Avery and his wife; after a Harvey lunch, dinner was often a testing time. At Spalding with the Gleeds it was nine holes of golf with father and daughter during the afternoon, and bridge after dinner into the small hours. Business was never discussed. Only after saying goodbye the next morning, Mr Gleed would slip a piece of paper into my hand. I would read it later: 'Ship me three butts of sherry and a pipe of port.'

Change is inevitable; the AOC laws, supermarkets and brewer-controlled multiples ensure that the public now has a better and a far larger choice. But it is sad that the shipper, who imported his wines in bulk, has all but disappeared.

* * *

Barbara Castle will forever be remembered:

> If you're barred from all driving by Castle's contriving
> And now you are sadder and wiser,
> With a wife who can drive you still may survive
> And laugh at the police breathalyser.
>
> So think of the joys when you join with the boys
> In a bitter, a lager or shandy,
> And go on to dine with a choice of good wine
> Ending up with a Cointreau or brandy

J W McFeeters, Wine Mine 1974.

* * *

1965-1985 by James Long

Whether it was the brewers or the breathalyser, the days when buying and selling were largely formalities that preceded long luncheons and lost afternoons have certainly gone. The wine trade today has become Big Business — with all the advantages and, inevitably, some of the disadvantages that the term implies.

Wine-drinking — a thirteen fold increase

This transformation has been closely linked to the increase in wine-drinking from not much more than half a bottle a head in 1930 to around thirteen and a half bottles a head in 1984. A colleague who started work in the 1930s told me recently that at that time almost the only people who bought wine regularly were 'the clergy, the doctors and the rich landowners' — and even they seemed to prefer port and sherry to light wines. Sir Stafford Cripps started the boom with that two-shilling-a-bottle reduction on table wines in his 1949 budget. Fuelled by the reaction to wartime and post-war austerity, the growing fashion for holidays abroad and the spread of wine knowledge through articles in newspapers and magazines, the trend gradually gathered momentum and still continues.

To cope with this new and welcome demand the wine trade had fairly quickly to adjust and improve a host of long-established practices in relation to shipping, quality control, range extension, etc. Furthermore, at the same time the trade had to come to terms with the problems of inflation and a mass of new and complicated domestic, foreign and latterly EEC legislation.

These changed circumstances have led to a much greater degree of specialisation so that, certainly within the bigger firms, key functions such as buying, marketing and distribution all have their separate departments to ensure that the customer receives what he wants when he wants at an acceptable price and in the best possible condition. Another difference between the old wine trade and the new is the importance attached to training. Employees from the Managing Director downwards, are encouraged — and indeed on occasions obliged — to acquire new skills and to sharpen up old ones by means of a wide variety of internal and external courses. For example, however knowledgeable a wine buyer may be about wine, to do his job properly he may well need to hear about the latest practices of negotiation or to learn how to use a computer or to speak another language.

New forms of transport

Turning to specific subjects, before the Second World War virtually all wines — including second and third growth clarets and most of the top burgundies — were shipped to the United Kingdom in cask and bottled here. The small quantity imported in bottle arrived in loose wooden cases. Today approximately 70 per cent is transported in bottle either in separate cases or in cartons or on 50/60 case pallets; the majority in huge forty-foot containers or 'boxes' with a total capacity of up to 1500 cases. Bulk wines normally travel in stainlees steel tanks of up to 25,000 litres capacity, on the backs of trailers, in built-in ships' tanks or increasingly, where access permits, in bulk rail wagons. All these methods have helped considerably to reduce costs.

Higher quality

Whereas in the old days the selection of wines was mainly confined to the classic regions of France and Germany, with a very limited number of well-known names from Italy, sherry from Spain and port from

Portugal, demand in recent years has resulted in a vastly increased range both from the lesser-known areas of the traditional countries and from Eastern Europe, the Americas and elsewhere. More exacting standards, expected by the consumer and imposed by the relevant authorities, have achieved better viticultural and vinification techniques and, aided by a battery of sophisticated instruments and equipment, more stringent checks by the importer to guarantee the required high standard of consistency and quality.

Liaison between specialists

Fast and frequent communications are maintained between shipper and supplier by telephone and telex. It is also now common practice for the wine-buyer and, as necessary, the oenologist, the marketing manager and other specialists to visit suppliers *in situ* regularly to oversee production, to gather product knowledge, to seek new products and to discuss new ideas.

No trade — or member of that trade — can afford to stand still; low strength, low calorie wine, de-alcoholised wine (wine with the alcohol removed), spritzers (wine and mineral water) and wine coolers (wine, fruit juice and mineral water) are just some of the wine trade's novel contemporary projects.

Brands for mass market needs

Any article concerning the modern wine trade must not overlook wine brands. These have all been carefully researched and chosen to meet mass market needs. Strongly supported by advertising and promotions, the name and presentation are often as important as the source of origin. Classic examples of this mainly post-war,

and currently rapidly escalating phenomenon, are Blue Nun, Mateus Rosé, Hirondelle, the Paul Masson Carafe and Le Piat d'Or. Closely allied to brand development is the subject of packaging. For many years the glass bottle, albeit in different sizes, was the only handy container for wine. During the last decade, however, a lot of progress has been made in developing practical, effective and convenient alternatives — notably the bag-in-box, the tetrabrik, the PET (a type of plastic) bottle and the can.

There will always be people who mourn the days gone by. Some claim that, because they received less treatment, the wines of former times had more character than those of today. This may have been true, but their quality was very inconsistent. Times change and needs change too. Building on the traditions of the past, the modern wine trade has adapted it's ways to meet the demands of the present and to anticipate those of the future.

What and where to buy

What the public chiefly wants of the modern wine trade is advice on what to buy and where to buy it. Trying to cover the former thoroughly, *Everybody's Wine Guide* has little space left for the latter. Just as well; that comprehensive annual, *Which? Wine Guide** needs no less than 200 pages to describe all the specialist wine merchants, chains, supermarkets and auctions at your service in Britain. (A new

---

*1985 Edition, editor Kathryn McWhirter £7.95.
**Webster's *Wine Price Guide* £9.95.

210

Christmas 1984 publication** even compares regional prices of a hundred British merchants.)

With few exceptions the quality of wine nowadays is very good. It should be; many of the buyers and other leading lights were trained in our group, International Distillers & Vintners! There are of course bargains for those with the time, money and knowledge to 'shop around', but statements that this firm, or that supermarket, offer the best *overall* value, I believe are misleading. I form my judgement in Chichester, on my own shopping rounds, where four licensed supermarkets and seven specialist wine merchants within ten minutes' walk of my house constitute an off-licence concentration comparable to 'the on' outside a Royal Naval Dockyard gate, where pubs lie thick as Wardroom Windsor Soup.

People's wine and food shopping is largely a matter of personal convenience, where to park, weight to carry and how far; and for those as impatient as I am, how long we are kept waiting at the checkout point. But the more we become interested in wine the greater our need for informed opinion since we cannot try them all at once ourselves. A friend, brought up in Spain, looking for the cheapest acceptable wine for daily drinking told me she gave the go by to Rumania and Bulgaria along her supermarket shelves. 'If only you had asked a wine merchant', I said, 'I think you'd have been well satisfied with Bulgarian Sauvignon by now. Managers and staff attend tastings and pass exams nowadays.' She seemed surprised.

Women I read — though I rather doubt it — now buy more wine than men. I foresee tasting rooms being extended to wine shops. Who will want morning coffee in the High Street when there are Bordeaux and Bulgaria, Napa and New Zealand Cabernets to taste and compare in their Peter Dominic round the corner?

A Flute glass for Champagne and Sparkling Wines

A general-purpose glass for fortified wines (Sherries, port, etc.). Also useful for liqueurs

A Balloon for Brandy. Also good for liqueurs

A general-purpose glass for table wines

A long stemmed glass for table wines, usually used for Hock and Mosel

Part 3

The Wine~drinkers

TASTING

A: Do you detect a certain *malice* in this wine?

B: A touch of *gout de terroir?*

A: *(Vaguely)* Yes. I thought that I had noticed an alien glint in the *robe* and then again in the nose — and my sense of uneasiness has been growing since. It's almost frightening.

B: I like it though. I like a wine that you can taste with your teeth. You can feel the sharp edges of the flinty vineyard soil clicking against your molars. The peasants, I believe, drink this stuff with their mouths full of pebbles. I think one can see what they mean.

A: Oh yes — what's the grape do you think? *Kabinet semolina?*

B: Possibly, although are we not too far south for that? More likely a *pompidou noir.*

A: But surely we're north of the river?

B: ...but south of the petrol station...

A: ...but facing *east* on that slope between Henri's bistro and the cross-roads.

B: Even so, until Jean-Jacques went down with his *foie troublé* most of this wine was made from the vines beside the *abattoir* — which were, of course, pre-haemophilia *pompidous.*

A: (Suddenly) Have another look now: I think the wine is trying to tell us something (swill swill, sniff sniff, sip sip, gurgle gurgle, gargle, cough, splutter, choke...)

(**A** falls to the floor. His face assumes the colour of a *cru supérieur Châteauneuf-du-Pape* in an off-year. He expires.)

B: (Sniffing with great concentration) Yes, *pompidou noir*, definitely.

A. G. Cairns Smith
Wine-snob dialogue competition, set and judged by Arthur Marshall, *Wine Mine*, Winter 1970.

Drinking means thinking! As can be seen any Sunday morning at 'nineteenth holes' throughout the land, drinking means nothing of the kind. Unless, of course, the drinker wants to make the most of wine. Some wine-drinkers don't; very sensibly they drink with their meals what they can afford and are not really interested when given anything better, which is disappointing for their hosts and, of course,

for their wine merchant.

There was also the case of the Englishman in the hotel in France, who drank Mouton-Rothschild for dinner each night, retiring as quickly as possible to the bar to gulp down a large Coca-Cola. Asked why, he explained that wine was customary in France and he always had to have the best, though unfortunately he preferred Coca-Cola.

Two little books That many people are curious and do want to learn is evident from the huge sales of two small books, Michael Broadbent's *Wine Tasting* and Jancis Robinson's *Masterglass — A Practical Course in Tasting Wine.*

Almost twenty-five years ago, conducting weekly tastings at Bristol for his colleagues in Harveys, Michael Broadbent decided that few of them knew the first principles of tasting and — delving deeper — that in English there was neither a book nor a chapter on the subject. So, in 1962, he wrote a paper, expanded into *Wine Tasting* in 1968 after it had become indispensable for staff training in the wine trade.

Two years before, in June 1960, the Wine Mine Club had broken new ground by offering the public tastings of fine wines upon payment in the recently acquired 2-8 Orange Street 'cellar shop'. The first meeting was 'Claret — A Comparison of 1953 and 1955 Vintages'. Including only a few words on how to taste in the programme, my own view was that, like sex, people would soon learn how to do it without a *Kama Sutra* from me. In the event, the series continued unbroken with up to five meetings a year until the venue in 1984 moved to the Royal Festival Hall.

Michael Broadbent, conducting wine auctions throughout the English-speaking world as Head of Christie's Wine Department, has since won renown for *The Great Vintage Wine Book,* a record of tasting wines over twenty-five years. But for amateurs wanting to organise tastings, or just to discuss wines at the dinner table, the original *Wine Tasting* is still invaluable.

Three times longer, *Masterglass* (1983) is indeed a thoroughly detailed practical course, with everything Jancis Robinson wants her readers to learn merrily arranged down the left-hand columns, supported by all sorts of Teach Yourself experiments in contrasting italic print down the right. *Vin* 'O' Levels, at the very least, should be achieved.

In the trade Wines are judged by their colour, bouquet and taste. In the trade where large sums will be spent in buying them, tasting requires a considerable degree of concentration, even in a light, comfortable tasting room built for the purpose. Elsewhere, in freezing February along the Loire for example, tasting young, acid Muscadets from cellar to cellar and cask to cask, this concentration merits the description 'heroic attention to duty'.

Nowadays, the tasters are usually Masters of Wine, speaking two or more languages, who are probably away from home for fifty to sixty nights in an average year. Work in Bordeaux is always the most interesting; confronted with a dozen raw purple samples, all the same appellation and hardly six months old, the taster's palate has to tell which are likely to please the customers ten years hence.

At home, the quality controllers must taste samples from all incoming containers and in the large, clinical tasting rooms of the big groups, such as Gilbey House, Harlow, sample bottles sent from all parts of the globe quickly build up by the score. There are tastings too for training purposes. The man or woman behind today's wine counter has a certificate, a higher certificate or a diploma, and exhorting the retail staff from headquarters there is likely to be a man or woman Master of Wine, the highest professional distinction in the British wine trade.

Emulating 'Oxbridge' The layman's opportunities for tasting are restricted to what he buys, which costs money and to functions organised by wine merchants, societies, and his friends. Some people undoubtedly have better eyes, noses and palates and — of great importance — taste memories than others. But do not despair! Given intensive coaching by the wine trade over what must perforce be a short time, the standard achieved by the Universities' young wine-tasting teams is extremely high.

Of course, as I hope I have emphasised throughout this book, 90 per cent of wine is for gullet, not palate, slipping down the old red lane without sniffing, sipping or rolling it round the tongue as it if were Masefield's 'Dirty British coaster with a salt-caked smoke stack, Butting through the Channel in the mad March days'. The allusion is not inappropriate; such are the locations of our taste buds that the sides of the tongue detect the salt, the back the bitterness, the upper edges the acidity and the tip the sweetness.

Let's do it For what is an appraisal by eye, nose and tongue, only a plain tulip-shaped glass, curving inwards at the top to retain the bouquet and filled less than half full of wine is needed. If held by the base between the thumb and the fingers the eye can see all the wine, noting it's colour and limpidity.

1. Colour. A clear bright colour should mean a healthy wine. Red wines, as they age, change from deep purple through ruby to tawny. To study closely, tilt the glass away from you at an angle of 45° against a piece of plain white paper. White wines, some almost colourless, turn through very pale to full straw and finally brown when maderised and undrinkable.

2. Smell. Twirling the glass lightly, allowing the wine to coat the inner sides will accentuate the bouquet, 'nose' or smell. It should be pleasurably fresh and fruity, probably 'grapey', though professionals have different private descriptions such as 'blackcurrants', 'cedarwood', to help them recognise different grapes. Make a good sniff, with the nose just above the glass and record your reaction. Try again if necessary.

3. Tasting. Take a small mouthful, sucking in a little air with it, which will release esters, accentuating flavour. Swill thoroughly round the tongue and the mouth. Spit out the wine and breathe out the vapour through the nose. Record your impressions as to sweetness, acidity, tannin, body, mellowness, age, grape, place of origin as you feel inclined.

If there are any others present — including an expert ideally — with whom to discuss them, so much the better. To assess quality, professionals use a twenty-point system, maximum points being Colour 2, Nose 6, Palate 10, and Finish 2.

Hosts at home In practice every host should taste before decanting, or having just opened a bottle, before guests arrive, to be sure that the wine is in good condition. Doing it properly, notebook at the ready, is only a matter of seconds. Dining out as a guest or at a picnic, the procedure obviously has to be modified but by adopting my slogan — 'Drinking means Thinking'! — that useful note can be added to your tasting notebook later.

Order of tasting The following rules exist to show each wine at its best.

1. Young wines before old; dry before sweet; weak before strong; white before

red, though some experts prefer the reverse.

2. Tasting clarets, Médoc and Graves should precede St. Emilion and Pomerol which, though weaker, have more tannin. Burgundies should come after Bordeaux.

3. Aromatic wines like Gewürztraminer and strong Sauvignons should come after the dry, but before the sweet, in any white wine tasting.

Blind tastings To see or not to see, that is the question! Blind tastings are obviously essential for panels assessing a large number of wines for press articles. At home decanting into plain bottles or inventing masks of tin foil or cardboard to fit over existing bottles is laborious. Beginners might prefer to start with a range of up to six bottles of a kind, Rieslings, Cabernet Sauvignons, etc. with the aim of learning to recognise the principal grapes. Clarets of one year now constitute 'a horizontal tasting'; clarets of different years, 'a vertical tasting'. (The taster one hopes remains vertical at both.)

Social Tastings A pleasant lunch or supper tasting where only the car drivers might have to spit out can be for six to eight people sitting informally round the dining-room table with two kinds of paté, two kinds of bread, butter, three or four cheeses and up to six wines. Allow half a bottle a head and borrow glasses from your wine merchant. One village group I know meet in each others' houses, each host showing three or four wines of interest from his cellar. It might be two white burgundies, two red and finally an old Sauternes.

Cheeses keep well in a cold larder or in the coolest part of a refrigerator; the cut surfaces should be covered, the rind uncovered to allow the cheese to 'breathe'. To taste their best, two hours at room temperature before serving are essential.

Simple rules Professionals taste in the morning when the palate is fresh; amateurs working all day are usually restricted to evenings when tastings become less commercial and more social. The general rules are the same.

Refuse invitations if you have a cold or catarrh. Avoid scent or hair lotion. No smoking. Invite only people seriously interested. If tasting to decide what to buy, don't go to the buffet before you have finished or suck a cough lozenge half-way through. Like the nurse's thermometer, the palate must be normal for each patient.

Guessing games Connoisseurs (which only means knowledgeable people) in and out of the wine trade can sometimes guess the wine around the lunch or dinner table. But it is an embarrassing exercise for the expert if he guesses 1980 when it proves to be 1970, both for him and the host. Moreover, if he has never drunk that particular wine before, he can hardly be expected to guess the vineyard, vintage and what the cellar master drank for breakfast all in ten seconds. In reality, unless every person present is very wine-minded, the process of intellectual elimination is so slow that guests become bored and the hostess upset.

GOOD HEALTH
Good Health! Bonne Santé! Zum Wohlsein! Buena Salud! Drinking a toast to the health of relations, friends, honoured guests is a charming universal custom which must be almost as old as wine itself. The wish is sincere and it does not occur to us that should glasses be raised rather too

often, it might not be fulfilled.

Alcohol is a drug and those who drink too much of it can harm themselves and other people too, if their impaired judgement causes accidents. Consequently taxation, rising in proportion to alcoholic strengths, aims to curb consumption and special restrictions are imposed on car drivers.

A wine trade slogan Moderate drinking, however, is generally beneficial to health and happiness. Moreover, regarded solely from the commercial angle, 'Moderate drinking for the many' should be the slogan of the wine trade, particularly in Europe where the average expectation of life is now nearer four score years than three and the quality of riper years is improved by a little wine or spirit daily.

But what is moderation? An unusual 1982 Penguin paperback called *Same Again — A Guide to Safer Drinking* by Marcus Grant, gives a pretty good answer from the results of recent international research. The author, a forty-year-old Scotsman by no means averse to a glass, became the first Director of the Alcohol Education Centre and now works for the World Health Organisation in Geneva.

Everyday Pleasure or Drug? This research shows that not only the quantity we drink but the frequency and the style of our drinking habits relate to whether 'Drinking — The Everyday Pleasure' becomes 'Alcohol — The Everyday Drug', these respectively being the titles of the first two chapters. In the wine trade, regrettably, it is our products that, like tobacco, are a health risk; though I should emphasise that they are not comparable to tobacco in that drinking (unless the drinker is drunk) does

not upset other people and moderate drinking is good, while all forms of smoking are bad.

Results of Research Conveniently drinks divide into four strengths, Beer and Cider, Light Wines, Fortified Wines, Spirits. The table on page 219 comparing them shows that, very roughly, fortified wines are half the strength of spirits, light wines half the strength of fortified wines, beers and ciders less than half the strength of light wines.

Since most of us imbibe a mixture of them in the course of a day or a week from different sizes of bottles and glasses, discovering how much we consume is difficult. However, the amount of alcohol in the usual measures happens to be approximately 1 centilitre in each case, which suffices for a rough calculation.

More precise figures are:

One half pint of beer	1.05 centilitres
Single measure of spirits	
6 out (of a gill)	0.94 centilitres
(Scotland 5 out slightly more)	
A glass of light wine	1.04 centilitres
A glass of sherry, port or vermouth	1.12 centilitres

and each of these can be regarded as one standard drink.

The findings in terms of standard drinks were:

Up to 20 a week A low health risk assuming not concentrated into one or two bouts.

21-30 a week At risk. Consider reduction seriously.

31-50 a week Probably doing yourself harm; reduce to a safer level.

Over 50 a week It is very rare for anybody drinking as much as this not to be harming themselves. Your physical and mental health will be deteriorating. All sorts of social problems may be accumulating. Take urgent steps to cut down drastically.

The book then suggests that by looking at quantity and frequency together, a pattern of drinking emerges that may need changing. For me this recalled my own innocence when at 43 I joined the wine trade.

Mineral Water in Beaune Real wine merchants, I thought, drank nothing but wine (with an occasional Cognac) and came to no harm. I had not heard of congeners, those substances in wines and spirits that are close allies of ethyl alcohol, nor of liver cirrhosis that every Frenchman fears. Lunch in those Horsham days was a plate of sandwiches in the local with a pint of bitter (two standard drinks). Home at 7.30 p.m. two sherries before and two tawny ports after two glasses of table wine at dinner gives me a total of eight standard drinks, or fifty-six weekly.

All went well for four years. Then one day my wife and I arrived in Beaune to lunch with old M. Louis Latour after spending two nights on champagne at Moët & Chandon's hospitable Château Saran. Awaiting us on the restaurant table were two bottles of Burgundy, one red, one white, and a large bottle of mineral water. I was feeling slightly dizzy and longed to change my 'pattern of drinking' by disposing of that mineral water in one gulp leaving the wines to our host. 'Now', he said, pouring the white burgundy into two glasses and the mineral water into his own, '*You* must eat and drink all the specialities of Burgundy; alas, I am too old'.

Going on to Majorca I tried to swim it off and drank tonic water, creating a social problem for our hosts because it was more expensive than wine. Just a touch of *le foie* but it took total abstinence for a month to wear it off when I came home!

Take a break The long-term effects of overdoing the drinking — cancers, ulcers and other alimentary afflictions — make painful reading. Taking inadequate precautions, I am lucky at 72 to be fit, having avoided them so far. Prudent mariners on a collision course with hazards ahead make a bold alteration of course for a time, and this is what the researchers recommend.

Rest the system, give up drink at intervals for a week, fourteen days or a month; only then can you be sure that you are not dependent on alcohol!

Men's bodies it seems are 55/65 per cent water; women's only 45/55 per cent, which makes them that more vulnerable. Sad that! How can a gentleman ask his wife to drive if she has to drink even less at every party than he does?

The following exist to be helpful:

National Council on Alcoholism,
3 Grosvenor Crescent,
LONDON, SW1.
Tel. 01-235-4182
with a network of over forty advice centres.

Al Anon Family Groups,
61 Great Dover Street,
LONDON, SE1 4YF.
Tel. 01-403-0888
Associated with Alcoholics Anonymous;
helps families and friends of those in
difficulty.

Alcoholics Anonymous,
11 Redcliffe Gardens,
LONDON, SW10.
Tel. 01-352-9779
and at: Cardiff (0222) 373939
          Belfast (0232) 681084

Accept, Western Hospital,
Seagrave Road,
LONDON, SW6 1RZ.
Tel. 01-381-3155
Associated with the recently formed
Drinkwatchers.

Alcoholic strength Within the EEC
alcoholic strength of wines and spirits has
been greatly simplified since 1 January
1983 by scrapping the British Sikes Proof
Scale and adopting the metric scale of
Gay-Lussac, French physicist (1778-1850),
long used for wines on the Continent. This
scale, running from 0° (water) to 100°
(absolute alcohol) measures volume at
15°C/59°F. The Americans still retain their
proof scale 0° to 200° (absolute alcohol)
making all strengths double that of the
metric scale, i.e. light wines 8°-15° (metric)
= 16°-30° (American proof).

Below, the British Sikes Proof Scale
is still included for comparisons; any
number of degrees Sikes can be converted
to metric by dividing by 7/4, e.g. 70° Sikes
= 40° metric.

Strength and quality Light wines that are

COMPARATIVE SCALES – WINE AND SPIRIT STRENGTHS

Water	Beer Cider	Light Wines	Fortified Wines		Normal Spirits		Proof		Absolute Alcohol

Metric (Gay-Lussac) Scale (Percentage of Absolute Alchol)

| 0° | 3.7° | 8° | 15° | 21° | 40° | 50° | 57° | | 100° |

Sikes Scale (Percentage of Proof)

| 0° | | 14° | 26.25° | 36.75° | 70° | 87.7° | 100° | | 175° |

U.S. Proof

| 0° | | 16° | 30° | 42° | 80° | 100° | 114° | | 200° |

too weak (under 8°) neither travel nor last and are prone to oxidisation and other diseases. Light wines that are too strong (over 15°) tend to be unbalanced; the alcohol, predominating over acidity, tannin, and sugar, is disagreeable to the palate, particularly with food. If a mere reviver is required, spirits — a whisky and soda perhaps — could be better.

Variation in Light Wines This variation from 8° to 15°, nearly double, is worth noting. Low strength includes German Tafelwein and Kabinett, Beaujolais and Vinho Verde. High strength includes Barolo, Châteauneuf-du-Pape, Chianti, many Californias, Australian Shiraz and fine Sauternes. Bordeaux, Loire and other French regions are intermediate at 10.5° to 12.5°.

WINE WITH FOOD

Do you live to eat or eat to live? (schoolboy joke).

In my youth this was a question, spoken rapidly, that one schoolboy would fire at another. And if, unthinking, Forte minor retorted, 'Live to eat', there was a chorus of 'Glutton' and derisive laughter. Today, in our enlightened times, a caring master would immediately enrol him into Anna Best's Young Cooks' Club with a view to this possible prodigy winning the Mouton Cadet Amateur Chef competition and tasting for 'Oxbridge', even before he needed a razor.

To form the basis of a syllabus, I have taken André Simon's wines with food guidance† adding further comment as we go along.

†André Simon: *A Concise Encyclopedia of Gastronomy* 1952 & 1983.

Before the meal Dry vermouth, plain or with a little gin; dry sherry (fino or amontillado) or Montilla, slightly chilled; dry champagne or sparkling wine, iced; any dry still wine, cool; a vin rosé, iced.

The object of the aperitif is to cleanse the palate and sharpen the taste buds. Serving cocktails when wines are to follow, make it only one (avoiding rum and whisky which — though otherwise admirable — impose too strong a flavour).

With oysters and other shellfish Chablis, cool but not iced. Chablis, relatively light and the driest of the white burgundies, would allow the fuller Montrachets and Meursaults to come in later, with a fish entrée at the formal dinners of pre-war days. But Muscadet, Silvaner, Mâcon, Sancerre, Pouilly Blanc Fumé, Bergerac, Soave, Verdicchio — indeed any white wine below 4 on the new 1-9 dry to sweet scale — would be good.

With hors-d'oeuvres Dry white wines, chilled or a dry Rhône rosé; medium dry wines of the Mosel, Alsace, Graves. Hors-d'oeuvres invariably include strong flavours, from onions, garlic, soused herrings, eggs and egg sauces. Serve sound, inexpensive wines, such as Sauvignon Blanc, Graves, Spanish, Austrian or Hungarian white wines. Dry sherries, popular with *tapas* in Spain, are good.

With the soup A *vino de pasto* sherry or a dry Madeira, Sercial or Verdelho. Soup should be very hot or very cold; this leaves the palate too stunned or too numbed to appreciate wines lighter than sherry or Madeira.

With fish A fuller white wine than with the

hors-d'oeuvres, either a white burgundy or else a dry champagne, chilled but not iced. Chardonnay, Chenin Blanc and Soave are very suitable; German wines for those who want them less dry. A Paul Masson dry white carafe would go well with any fish from oysters to salmon. With smoked fish the powerful spicy Gewürztraminer is ideal. But white wines are by no means obligatory. Jancis Robinson in *Masterglass* makes the point that fish needs acidity (lemons, capers, vinegar), so white wines, having more acidity than red, are always recommended. But *maceration carbonique* reds are low in tannin and high in acidity so our salmon, bass and brill are all the better for Beaujolais, many Côtes du Rhône, *Vins de pays*, reds of the Loire, Veneto and Alto-Adige, Germany and New Zealand. All the light ones, in fact, that we serve chilled.

With chicken, turkey, veal or light entrées The same as with fish. These give the widest choice from full-bodied white wines to red of all kinds.

With beef, lamb and mutton Médoc, red Graves, Beaujolais, Loire or any other light red wines served at the temperature of the room.

With duck, goose, pork and venison St-Emilion, red burgundy, Côtes du Rhône or any other of the fuller red wines from Italy, Spain or Portugal, served at the temperature of the room. The convention is that the lighter meat (first above) gets the lighter wines. Game birds, duck, venison, etc. have more flavour and need something more assertive. Many people nowadays settle for Bulgarian Cabernet Sauvignon with either.

With the sweets Sauternes, Saumur, Palatinate, or any other sweet wine, still or sparkling and iced. André Simon makes no provision for cheese (wine's perfect partner) coming *after* the meat course to finish any red wine still remaining. A fine Sauternes can begin with the cheese and continue through the sweet course. It is best really cold with a peach, nectarine or summer pudding rather than soft fruit and cream. A bottle between six to eight people gives each at least one glass and is always acclaimed by all present who have a sweet tooth.

With the dessert Port, Madeira or one of the fuller types of sherry. Though a variety of late-bottled ports, ready to drink, are made nowadays, there is no substitute for tawny port, long aged in cask or, for the special occasion, a bottle of old vintage or crusted port long aged in bottle.

With the coffee Brandy, never in a heated glass, or liqueurs, chilled or served in iced glasses.

Imperfect partners There are of course foods that do not go with wine at all. With curry the only possible drink is lager, or water by the bucket if it's too hot. The tart taste of apples (malic acid) spoils wine and the old piece of wine trade advice, 'Buy on apples, sell on cheese', means that any wine tasting good with an apple is worth buying, while cheeses, making them all taste better, are good for sales. There are always one or two exceptions: Gorgonzola is too fierce, Roquefort too salty and an old Camembert can be too ammoniac.

Asparagus and globe artichokes want for a suitable wine partner and salad dressings with vinegar are to be avoided. At Château

221

Loudenne there is always a green salad in the offing, made with the slightest touch of lemon juice added to a best olive oil dressing.

For eggs there are two proper places — the breakfast table and the bar, where Flips, Noggs and Possets are part of the bartender's art and, incidentally, of my book, *Cocktails and Mixed Drinks*. Eggs coat the mouth and are not worth a bottle of wine — not even one of Rhode Island Red. Lastly, chocolate is on the wine buff's index — except (if you'll pardon the pun) when the meal is over — After Eight.

Of all the Adult Education courses available in Britain, cookery seems to be the most popular subject (no less than nineteen are being offered by Chichester College of Technology alone in 1984-5). In two I have attended myself, wine with food was not discussed, so I hope these notes will interest lecturers and students alike.

BUYING WINE

Every man, no matter how unprepossessing, finds some woman whom he thinks is the last word in finesse . . . and so it is with wine. Somewhere there will be someone whose eyes mist over at the fragrance even as you begin to retch ... somewhere there is someone who actually likes the stuff.

—Clement Freud:
A Wine Guide Review(1976)

Buying wine, says Section 169 of the Licensing Act 1964, has to be done by persons over the age of eighteen, so if you can dissuade your fifteen-year-old honey-child from disguising herself as Elizabeth Taylor and do it for her, the wine trade would be much obliged. The licensee, who must not 'knowingly sell', usually gets the blame in Court in these 'dare-devil Deirdre' cases.

The first bottle Otherwise the first purchase should be the sort of wine the eighteen-year-old has enjoyed in pub, club, wine bar, at home or in other people's houses. It is likely to be white with some sweetness, numbered 4, 5 or 6 on the new dry-to-sweet 1-9 scale, which the majority of retailers and supermarkets should now be displaying to help people choose what they want.

The wrong way to choose wine (says a booklet which might do just as well for the Marriage Guidance Council as the Wine Development Board) is:
1 Because you like the shape of the bottle.
2 It has a pretty label.
3 It is expensive.
4 You've seen it advertised on television.

Wine to lay down Why not make a start, tasting anything that comes your way and learning about wine as you go along? But first you will need to lay down some good bottles to drink in a few years time when you have become a connoisseur.

Never has there been a better time to start a cellar, which can be anything from two dozen bottles under the stairs to the spiral cellar that fits on a 3 metre base and holds 900 bottles (as illustrated). Already thousands of cases of 1982 clarets in bond have been offered and sold, long before 1984 the year of bottling and delivery. 1983 turned out to be almost as bountiful a year; in Sauternes, never had the rot been nobler and offers for laying down Climens, Coutet and other *crus classés* were a feature of 1984.

Port shippers have declared 1982 or 1983 as vintage years and their predeces-

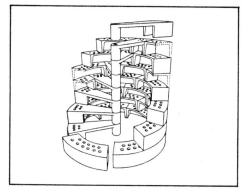

The spiral cellar. The invention of a Monsieur Harnois, a French civil engineer, it provides a cellar cum larder on any floor base 3 metres square, by means of special concrete modules fitted together. Capacity is governed by the height, eg. 2 metres high holds 900 bottles; price £1600. 3 metres holds 1600 bottles; price £2100.

4000 have been built in France, 1000 in Holland. There is no doubt any wine drinker building a new house or able to extend an existing one should study this carefully in conjunction with his accountant for it could well pay for itself in time.

sors, 1980, 1977 and 1975, are still listed by good merchants. Other wines worth laying down for just a few years are the best white burgundies, hocks and Mosels and the best reds of Côte Rotie, Hermitage and Châteauneuf-du-Pape. People disparage vintage charts, but not being a walking wine list myself, I like them, frequently referring to the one in my diary to check the ratings of years like 1980 and 1981, only good in some parts.

Unit investment plan Run for many years by Justerini & Brooks of St James's Street, London and George Street, Edinburgh, this plan includes free storage in proper conditions and insurance against theft or loss. In 1984 there was a choice of four units. Three hundred customers chose the first, paying £18 a month (£216 outright) for five dozen bottles — 2 dozen 1981 clarets, 1 dozen 1982 clarets, 1 dozen Mâcon Villages and 1 dozen Mosel. The monthly paymments for the three others were £25, £40 and £83 (£996 outright); this the No. 4 attracting forty buyers, included first growth clarets. The outright payers received quite a discount on the bracketed totals above.

Storage The perfect place in which to keep wines and spirits is cool, dark, dry and free from draughts and vibrations, with a constant temperature of about 13°C/55°F. Lying thus undistrubed, wines age slowly but surely and are often found in cellars of great châteaux and British country houses in their prime after many years.

If intending to lay down, for many years, a substantial 'cellar' of vintage port, fine claret, burgundies and Sauternes, it is advisable to use the 'Customers' reserve cellars' of a wine merchant, accepting the small annual rental, if these conditions are not available otherwise. Having done so, it is also important that you or your descendants should remember they are there (in 1983, Peter Dominic had to advertise widely in legal columns to trace customers who had moved or died, yet many cases were never claimed).

For lesser wines, quantities or periods, such perfection is hardly necessary. Most private houses have some nook or cranny large enough for a small wine bin, where wines will age satisfactorily for up to ten years, being none the worse for the slow temperature changes 13°C/55°F to

24°C/75°F likely to occur between winter and summer. Usually the only trouble is damp, destroying labels, though harmless to wine.

Corks Wine bottles should be binned on their sides so that their corks are kept moist. Dry corks shrink, admitting air to the detriment of the wine, and becoming hard, they are difficult to extract. The life of a cork is about twenty-five years; wines of this age should be professionally examined and bottles re-corked as necessary (in 1981 the *Maître du Chai* of Château Lafite came to London to do this service for appropriate holders in Peter Dominic's Orange Street cellars).

Bottles laid down should lie with labels (or in the case of vintage and crusted ports, the white splash) uppermost. This universal practice ensures that any sediment or crust forming on the lower side of the bottle remains there.

Stopper corks Fortified wines, such as wood ports and sherries, bottled for immediate drinking, are fitted with stopper corks or 'filter proof' caps removed by hand. In either case, these wines are best kept upright to drink at their best in a matter of weeks not months; stopper corks are short and can leak.

Cold weather White wine, particularly sherries, can develop crystalline deposits or become hazy in cold weather. These have no effect on flavour and are in fact beneficial tartrates. Nevertheless, the bottle should be exchanged by the supplier on request.

Spirits Unlike wines, spirits can be tainted by cork so that bottles have always been kept upright. With present day 'pilfer-proof' metal caps, this precaution is no longer necessary. No spirits *improve* in bottle.

To drink or to sell? Wine of course is for drinking; but there are people more interested in profit for pocket rather than palate, and others who try to achieve both by buying twice what is required and selling half at auction when the wine has matured.

Certainly fine wines become more valuable as they grow scarcer and older, the first growth clarets plus Châteaux Petrus, Cheval Blanc, Ausone, Yquem and the red burgundies of the Domaine de la Romanée-Conti reaching prices at auction at least three times more than those of the other classed growths. Vintage port and a little vintage champagne also feature at auction sales and in November 1984 Sotheby's held their first-ever New World Sale, mainly California and Australia.

At Christie's in October 1984, £330 was paid for just one bottle of Château d'Yquem 1921, £820 for two bottles of Mouton-Rothschild 1945 and £1550 for a dozen Taylor vintage port 1945. Many of these old gems are bought for publicity by small-town American wine-merchants. There is no pre-tasting and nobody knows how many owners there have been or how the bottles have been kept. I begin to wonder whether the great *grands crus* should not have a history sheet, like naval torpedoes liable to be fired and recovered for practice by different ships in turn.

I seldom go to auctions myself but in December 1977 I did buy a case of Sandeman 1966 for £48. If I sold it now, after seven years, I might get £135, less £20 auctioneer's commission. Had I invested in Grand Metropolitan ordinary shares instead, my £48 would now be worth £175.47 and I should have had dividends too each year.

SERVING WINE

> T'was Leporello, the servant, who said:
> My master's not right in the head.
> The appropriate manner to woo Donna
> Anna
> Is Carafino in litres in bed.
> > R.K.Spurrell: *Wine Mine* 1965
> > Wine & Music Limerick competition.

Wine can either be served from it's bottle or decanted into a jug or decanter. The object of decanting is to separate the wine from it's sediment (lees) and, with red wines, to let them take the air and the temperature of the room. Since white wines usually have no sediment and are drunk cold, decanting them is not obligatory, though they may look better on your table in a decanter.

Nowadays, most cheap red wines also have no sediment due to changes in vinification and people find that the stronger they are, the more they mellow given an hour or so in a decanter before they are drunk. Experiment for yourself with Bulgarian Cabernet Sauvignon, Rhône, Australia, California and others; the reason is not known, you might discover it.

Temperatures The maximum flavour of all wines is brought out when their temperature is 18°C/65°F, a point to remember particularly when serving white burgundies and other Chardonnay wines with good fish cooking. Too cold, that subtle bouquet and flavour is lost; you might as well have saved your money with a jug wine. Red wines are normally served at room temperature 18°C/65°F to 21°C/70°F; in a heat wave they may need chilling in an ice-bucket.

Lighter red wines, Beaujolais, Loire and others associated with *maceration carbonique* are better slightly chilled. Rosé wines, white wines, sparkling wines are preferred chilled (about 5°C/40°F to 10°C/50°F), the sweeter, the colder. While a short sharp shock (thirty minutes) in the cold compartment of the fridge or sixty minutes in the larger part does the job, there is no doubt that a mixture of ice cubes and cold water in an ice-bucket does it better. Immersed up to the neck the temperature will go down from 65°F to 55°F in eight minutes, which takes an hour in the fridge.

Vinicool In summer the fridge is a useful place to keep, before and after opening, a ready-to-use bottle of dry sherry, wood port or white port for any unexpected caller. When in use out of the fridge, stand the bottle in a Vinicool, a double-glazed perspex container that keeps it cool for hours and may save a wet bottle marking your furniture. The price is high but the Vinicool should last forever and it can be used as an ice bucket. The makers are Spong and Co., Repton Close, Basildon, Essex. Tel. 0268-3341.

Opening sparkling wines Remove the foil over the cork and then the wire muzzle, tilting the bottle away from you at an angle of 45°, with one hand round the neck, holding the cork in. With the other hand on the base, turn the bottle around the cork, which should ease out gradually. A glass to take the first fizz and a pair of champagne pliers to grip difficult corks are useful aids. Kept in the fridge, sparkling wines in part-drunk bottles, if fitted with the special spring-loaded champagne stopper

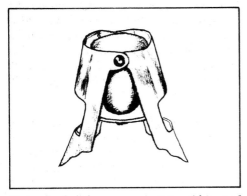

Spring-loaded champagne stopper; with one of these fitted, partly drunk bottles of sparkling wine will keep in a refrigerator for up to a week.

To fit: Hold bottle upright on firm surface. Hold stopper over neck, press down allowing the two arms to engage under the bottle's flange.

OPENING SPARKLING WINE

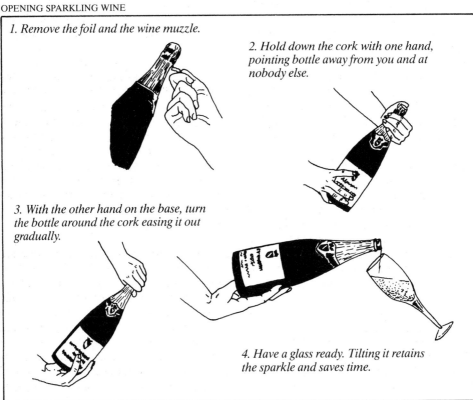

1. Remove the foil and the wine muzzle.

2. Hold down the cork with one hand, pointing bottle away from you and at nobody else.

3. With the other hand on the base, turn the bottle around the cork easing it out gradually.

4. Have a glass ready. Tilting it retains the sparkle and saves time.

illustrated retain their sparkle and remain good to drink for up to seven days.

Decanting If possible, first stand any bottle of fine red wine or vintage port upright for 24-48 hours at room temperature. Alternatively, keeping the bottle horizontal, move it gently from it's bin into a wine basket and extract the cork with the basket horizontal. When decanting, baskets screen the level of the wine so that one cannot see when to stop pouring; they are generally out of favour.

Taking care to insert corkscrew centrally, pull gently and smoothly. Then wipe the lip and the inside of the neck with a clean cloth. Check that the decanter is clean and that there is neither a trace nor a smell of detergent inside it. Pour yourself a sample and taste it to be sure the wine is satisfactory.

Now place a light (candle, torch or bare bulb) behind the shoulder of the bottle and pour steadily into the decanter, tilting it with the hand not holding the bottle. The light will illuminate the contents and the moment to stop pouring is when the leading edge of the sediment reaches the neck. Do not use muslin to try and strain the muddy liquid that remains; some sediment always gets through. The proper place for the *lees* is in the cook's bottle in the fridge. The only proper use for muslin when decanting is to exclude fragments of a broken cork or that wispy, floating substance called 'beeswing' sometimes found in vintage port.

Timing Once decanted, very old clarets and burgundies can die within an hour or so; decant only a few minutes before drinking, or serve them direct from the bottle. Big wines, like Barolo and Châteauneuf-du-Pape may need four to six hours in a decanter to show their quality. As to clarets, up to two hours beforehand is about right for five to ten-year-olds of a good year, although I am quite aware that Professor Emil Peynaud, the Bordeaux authority, is against decanting, if at all, until the last possible moment.

Vintage and crusted port Matured for many years in the bottle, these wines form a crust which is unsettled when, for example, a bottle is bought and taken home for Christmas. If the bottle is stood up for 48 hours, the crust should resettle at the base and the bottle can be left upright for opening when required. The sealing wax over the corks prevents *Oronico flavius*, a fly, laying it's eggs in the cork and gradually eating it's way through to a glorious death in the wine.

With vintages over twenty years old, the cork may crumble and get pushed into the bottle. To rid the port of all the bits, I find it necessary to decant twice. First into a jug through an old silver funnel which has a strainer; secondly from the jug into the decanter through a clean piece of muslin or handkerchief material. The alternatives, decapitation at the neck with a hot flame and special tongs or by a sharp blow with the edge of a heavy carving knife, are skills I have never acquired.

In the restaurant A good hotel or restaurant wine list should be legible, easy to understand and up to date. Some may have a grandiose printed list, others a simple typewritten one in a loose-leaf folder with a plastic cover, easy to keep up to date and presentable. There should be plenty of copies, including some at the bar for pre-ordering and at the table the list should be presented with the menu. Each wine should have a number corresponding to that of it's bin. Ordering by number obviates difficulty and misunderstanding in attempting to pronounce their names. Fine mature wine, for example a ten to fifteen-year-old claret, needs to be ordered 24 – 48 hours in advance and an arrangement made to decant beforehand.

Having ordered, you should be shown the chosen bottle before it is opened in your presence. Check that the year is the one you ordered; if different, there may be some satisfactory explanation — stocks do run out and many wines do not differ much from year to year. But with a fine claret, a substitute for a 1975, 1976 or 1978, particularly at the same price, would not be acceptable.

After extracting the cork and wiping the lip of the bottle with a clean napkin, the wine waiter (who may know little about wine, though some know a lot), pours out some wine solely for approval. You may need only swirl and 'nose' — though you can taste as well — to decide whether it is in good condition. If doubtful, ask the wine waiter or the head waiter to taste it too. They should know that they can debit their supplier and that it makes sense to offer a different wine if nobody is quite sure.

On no account complain angrily like the diner who said, 'Take this away — it's vinegar!' The proprietor himself came with another bottle, pouring the sample deferentially. The diner swallowed and nearly choked to death. 'That is vinegar,' said the proprietor. 'I thought you should learn to tell the difference.'

THE CONTAINERS: BAGS, BOTTLES, CANS AND GLASSES

Let Misers in Garrets hide up their gay Store,
And heap their rich Bags to live wretchedly Poor.
'Tis the Cellar alone with true Fame is renown'd.
Her Treasure's diffusive, and cheers all around.
The Gold and the Gem but the Eye's gaudy Toy,
But the Vintners' rich Juice gives Health, Life and joy.
E. Settle: *Song to the Vintners* 1702

The bag-in-box, evidently, is so easy to carry home and the white wine on tap so easily kept cool for weeks in the fridge, that by the end of 1984's glorious summer, twelve out of every hundred glasses of wine drunk in Britain were coming out of one.

Inspired by marsupial pouches, a jolly bagman down under in the late 1960s developed this new container, now in 5 and 3 litre sizes, with a 10 litre for bars and restaurants. Unfortunately, bags burst and oxygen, penetrating the plastic, spoilt the wine. The present models, with these faults corrected, reached Britain in the summer of 1981, led by Stowell's *Vin de table*, an excellent brand. Soon there were forty others from ten different countries, which independent tasting panels found to be of disgracefully low quality.

In the spring of 1984, a new tasting panel carried out another careful examination tasting blind twice, before and after an interval of seven days. They were also able to compare wines in these boxes with identical wines also available in bottles. They found that the majority of those in the box deteriorated over the seven day period and were inferior to those in bottle. In their opinion, producers should replace these wines with others of higher quality that should stand up better to bag-in-box treatment.

As it happened, Peter Dominic had already done this in August 1982 making their debut with two *vins de pays*, the quality strictly regulated by French law.

To summarize: on the evidence so far, (i) wine is no cheaper in bags-in-boxes than the same wine in bottles, (ii) whenever possible, try a bottle before committing yourself to the bigger container, which could cost £10-£20, (iii) the tap allows you to have one, two, three... glasses as and when you like (cooking the *coq-au-vin* perhaps?) (iv) the contents being hidden, so can others without your knowledge (v) what if our friend 'dare-devil-Deirdre' (page 222) is around?

Cans So long as wine competes in price with beer and cider, there is bound to be a market for wine in cans, which are easily carried, stored and kept cold in the home. Holding two glasses, a 25-centilitre can is ideal for picnics and drivers should be safe with one can and some food. Any doubts Peter Dominic may have had about cans were dispelled at the 1984 Country Landowners' Game Fair held at Broadlands, the Mountbatten home on the Test at Romsey in Hampshire. In their tent 100 dozen cans of La Sonelle were sold in the three July days, so hot that the red had to be chilled. I found the manager singing that rumba number:

> We're having a heat wave,
> A tropical heat wave,
> Sonelle sales are climbing,
> Country gents are all dining,
> They certainly can can can.

Bottles: sizes and contents Having regulated wine descriptions, the EEC turned it's attention to sizes and contents of beverage containers from milk to wine. The standard wine bottle is to contain 75 centilitres when filled and corked. Formerly the French standard held two or three centilitres less and some regions reduced to 70 centilitres holding less still. For Britain the 75-centilitres size has the advantage that six bottles (6 x 75 cl) equals 4.5 litres, virtually one gallon. Thus a dozen case has always been regarded for practical purposes, including duty, as being two gallons of wine.

By 1989 wine and spirit bottles in the EEC should have been reduced from nearly sixty sizes to under forty as shown on page 230.

Carafes EEC regulations require these to be in the following sizes:
Metric: 25, 50, 75 and 100 centilitres
Imperial: 10 fl oz (28 cl) and 20 fl oz (56 cl)

Small bottles A few empty half-bottles and quarters can be useful to 'waste not, want not' in any household. Whenever wine is left over, if put into a bottle of suitable size, filled to the top and lightly corked, it will keep indefinitely for drinking later. Half-litre Paul Masson carafes and quarter litre Carafino carafes may be easier to obtain than half and quarter bottles. Other surplus can go in cook's bottles, red and white, best kept in the fridge.

Extra large bottles Magnums (2 bottles) of champagne, claret and burgundy are often obtainable, but the larger sizes from Jeroboam to Nebuchadnezzar are usually made for national events like a Royal Jubilee or an occasion such as a wine firm's centenary. Their *Old Testament* names and

Bottle capacity in litres	Light Wines	Fortified Wines	Sparkling Wines	Spirits
0.02				•
0.03				•
0.04				•
0.05				•
0.10	•	•		•
0.125			•	
0.20		•	•	•
0.25	•			
0.375	•	•	•	
0.50	•	•		•
0.75	•	•	•	
1.0	•	•		•
1.5	•	•	•	•
2.0	•			•
2.5				•
3.0	•		•	•
5.0	•			

Bottles — EEC Final Sizes

Permitted temporarily
Until 31.12.85 for light wines 0.73 litres
Until 31.12.88 for light wines 0.35, 0.70 and 1.25 litres
Until 31.12.88 for liqueurs and spirits 0.35, 0.375, 0.70 and 0.75 litres

Extra Large Bottles	
Magnum	2 bottles
Double Magnum or Jeroboam (Champagne)	4 bottles
Jeroboam (Bordeaux)	5 bottles
Rehoboam	6 bottles
Imperial or Methuselah	8 bottles
Salmanazar	12 bottles
Balthazar	16 bottles
Nebuchadnezzar	20 bottles

capacities (a favourite topic in wine quizzes) are tabulated above.

Glasses Wine glasses need to be of clear glass so that the colour of the wine can be seen and enjoyed. They should be large enough to hold a good measure of wine when half full and should narrow towards the top, the better to concentrate the bouquet. The general purpose glass is known as a Paris goblet and there are sizes from $12\frac{1}{2}$ to 5 oz, the figures being capacity in fluid ounces. The 8 oz size, filled half to two-thirds full is ideal for light wines, the 5 oz size for sherry and port.

For champagne and sparkling wines, the flute shape is recommended because the bubbles are well displayed and will last longer. The shallow saucer-shaped glasses, fashionable in Victorian times, are unsuitable; one jog of the elbow at a crowded reception and the wine is spilt, as like as not down a dowager's dress.

Of the five glasses illustrated on page 212 many households manage with three; table wine, champagne and port. When buying, be sure the length of the stem is suitable for any kind of dish-washing machine. Old glass, easily cracked by the very hot water in these machines, should be hand washed. To clean wine glasses and decanters, fill with hot water, add half a denture cleaning tablet per glass and leave overnight.

Wines by the glass These need to be strong enough to remain in good condition from opening the container until it is empty. In this respect wines from bags-in-box should be better than the same wines in jars or bottles exposed to the air after opening. At closing time any ullaged bottles should be topped up from others and corked.

When you go to places serving wines by the glass, inquire about the notice saying what measures they use and the prices charged. It is not obligatory to have one, but after long talks between trade and government, this voluntary code began on 1 May 1984. It's object is 'to ensure, as far as possible, that anyone wanting a glass of still table wine will know the quantity and the price'; and there should be specific notices in 'readily discernible positions'.

The Code recommends that licensed premises should select only two sizes from either the imperial or the metric system, given as appropriate for the sale of wine in the Weights and Measures Act (Part IV of schedule 3). These are:

Metric in centilitres	Imperial in fluid ounces	
10.0	—	
12.5	4	= 11.4 fl. oz.
15.0	5 (1 gill)	= 14.2 fl. oz.
17.5	6	= 17.0 fl. oz.
20.0	6⅔ (⅓ pt)	= 19.0 fl. oz.
25.0	8	= 23.0 fl. oz.

The capacity of the two selected must differ by at least 5 centilitres or 2 fluid ounces. 'Discernible positions' are on wine lists and on the menu outside restaurants.

A standard glass? Within this framework, Stowells and Whitbreads, supported by the Wine and Spirit Association, have declared 12.5 centilitres as a standard measure, hoping others will follow and that it will become law in time. This would mean six standard measures to the 75-centilitre wine bottle, making it easy to check the mark-up on one glass, knowing the retail price of a bottle. Places like El Vinos for example, would be entirely free to use larger sizes, just as for spirits some bars adopt a four or five out (of a gill) measure as standard in place of the usual six. This standard glass, a 5 oz Paris goblet with a line at the 4 oz level, has been developed by Stowells.

At table, at home or in restaurant, the larger 8 oz Paris goblet filled two-thirds full is best, giving six to eight glasses from a 75-centilitre bottle and about ten from a litre bottle.

TAXATION

Dulce et decorum est pro patria bibere?
Drinking for one's country has always seemed to me sweeter and more decorous than dying for it and in the first *Wine Mine* of 1959 I recorded the drinkers' contribution to the Exchequer at that time. Figures per bottle, then were:

Champagne and sparkling wine		
	6s 3d =	31p
Foreign table wine bottled in UK		
	2s 2d =	11p
Foreign table wine bottled abroad		
	4s 7d =	23p
Port, sherry, Madeira	6s 4d =	32p
Spirits: whisky, gin, vodka, etc. 40°		
	24s 8d =	£1.23p
Brandy	22s 11d =	£1.15p

Historically tax reductions on light (table) wines have been few and far between. In 1860 Gladstone, the great Liberal, bringing it down to 1s a gallon (2d a bottle) set French wines on the road to popularity. In 1949 Sir Stafford Cripps, Socialist, brought it down from 25s a gallon (4s 2d a bottle) to 13s a gallon (2s 2d a bottle). In 1984 Nigel Lawson, Conservative, brought it down 108p a gallon (18p a bottle). Otherwise scores of Chancellors, carrying Gladstone's dispatch box to this day, have put it up and up.

Ups and downs In 1984 the reduction came about because Italy's plea, that British taxation discriminated against wine by 4 to 1 in favour of beer, had been upheld by the European Court of Justice. Britain, having previously convinced the same Court that Italy's whisky taxation was unfair in relation to grappa, had no alternative but to redress the balance. Thus, light wine tax went down by 18p a bottle; beer tax went up by 2p a pint. Barely noticed by wine drinkers celebrating their rare reduction in duty, 10p a bottle was put on sparkling wines, sherry, port, vermouth and spirits.

Ironically this heavy taxation causes us to spend more on drink than people in any other Western European country — wine producer or not — although they consume far more than we do. Once beer was our 'wine of the country'; at 90p a pint, can it still be so called? In *The Guardian*, John Arlott summed up the impasse: 'So the factor which raises the worker's meal to the level of gastronomy right across Europe from France and Portugal to Rumania and Bulgaria remains barred to his or her British opposite.*But another report by the Consumers' Association found that the price of beer had gone down compared to wages between 1950 and 1976, while the price of a loaf had gone up.

Better wine is better value Taxes on wines and spirits go back to the days of King Alfred; *excise duty* being paid on articles

---

* The Guardian 7.7.84.

TAXATION PERCENTAGES ON WINES AND SPIRITS

Low strength wines	Table wine	Quality wine	Sparkling wine	Champagne
WINE	£0.28	£1.24	£0.56	£3.12
Distribution retailing	0.52	2.12	1.45	2.35
Bottling shipping	0.31	0.36	0.36	0.38
EXCISE DUTY	0.63	0.63	1.11	1.11
VAT	0.26	0.65	0.52	1.04
RETAIL PRICE	£2.00	£5.00	£4.00	£8.00
Taxation	44.5%	25.6%	40.7%	26.9%

Higher strength wines	Vermouth	Sherry	Port	Premium Port
WINE	0.32	0.48	1.10	4.36
Distribution retailing	0.43	0.65	1.13	2.54
Bottling shipping	0.32	0.34	0.42	0.52
EXCISE DUTY	1.10	1.10	1.28	1.28
VAT	0.33	0.38	0.57	1.30
RETAIL PRICE	£2.50	£2.95	£4.50	£10.00
Taxation	57.2%	50.2%	41.1%	25.8%

Spirits	Gin	Vodka	Whisky	Brandy
SPIRIT	0.38	0.38	0.44	0.45
Distribution retailing	0.82	0.90	0.98	0.67
Bottling shipping	0.46	0.46	0.46	0.76
EXCISE DUTY	4.64	4.35	4.64	4.21
VAT	0.95	0.91	0.98	0.91
RETAIL PRICE	£7.25	£7.00	£7.50	£7.00
Taxation	77.1%	75.1%	74.9%	73.1%

made within a country, *customs duty* on imported articles of foreign manufacture. The system is based on alcoholic strength — the stronger the liquor, the greater the duty.

With wines this means that a bottle of the cheapest claret attracts the same excise duty as the *grand cru* (63p a 70 centilitre bottle at present) but a very different VAT at 15 per cent is added to each of them. Thus, the duty on the cheaper wine forms a higher proportion of the total price. In short, better wine is better value, provided the individual can afford it.

For us *Excise* has now become the duty on goods produced and sold within the EEC and the imposition of Value Added Tax on top has made the arithmetic of *Dulce et decorum est pro patria bibere* rather complex. VAT is 15 per cent of the retail value (virtually 13 per cent of the total you pay on any VAT rated goods). Excise duty varies with alcoholic strength, and with content, for example 70, 75 or 100 centilitres bottles. Other components of the price also vary with country of origin (EEC or non-EEC), production (whether large or small of the item concerned) and with the type and policy of the retailer.

The figures on page 232 opposite aim to give a general idea. I confess the taxation percentages seem rather odd. Does the true patriot drink himself rapidly to death on gin (77.1 per cent to the Chancellor) or hope to make a 100 with a daily *coupe de champagne* (26.9 per cent to that same Exchequer)?

LEARNING MORE

Lines received after a Wine Appreciation week-end at the Links Country Park Hotel, West Runton, Norfolk.

> Examine the colour, breathe in the bouquet
> Roll over the palate, decide what to say,
> And then spit it out in a ladylike way,
> Like the West Runton Wine Mine wine
>   tasters.

Declare that you find the aroma elusive,
The flavour assertive, the tannin intrusive,
So praise what you can, then be roundly
    abusive,
Like the West Runton Wine Mine wine
    tasters.

We hold up our glasses and look at the hue,
"They say it is sherry but can that be true?"
"So murky and turgid we think it is glue!"
Say the West Runton Wine Mine wine
    tasters.

Quite pleasantly sound but, perhaps, past
    it's prime?
A claret? Rioja? A red Rudesheim?
Italian! Chianti! We knew all the time!
Boast the West Runton Wine Mine wine
    tasters.

A glorious colour, an aroma inhalable,
Magnificent flavour and style unassailable,
A wonderful wine but, alas, not available
To the West Runton Wine Mine wine
    tasters.

W.R.W.M.W.T.   by G.H.N.

'How do I learn more about wine?' People never cease to ask this question, so here are some ways.

Books   Ever since André Simon, a Frenchman who settled in England but never lost his French accent, decided in the 1920s to teach the British all about French wines in their own language, the written word has been prominent in wine education. A general guide to wines in any wine-drinking home is a useful book of reference and there are usually several at different prices in print. Currently there is at least one book on almost every wine country or region that warrants one. Up-to-date books are important because

233

the world of wine is changing rapidly and existing books are difficult to revise, due to the prohibitive cost of resetting print.

For prompt reviews one could formerly rely on John Arlott's regular Friday articles in *The Guardian*. Wine correspondents of comparable Dailies and Sundays tell me that they are not encouraged to review books, except the *Financial Times* in which Edmund Penning-Rowsell's highly informative articles appear on Saturdays frequently.

In London Hatchards, 187 Piccadilly, have their separate wine book corner, while Blackwell, Bowes and Bowes, George's, Hammicks, Hooks and Websters are all booksellers whose branches in many parts of the country offer a good selection. Club at Vintner House, Templefields, Harlow, Essex, also have book lists and supply by post.

Students particularly may like to be reminded that public libraries also keep wine books, for lending and for reference, and there are numerous magazines, newsletters and price lists, mostly free for the asking from points of sale in every High Street.

Television Wine and food programmes are on the increase and there is Hugh Johnson's wine video ('How to handle a wine' (£14.95 plus £1.45 p&p) from Mulberry House, Canning Place, Liverpool, L1 8HY).

Clubs, courses and tastings There are about a dozen wine clubs in Britain, mostly small mail order firms. The only ones of use to the learner are those associated with courses and tastings. For these, the best sources of information are:

1 The annual *Which? Wine Guide*: 600 pages on where to buy, what to buy, etc. published by the Consumers' Association each autumn.

2 *The Sunday Telegraph Good Wine Guide*, also an autumn annual.

3 *Webster's Wine Price Guide Consumer and Professional Handbook*.

4 *Decanter:* the monthly wine magazine, which includes a diary of tastings, wine weekends, courses, exhibitions and festivals, mainly in Britain but some of them abroad.

October to March is the high season for most of these activities; Christie's and Sotheby's, besides being wine auctioneers, hold wine appreciation courses in London, but there are, too, a surprising number outside London costing less, some Technical Colleges having added wine to their evening classes.

Ecole du Vin The 'school' is Gilbey's Château Loudenne in the Médoc where the vines surround the house and the lawn slopes down to the Gironde, an hour by car from Bordeaux airport. During 1985 (March to October) there were five 5-day courses directed by Charles Eve M.W., each for twelve people, accommodated at Loudenne and neighbouring châteaux. A sybarite's dream for £625, excluding travel there and back! For 1986 information, write to Charles Eve M.W., Vintner House, Templefields, Harlow, Essex.

Travel Organised wine tours include the popular Rhine and Mosel K.D. cruises, Blackheath Travel's different 'Wine Trails' to Portugal, Madrid and Rioja, Italy, Madeira, Champagne and Alsace. The Wine Club, associated with the Sunday Times, runs European wine tours for its members, who pay £3 a year subscription (£35 for life membership). Brittany Ferries are trying out a four-day Bordeaux wine-buying trip, travelling by luxury coach via their Portsmouth — St-Malo service. Details of these and other tours from travel agents.

For those travelling independently by car in Western Europe, there are a series of wine establishments that welcome visitors, the large concerns, particularly in Champagne, requiring no prior notice. My *Guide to Visiting Vineyards* is helpful for those not knowing who to visit or how to go about it.

Grape picking During the sixties Peter Dominic helped many young people to earn a little money at this arduous job during the long summer vacations. Later, in 1977, the free leaflet *Holiday Work Abroad* was embodied in *Off The Shelf*, Gilbey Vintners' *Guide to Wines and Spirits* sold in Peter Dominic shops.

Since then, opportunities have been considerably reduced by mechanical harvesting; the French employment agencies, which applicants were previously recommended to contact, are now bound to give French people priority in filling vacancies. Nevertheless, there are two reputable British organisations which will only send pickers where jobs are guaranteed. This is very important.

Vacation Work International, 9 Park End Street, Oxford, OX1 1HJ (Tel. 0865-241978 or 243311) bring out their annual programme each January. They also publish a dozen different directories of jobs in Britain and abroad, some of which should be in public libraries.

In France the vintage lasts for three weeks, normally starting at any time between 14 and 28 September. If you are free, over sixteen and this is 'your scene', write to Vacation Work International for their programme in January, from which you can apply for membership £5 and book one of their grape-picking holidays at the same time.

Alternatively, write with stamped, addressed envelope to Concordia Youth Service Volunteers Ltd., 8 Brunswick Place, Hove, Sussex BN3 1ET (Tel. 0273-77086). Concordia, a charity organisation working with an 'opposite number' in France, places pickers in Champagne, Chablis, the Côte d'Or and Beaujolais for a registration fee of £25 (1984). They then travel there independently at their own expense.

There are other jobs — hotels, agricultural, archaelogical — and other agencies. Apply in January and be sure where you are to work, for how long, what you will be paid and that you are insured.

Buying wine abroad For Customs purposes within EEC countries a distinction is made between duty paid liquors bought from a supermarket, shop, firm or grower and liquors bought duty free in the air, at airport shops or at sea. If bought duty free, anyone over the age of 17 entering Britain has an allowance of:

One litre of spirits over 22° volume   OR

Two litres, either sparkling or fortified wine, under 22° volume

PLUS

Two litres of still wines (other than fortified)

But if bought duty paid, the allowance is increased to:

One and a half litres spirits   OR   3 litres sparkling or fortified wine
PLUS
Four litres of still wines.

Bottles bought in non-EEC countries rate as Duty Free. Purchases of Duty Free and Duty Paid cannot be mixed, except for a concession of 7 May 1985 — see next paragraph. Even so, for two people — one choosing Duty Free, the other Duty Paid — this gives a score of combinations, as this table shows. With seven litres of wine each, a couple touring France have an allowance of fourteen litres, regarded by a generous UK customs as nineteen 75 centilitre bottles. If the couple have two dozen bottles, only five will be dutiable, at about 80p each, i.e. 75p + VAT.

The concession of 7 May 1985 entitles travellers from EEC or other countries with alcoholic drink, *other than still table wine,* purchased Duty Free, to four litres of still table wine if bought Duty Paid within the EEC. Thus a person buying a litre of whisky in a Duty Free shop, ship or plane can now bring in four litres of light table wine duty paid from a French supermarket as well. This consession is not shown in the table. If you speak a little French (or German) buy your wine, not at a supermarket nor at the first 'Vente Directe' sign you see on a main road, but from a reputable grower in a wine village or town. Hugh Johnson's *Wine Companion,* my own *Guide to Visiting Vineyards* and the Companion Guide to Burgundy, the Loire and other regions should lead you to them.

BUYING WINE ABROAD

HM Customs concessions for two in Litres

Serial No.	Table Wine Dp Df	Fortified or Sparkling Wine Dp	Df	Spirits Dp	Df	Total	
1	14					14	EEC Duty Paid
2	11	3					
3	8	6					
4	11				1½	12½	
5	8		3		1½		
6	8				3	11	
7	7+4					11	Duty Paid & Duty Free
8	7+2		2				
9	4+4	3					
10	4+2	3	2				
11	7+2				1	10	
12	4+2	3			1		
13	4+4				1½	9½	
14	4+2		2		1½		
15	4+2				1½+1	8½	
16	8					8	Duty Free
17	6		2				
18	4		4				
19	6				1	7	
20	4		2		1		
21	4				2	6	

Dp = Bought duty paid in EEC
Df = Bought duty free

Publisher's note:
If you have enjoyed this book, why not buy the other Peter Dominic guide, *Practical Cocktails* by John Doxat (Quiller Press £3.95)?

Training Vines

Hard winter pruning produces high quality grapes; these diagrams show the more popular methods used today.

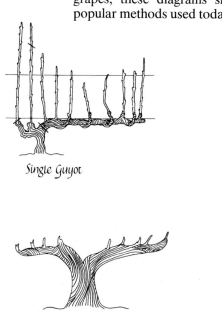

Single Guyot

Cordon Cane

Eventail

Gobelet

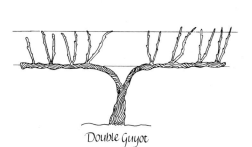

Double Guyot

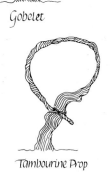

Tambourine Prop

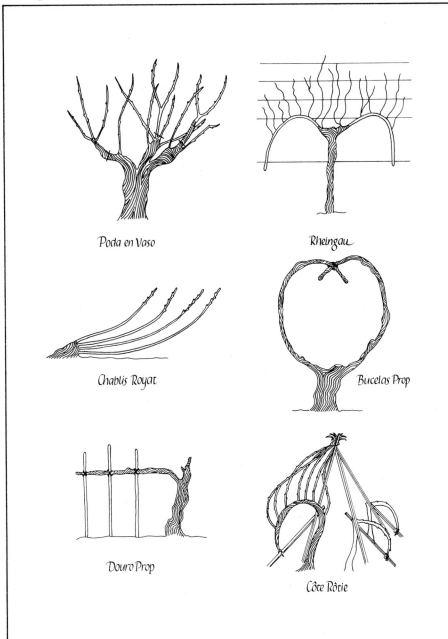

Poda en Vaso

Rheingau

Chablis Royat

Bucelas Prop

Douro Prop

Côte Rôtie

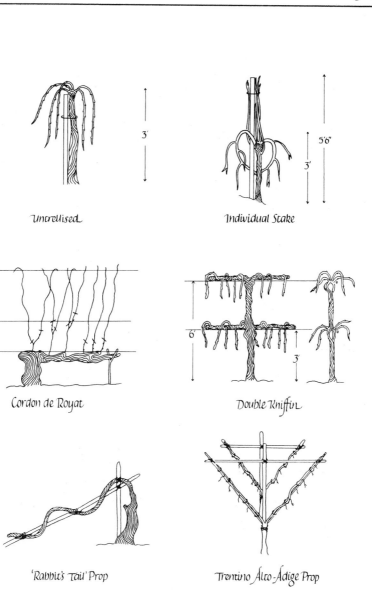

Untrellised

Individual Stake

Cordon de Royat

Double Kniffin

'Rabbit's Tail' Prop

Trentino Alto-Ádige Prop

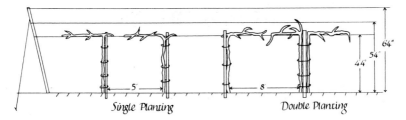

Single Planting   Double Planting

Lenz Moser High Culture System

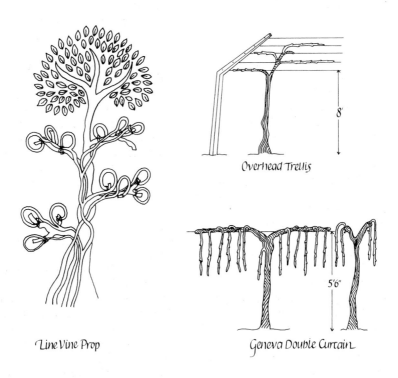

Line Vine Prop

Overhead Trellis

Geneva Double Curtain

Bibliography

The following books have been helpful to me and are recommended for further reading. The dates given are those of the latest editions, likely to be in bookshops and public libraries. John Lyle, Bookseller, Harpford, Sidmouth, Devon, Tel. (0395) 68294 specialises in second-hand wine books.

General

Wine Companion, Hugh Johnson (Mitchell Beazley, 1983)   £15.95.
Wines of the World, André Simon (George Rainbird, 1967).
Wines of the World, Second Edition, Ed. Serena Sutcliffe (Macdonald, 1981)   £18.95.
Drinking Wine, David Peppercorn, Brian Cooper & Elwyn Blacker (Macdonald, 1984)   £7.95.
The Great Vintage Wine Book, Michael Broadbent (Mitchell Beazley, 1980)   £13.95.
The World Atlas of Wine, Hugh Johnson (Mitchell Beazley, 1982)   £17.95.
The Penguin Wine Book, Pamela Vandyke Price (Allen Lane, 1984)   £8.95.
The Wine Book, Jancis Robinson (Fontana Paperback, 1983)   £2.95.
The Great Wine Book, Jancis Robinson (Sidgwick and Jackson, 1982)   £15.00.
Great Vineyards and Winemakers, Ed. Serena Sutcliffe (Macdonald, 1982)   £15.00.

The Wine Drinker's Handbook, Serena Sutcliffe (Pan Books, 1982)   £5.95.
The New Wine Companion, David Burroughs & Norman Bezzant (1980)   £5.25.
(Heinemann on behalf of Wine and Spirit Education Trust.)
Wine Regions of the World, David Burroughs & Norman Bezzant (1979)   £5.90.
(Heinemann on behalf of Wine and Spirit Education Trust.)
Alexis Lichine's *Encyclopedia of Wines and Spirits* (Cassell Ltd., 1979)   £20.00.
Same Again: A Guide to Safer Drinking, Marius Grant (Penguin, 1984)   £1.95.
Tread of Grapes: The Autobiography of a Wine Lover, Edward Ott   £3.50.

France

Guide to the Wines and Vineyards of France, Alexis Lichine (Papermac, 1982)   £6.95.
Bordeaux, David Peppercorn (Faber & Faber, 1982)   £5.50.
The Wines of Bordeaux, E. Penning-Rowsell (Penguin Books, 1985)   £12.95.
The Wines of Saint-Emilion and Pomerol, Jeffery Benson & Alistair Mackenzie (Sotheby Publications, 1983)   £19.95.
Sauternes, Jeffery Benson & Alistair Mackenzie (Sotheby Parke Bernet, 1979)   £9.95.

241

Victorian Vineyard: Château Loudenne and the Gilbeys, Nicolas Faith (Constable, 1983) £9.95.
Alsace Wines and Spirits, Pamela Vandyke Price (Sotheby Publications, 1984) £16.95.
Burgundy, Anthony Hanson (Faber & Faber, 1982) £4.95.
Burgundy Vines and Wines, John Arlott & Christopher Fielden (Quartet Books, 1979) £3.95.
The Wines of Chablis and the Yonne, Rosemary George (Sotheby Publications, 1984) £14.95.
The Wines of the Rhône, J. Livingstone Learmouth & Melvyn Master (Faber & Faber, 1983) £5.25.

Germany
The Wines of Germany, Frank Schoonmaker (Faber & Faber, 1983) £4.95.
German Wines, Ian Jamieson (Mitchell Beazley Pocket Guide, 1984) £4.95.
The Wines of Germany, Cyril Ray (Allen Lane, 1977) £4.25.

Italy
Italian Wine, Victor Hazan (Penguin Books, 1984) £6.95.
Italian Wines, Philip Dallas (Faber & Faber, 1983) £5.95.
Vino, Burton Anderson (Macmillan Papermac, 1982) £6.95.

Spain
The Wines of Spain, Jan Read (Faber & Faber, 1982) £3.25.
Sherry, Julian Jeffs (Faber & Faber, 1982) £3.95.

Portugal
Wines of Portugal, Jan Read (Faber & Faber, 1982) £5.95.

Portuguese Wine, Raymond Postgate (J.M. Dent, 1969) £1.25.
Rich, Rare and Red, Wine & Food Society's Guide to Port, Ben Howkins (Heinemann, 1982) £5.95.
The Story of Port, Sarah Bradford (Christie's Wine Publications, 1983) £7.50+.
Madeira, the Island Vineyard, Noël Cossart (Christie's Wine Publications, 1984) £10.90+.

USA
The Wines of America, Leon D. Adams (Sidgwick & Jackson, 1984)* £15.00.
Robert Mondavi of the Napa Valley, Cyril Ray (Heinemann/Davies, 1984) £9.95.

England and Wales
Vine Growing in the British Isles, Jack Ward (Faber & Faber, 1984) £5.25.

Wine tasting
Pocket Book of Wine Tasting, Michael Broadbent (Mitchell Beazley, 1982) £3.95.
Masterglass: A Practical Course in Wine Tasting, Jancis Robinson (Pan Books, 1983) £2.95.

Wine travel
The Wine Roads of Europe, Marc and Kim Millon (Nicholson, 1983) £4.95.
Guide to Visiting Vineyards, Anthony Hogg (Michael Joseph, 1984) £6.95.
Travellers' Portugal, Sea and Fly/Drives, Anthony Hogg (Solo Mio Books, 1983) £4.95.

+From Publisher, includes postage.
*Third Edition, first in UK.

Useful addresses

AUSTRALIA
Trade Commissioner
Australian High Commission
Strand, London WC2
(Tel: 438 8205)

AUSTRIA
The Commercial Counsellor
Austrian Trade Commission
1 Hyde Park Gate, London SW7
(Tel: 584 4411)

BULGARIA
The Manager
Bulgarian Vintners Co. Ltd.,
156 Caledonian Road, London N1 9RD
(Tel: 278 8047)

CYPRUS
The Commercial Counsellor
Cyprus Trade Centre
213 Regent Street, London W1R 8DA
(Tel: 437 3831)

FRANCE
The Director
Food & Wine From France
Nuffield House, 41-46 Piccadilly,
London W1V 9AJ
(Tel: 439 8371)

GERMANY
The Director
Wines From Germany Information Service
121 Gloucester Place, London W1
(Tel: 935 8164)

GREECE
The Commercial Counsellor
Greek Embassy
1A Holland Park, London W11 3TP
(Tel: 727 8040)

HUNGARY
Commercial Section
Hungarian Embassy
46 Eaton Place, London SW1
(Tel: 235 8767)

ITALY
The Director
Italian Trade Centre
37 Sackville Street, London W1
(Tel: 734 2412)

NEW ZEALAND
The Commercial Minister
New Zealand High Commission
New Zealand House
80 Haymarket, London SW1
(Tel: 930 8422)

PORTUGAL
The Director
Portuguese Govt. Trade Office
New Bond St. House
1/5 New Bond Street, London W1Y 9PE
(Tel: 493 0212)

SPAIN
The Director
Vinos de España
22 Manchester Square, London W1
(Tel: 935 6140)

U.S.A.
The Agricultural Officer
U.S. Agricultural Trade Office
101 Wigmore Street, London W1H 9AB
(Tel: 499 0024)

YUGOSLAVIA
The Director
Yugoslav Economic Chamber
Crown House, 143/147 Regent Street, London W1
(Tel: 734 2581)

Index

Compiled by Diana LeCore, Society of Indexers.